Environments, Ethics and Human Concern

Environments, Ethics and Human Concern

John Benson

The Open University

The Open University

Walton Hall, Milton Keynes
MK7 6AA

First published 1999

Edited, designed and typeset by the Open University.

Printed and bound in the United Kingdom by Alden Press Ltd, Osney Mead, Oxford, OX2 0EF.

ISBN 0 7492 8752 7

This text forms part of an Open University course A211 *Philosophy and the Human Situation*. Details of this and other Open University courses can be obtained from the Course Reservations Centre, PO Box 724, The Open University, Milton Keynes MK7 6ZS, United Kingdom: tel. (00 44) 1908 653231.

For availability of this or other course components, contact Open University Worldwide Ltd, The Berrill Building, Walton Hall, Milton Keynes MK7 6AA, United Kingdom: tel. (00 44) 1908 858585, fax (00 44) 1908 858787, e-mail ouwenq@open.ac.uk

Alternatively, much useful course information can be obtained from the Open University's website

http://www.open.ac.uk

1.1

20840/a221book3i1.1

Contents

READINGS

Preface

Acknowledgements

My greatest debt is to my colleagues in the Philosophy Department of Lancaster University with whom I have undergone a prolonged mutual education in environmental philosophy, and in particular to Jane Howarth, John O'Neill and Vernon Pratt who have helped me with particular parts of the book. I am also grateful for the comments of members of the course team, but most of all for the expert midwifery of the OU philosophy editor, Peter Wright, which has been exercised far beyond the call of editorial duty.

Grateful acknowledgement is made to the following sources for permission to reproduce material in this book: Warnock, G.J. (1971) *The Object of Morality*, Routledge; Hepburn, R. (1984) *Wonder and Other Essays*, Edinburgh University Press; Sylvan, R. and Routley, V. (1980) 'Human chauvinism and environmental ethics' in Mannison, D.S. et al. (eds) *Environmental Philosophy*, Australian National University; Norton, B.G. (1989) 'The cultural approach to conservation biology', from *Conservation for the Twenty-first Century*, Western, D. and Pearl, M.C. (eds), used by permission of Oxford University Press, Inc.; Wilson, E.O. (1992) *The Diversity of Life*, Penguin Books Ltd; Pearce, D. et al. (1989) *Blueprint for a Green Economy*, HMSO, Crown copyright is reproduced with the permission of the Controller of her Majesty's Stationery Office; Pearce, D. (1992) 'Green economics', *Environmental Values*, vol. 1, no. 1, Spring 1992, The White Horse Press; Hardin, G. (1968) 'The tragedy of the commons', *Science*, vol. 162, pp.1243–8, copyright © 1968 American Association for the Advancement of Science; Mackie, J.L. (1977) *Ethics: Inventing Right and Wrong*, Penguin Books, 1977, copyright © J. L. Mackie, reproduced by permission of Penguin Books Ltd; O'Neill, J. (1993) *Ecology, Policy and Politics*, Routledge; Howarth, J. (1996) 'Neither Use nor Ornament: A Conservationists Guide to Care', Lancaster University; Taylor, P.W. (1986) *Respect for Nature: a Theory of Environmental Ethics*, copyright © 1986 by Princeton University Press, reprinted by permission of Princeton University Press; Rolston III, H. (1979) 'Can and ought we to follow nature', Environmental Ethics; Naess, A. (1989) *Economy, Community and Lifestyle*, Cambridge University Press;

How to use this book

The subject matter of this book is to occupy you for four weeks. There are seven chapters. You should work through two chapters and the associated Readings in each of the first three weeks, leaving one chapter for the fourth week when you will be writing your TMA. As in the two previous books, the exercises are intended to be an integral part of the course. Some are intended to let you check that you have understood the main points of a particular passage. Others invite you to think about a problem in advance of reading the discussion of it in the book; these exercises are open-ended in the sense that there is likely to be no obviously right answer, so if you find yourself following a line of thought different from the discussion in the book, you should not assume that you have gone wrong somewhere.

Before you embark on the book spend a little time thinking about this problem.

A PRELIMINARY EXERCISE

> After the destruction of (almost) all human life in some global catastrophe – nuclear holocaust or celestial collision – one human being alone is left alive. He is the last man; there will not be any more, ever; and he somehow knows this. All the members of other species of sentient creature have also expired. He has a flame-thrower which is still working, so he spends his last hours or days destroying what he can of the still flourishing plant life, including some fine oaks.

Keeping within the stated assumptions – especially that he really is, and knows he is, the last man – what would be your moral judgement of the last man's behaviour? What does your judgement tell you about your view of the value of nature?

9

STUDY OBJECTIVES

By the end of Weeks 13–16 you should:

- Have understood the variety of ways in which nature and natural objects can be valued.

- Have a good knowledge and understanding of the opposition between radically different philosophical positions concerning the value of nature.

- Be able to offer arguments for and against the main positions discussed.

- Have had practice in the analysis and critical assessment of arguments.

- Have become acquainted with a variety of kinds of writing in environmental philosophy.

Study plan

The reading for each week is outlined below. It might be a good idea, before you start work, to put the bookmark at the end of each week's reading, so that you can see where you are aiming to get to.

Study Week	Chapters	Readings
Week 13	Chapters 1 and 2	(1) Routleys (2) Norton (3) Wilson (4) Pearce et al. (5) Pearce (9) Howarth* (16) Verses*
Week 14	Chapters 3 and 4	(6) Hardin (7) Mackie (8) O'Neill (9) Howarth (16) Verses*
Week 15	Chapters 5 and 6	(10) Taylor (11) Mill (12) Rolston
Week 16	Chapter 7 Revision test	(13) Naess (14) Plumwood (15) Fox (16) Verses*

*Readings marked (*) are either optional or read only in part.

The scope of this book and some suggestions for further reading

This book is not intended to be, and certainly is not, a comprehensive survey of environmental philosophy, nor even of environmental ethics. It is about one fundamental question: whether a concern with human well-being is an adequate basis for environmental ethics. So, in addition to the suggestions for further reading given in the separate chapters, here are some suggestions for general reading over the whole area.

A good general introduction, clearly written, is J.R. Des Jardins, *Environmental Ethics: an introduction to environmental philosophy*, Wadsworth, 2nd edn, 1997. A seminal work, by the American conservationist Aldo Leopold, is *A Sand County Almanac*, Oxford University Press, 1949, the last section of which, 'The land ethic', is the source of much subsequent philosophical writing on ecology and ethics. Two big, comprehensive, collections of readings representing a wide variety of views and problems are: *Environmental Philosophy* edited by Michael E. Zimmerman, Prentice Hall, 1993; and *The Ethics of the Environment* edited by Andrew Brennan, Dartmouth Publishing Company, 1995. A shorter collection of articles, mostly good and all in some way relevant to this book, is *Environmental Ethics,* edited by Robert Elliot, Oxford University Press, 1995.

CHAPTER I

Environments and Environmental Ethics

OBJECTIVES

When you have worked through this chapter you should:

- Appreciate some different aspects of the meaning of 'environment'.
- Have a grasp of what it means to ascribe *independent moral status* to a being.
- Understand the division between 'lighter' and 'deeper' green approaches to environmental ethics.

Environments

There is no such thing as *the* environment. As its derivation suggests (see any standard dictionary) the term is a relative one, meaning 'surroundings'. There is always to be understood some thing that is surrounded. An environment is always an environment of ... Consider the environment of a domestic cat. Its immediate environment is the household in which it spends most of its time, awake or asleep (when vets recommend environmental flea control they mean spray the house, not just the cat), but its environment is, more accurately, the area over which it ranges and the features of that area that affect the cat in some way, providing sources of food, opportunities for mating, challenges (rival cats, cars), safe places to sleep, and exciting places to prowl, skip and generally brisk about the life. Strictly speaking two cats in the same area do not have identical environments because each is part of the other's. Less strictly they can be said to share an environment because most of the features of the area affect each of them in the same way.

To speak of an environment in this way is to speak of it as a set of resources. That is to emphasize one side of a two-way relationship. The other side is the impact that individuals or populations have on their environment, and unavoidably – since that environment contains other living things – on the environments of those living things. When we speak of the environment we need to have in mind *whose* environment we mean. This is important because what improves a locality as the environment of one kind of organism, may spoil the environment of another. Draining a pond may be good for human beings but bad for mosquitoes.

The distinction between a creature's effect on its environment and the environmentalist's effect on the creature is not the only one we can make. Two aspects of an organism's relation to its environment are adaptation and familiarity. By 'adaptation' I mean the greater or lesser extent to which its surroundings are ones in which it is equipped, as a biological entity with a particular evolutionary pedigree, to flourish. This emphasizes the environment as a set of resources; an organism depends on its environment for the provision of its needs – a cat needs an environment in which there are small rodents and/or dollops of cat food – and any place with these resources will do as well as any other. But familiarity is importantly different. Animals that move around and whose movements are guided by their perception of their surroundings need to know their way around. A cat's environment, in an important sense, is not just the area in which its needs are met, but the area that it knows its way around. This relationship is a very particular one: it is to *this* place, not just to *a* place with these features.

Boundaries. Where do environments end? Where does my environment end? The answer depends on which aspect one has in mind. The area in which I feel at home, move around with ease, knowing its landmarks, may be quite small, say a few square miles. At the other extreme the area on which I depend for continued existence is very large, extending at least to the earth, with its atmosphere, soils, waters and living things – the *biosphere*. This comes close to saying that there is such a thing as *the* environment, but not quite. For one thing, this all-inclusive sense does not supersede the restricted local environments which remain important for the lives of particular individuals and groups. For another, we are still using 'environment' as a relative term – relative to particular individuals or groups. The biosphere is many environments, for the relation in which any individual, population or species stands to the biosphere is particular to it.

Throughout this book I shall try to keep in mind the relative nature of the term by avoiding the expression 'the environment' except in contexts where it refers to the global system which all living things share.

Environmental ethics

What is environmental ethics? Ethics is concerned with individuals and groups as subjects and objects of actions, that is as doers and as things to which things are done. Traditionally it has been most concerned with human beings as subjects and objects of doings. Many accounts present recent developments as extending this concern in stages, first to non-human animals, next to living things generally, and on to wholes such as populations, plant communities, ecosystems, lakes, streams and mountains; the move to each stage being more radical and problematic than the last. On this account environmental ethics begins where the ethics of concern for animals leaves off. But that is somewhat arbitrary: are not animals part of one's environment? Is it not more sensible to say that environmental ethics incorporates the ethics of animal concern?

Having accepted that, one might be struck by the thought that other human beings are also part of one's environment. Does that mean that environmental ethics incorporates the ethics of human concern? If so, environmental ethics becomes indistinguishable from ethics. But in practice it is convenient to recognize a subdivision of the field of ethics that is concerned with the rights and wrongs of our treatment of the non-human.

There is, however, another point that is worth bearing in mind. We have become in the recent past increasingly aware of the way in which living things form intricate relationships of interdependence within their shared environment. The saying 'It is impossible to do only one thing' draws attention to the often unpredictable ramifications of the effects of our actions. The implication for ethics that I want to point out is this: an environmentally informed ethics is one that takes full account of the fact that an individual organism, of whatever kind, is embedded in its environment, and gives full weight to this in deliberating about actions that are likely to affect the organism.

Thus environmental ethics considers not only natural, but also urban environments: how human beings are affected physically, mentally and spiritually by the design and materials of the buildings in which they live and work, the layout of cities, provision of public services, and so on. Cities, it should be remembered, are not only human environments, so a more comprehensive environmental view considers their effect on foxes and plane trees.

Environmental problems

The variety of environments is matched by the variety of problems that can be termed 'environmental'. Someone playing loud music near by can be an environmental problem if it is heard as an unwelcome intrusion. It is a problem because it causes distress and prompts the question 'What is to be done about it?' For there to be a problem there needs to be some feature of an environment that is seen as undesirable, and someone for whom it raises the practical question 'How can it be removed?' The spread of bracken on the Cumbrian fells is a problem (at least in part) because it reduces the area that can be grazed, and because it raises the question 'How can it be halted or reversed?'

Environmental problems can be quite local, like that one; indeed, even more local, like a loose slate that allows unwanted rainwater to spoil the fabric of my house. They can also be far-reaching, like the smog produced by large-scale forest fires. And, at the extreme, they can be global in extent like the effects on the earth's atmosphere of the emission of carbon dioxide. Such far-reaching problems constitute problems because of the harmful effects on human beings, though not only on human beings. Other species may be, and almost certainly will be in most cases, adversely affected, and that may be seen as part of the problem. Many of the most threatening environmental changes are brought about, intentionally or otherwise, by human agency. Intentional changes include such things as the rerouting or damming of rivers, the drainage of marshes, forest clearance for agricultural purposes, and so on. Unintentional changes include the pollution of air, soil and water by industrial emissions (where the act of emitting certain substances into the atmosphere or into a river is intentional, but its consequences not intended, or even foreseen), and the destruction of animal and plant populations (by forest clearance, for example). But changes not brought about by human activity at all can be seen as undesirable from some point of view. Whatever brought about the destruction of the dinosaurs – some cataclysmic change in their environment – was certainly a bad thing from the dinosaur point of view. It is debatable how much effect human activities have on climate changes, but certainly there are large-scale environmental changes, of which climate changes is one, which are independent of human activity. Such change may none the less raise problems for human beings. The causal origin of a change – whether or not it was brought about by human action – is irrelevant. The relevant considerations are whether a change has harmful effects on human (or non-human) beings, and whether human beings can do something about these effects. It is important to note here that the problem consists of three questions (a) are the effects really harmful? (b) can we do anything about them, either by controlling the changes or by remedying their effects? (c) if we can is it morally incumbent on us to do so?

I think it is fair to say that environmental ethics has been unduly crisis oriented. Its growth in recent years has certainly accompanied rising consciousness of, and anxiety about, the serious threats to human well-being, and, on the part of many, to the well-being of other species, posed by pollution and the destructive exploitation of natural resources. At least in the public consciousness there has been a tendency to concentrate on supposedly imminent catastrophes. (But not only global catastrophes; there is also gloom at the degradation of the countryside, the encroachment of concrete, as expressed in Philip Larkin's despairing poem 'Going, Going' (see Reading 16).) It is certainly good that people should become more aware of the ways in which humans and other beings can be harmed by actions which in themselves may be beneficial, but which disturb the unobvious mechanisms by which living things are supported. It may be a good thing that people should be scared into changing their behaviour by the threat of catastrophe (though there are dangers in crying wolf). But environmental ethics, though stimulated by crises, is not fundamentally concerned with what ought to be done in critical situations. What then is it concerned with?

The range of environmental concern

So far I have characterized environmental ethics as concerned with the relationship between morally aware subjects and the objects in their environments; with the latter considered as themselves having environments, that is, as beings-in-environments. But it won't do to leave it there. There is a significant narrower conception that needs to be recognized. So far I have said nothing to delimit the objects with which environmental ethics is concerned. Human beings, yes, other animals, yes, living things generally, yes – but nothing so far has been excluded. But for some of its practitioners it is conceived of as concerned with the natural world, with what is of value in nature, and with how the recognition of value in nature should regulate human behaviour. This is a narrower conception of environmental ethics, and one which raises some difficult questions. 'What should we understand by "nature"?' is one. This is a question that will be discussed at some length later in the book (especially in Chapter 6). For the present we can say that nature or the natural world is often understood to be the world of living things other than human, and their non-living setting.

Thus conceived, environmental ethics has to do with working out the principles that should govern human dealings with the natural world – what duties we have to refrain from harming or to protect from harm or to actively promote the good of ... – of what?

I'm going to borrow from Mary Midgley a convenient list of kinds of things, other than normal adult human beings, concerning which we may have duties.

Human sector	The dead
	Posterity
	Children
	The senile
	The temporarily insane
	The permanently insane
	Defectives, ranging down to 'human vegetables'
	Embryos, human and otherwise
Animal sector	Sentient animals
	Non-sentient animals
Inanimate[1] *sector*	Plants of all kinds
	Artefacts, including works of art
	Inanimate but structured objects – crystals, rivers, rocks, etc.
Comprehensive	Unchosen groups of all kinds, including families and species
	Ecosystems, landscapes, villages, warrens, cities, etc.
	Countries
	The biosphere
Miscellaneous	Oneself
	God

(Midgley (1983) in Elliot, R. (ed.) (1995), p.97)

This list of objects regarding which we may have duties, or have some sort of responsibility to treat as if they matter in some way and for some reason, raises a question that is answered in different ways by different parties within the ranks of those interested in working out the principles of environmental ethics (not confined to professional philosophers). The question is: 'Which of these kinds of thing have a claim to be considered *in their own right*?'

Independent moral status

The sort of distinction that is in question has been considered earlier, in Book 2, Chapter 3, where you were asked to consider two rather different arguments for the view that we have only indirect duties to animals. Each argument conceded that there are things that it is wrong to do to an animal but tried to show that the reason for holding the action to be wrong would be that it entailed a failure of duty owed to some human being or to humanity at large. Much as I can have a duty to post a letter, but not because I have a duty to the letter, so I can have a duty to feed the cat, but not because I have a duty to the cat. I have say promised you that I will post your letter, or that I will feed your cat, and so the duty in either case is a duty to you. Or I can have a duty to feed my own cat, not because I have a duty to the cat but because I have a duty to humanity at large to encourage myself to care for things I have taken on. The arguments in question were intended to show that animals can enter the moral arena only on the back of human beings, not on their own feet. In the absence of some relationship to human beings, letters and cats would not claim my attention from a moral point of view. The point may be made in this way: when I contemplate some action there is a whole array of other beings which it may affect. Some of these other beings *matter*: that is, how they are affected determines whether the action is right or wrong. Beings of some sorts matter in a way that can be explained only by reference to the way in which beings of some other sort are affected; but some matter in a way that requires no such further reference to explain why they matter: they matter in themselves. A list of the beings I need to consider in deciding whether to go ahead need include only items of the second sort, for in considering them I will automatically take account of what matters about the way my action affects beings of the first sort. The beings in this necessary list – those whose claim to be considered is independent of the claims of any other beings – are the ones that have a claim to be considered *in their own right*. Philosophers use various quasi-technical phrases to describe such beings, they may be said to be 'morally considerable', to have 'moral standing', or have 'independent moral status'.

The first two of the phrases I have just mentioned have some currency and you may well come across them in your further reading on the subject, but both have drawbacks. Take 'considerable': if you say that something is a considerable weight or has considerable importance you imply that it is really quite heavy or more than slightly important. To call a being morally considerable however is not intended to convey any degree of importance, but only to identify the being as one to be considered in a particular way. 'Considerable' means 'eligible for consideration', or perhaps more strongly, 'deserving of consideration'. Since this distinction is an important one it is a pity to use a term that blurs it. ('Standing' has gained currency, I believe, because of the work of the American lawyer and philosopher, Christopher Stone (Stone (1974)). The term has a particular use in the legal parlance of the US. To have standing is to be recognized by the court as entitled to make pleas in person or through a representative. Stone argues that it would be a good idea to grant legal standing to natural objects, for then it would not be necessary to show, for example, that other users of a stream are harmed in order to get a court to grant an injunction against someone who was polluting it. The notion of moral standing is a metaphorical application of this legal term. It has the merit of suggesting that a being is an independent source of claims; it has the defect, for many, of being an extension of an unfamiliar technical term. In what follows I shall use the phrase 'independent moral status', for which I make no claim to neatness.

Terminology apart, the important thing to note about being independently eligible for consideration is that it is not the possession of some *degree* of value, it is not a matter of being more or less eligible. Something is either independently eligible for consideration or it is not.

The question now is: 'To what categories of being is it correct to ascribe independent moral status?' We need some reason for attributing it. There must be some characteristic (a 'status-conferring' characteristic) or set of them that makes direct moral consideration appropriate. In Book 2 you were introduced to three quite different views about this. According to one, only human beings have this status; according to a second, all and only sentient beings have it; according to a third, subjects of a life have it. The first view needs to be clarified: being human is not usually offered as the status conferring characteristic; rather it is supposed that human beings are the most commonly encountered beings who possess some status conferring characteristic such as rationality. On any of these views most of the items on Midgley's list are excluded and can be considered only in relation to those beings that possess independent status. So, for instance, someone who, like Singer, regards sentience as the status conferring characteristic, will consider non-sentient things such as trees as having moral significance only insofar as they contribute in some way to the well-being of sentient things.

Is it important to draw this distinction? At one point Mary Midgley seems to say it is not:

> To speak of duties *to* things in the inanimate and comprehensive sectors of my list ... expresses merely that there are suitable and unsuitable ways of behaving in given situations. People have duties *as* farmers, parents, consumers, forest dwellers, colonists, species members, shipwrecked mariners, tourists, potential ancestors, and actual descendants, etc. As such,

> it is the business of each not to forget his transitory and dependent position, the rich gifts which he has received, and the tiny part he plays in a vast, irreplaceable and fragile whole.
>
> (Midgley, op. cit., p.101)

Consider the duties someone has *as* a farmer. Let us suppose that these include the duty to maintain the fertility of the soil, not to reduce biodiversity by grubbing up hedges, not to spoil the quality of the landscape by removing old buildings or erecting structures that are not in harmony with it (a list that would perhaps appeal more to conservationists than to farmers). If we ask what are the grounds for these duties it is apparent that the reasons for concern are different and not all related to human interests in the same way, or perhaps not at all. Maintaining the fertility of the soil is important because soil is a human resource, preserving landscape character is important for our sense of the historical continuity of a lived-in place. Biodiversity – why is that important? Does the maintenance of diverse animal and plant communities serve some interest of human beings (because of the possibility, for instance, that some inconspicuous plant species may turn out to have medicinal properties)? That such reasons are often urged against actions that result in loss of biodiversity implies that concluding something ought to be done because it benefits human beings has sufficient force to make it a justifying reason that will be widely recognized as such. But some conservationists would claim that we should care about biodiversity independently of its benefits to human beings, and this seems to imply that such non-human communities are owed consideration in their own right.

So it is not enough to say that speaking of duties to things merely expresses that there are suitable and unsuitable ways of behaving in given situations. This is to overlook the fact that behaviour can be suitable or unsuitable in different ways. Mary Midgley makes the point herself two paragraphs later when, speaking of the duties one has to one's country:

> Here the language of *fatherland* and *motherland,* which is so widely employed, indicates rightly a duty of care and responsibility which can go very deep, and which long-settled people commonly feel strongly. *To insist that it is really only a duty to the exploiting human beings is not consistent with the emphasis often given to reverence for the actual trees, mountains, lakes, rivers and the like which are found there.*
>
> (Ibid., p.102; my italics in the final sentence)

So it seems that it does matter that we not only have a duty not to pollute a lake – that this is unsuitable behaviour – but that it is *to the lake* that we owe this duty.

If this distinction between beings that have and beings that lack independent moral status were not important it would be difficult to understand the fact that philosophers and activists within the environmental movement have divided over the question whether our responsibilities towards our environments are ultimately responsibilities to human beings or are to non-human entities directly. One important reason for this division is that there is a division over what entities have independent moral status.

Shades of green

We will now look at this division within the environmental movement. In 1973 one of the founding fathers of environmental philosophy, the Norwegian philosopher Arne Naess published a short paper called 'The Shallow and the Deep, long-range Ecology Movement' (Naess (1973).

As a result of Naess's influence, the terms 'shallow' and 'deep' have become common currency amongst environmentalists. A shallow position is one that reduces concern for the environment to concern for the interests of human beings. A deep view is one that is committed to 'the equal right to live and blossom' of all forms of life. The use of this pair of terms is unfortunate. As applied to thought, shallow is bad and deep good, so anyone who wishes to defend a shallow view seems self-condemned by the very label. Alternative labels that are sometimes used are 'reform' and 'radical' environmentalism. But another alternative ready to hand is the term 'green', which allows us to speak of light green and deep green variants. This has the advantage over the shallow/deep terminology of having less prejudicial overtones, and the advantage over the reform/radical terminology of suggesting the possibility of degrees, intermediate positions between light and deep green ones.

First, the shallow or, less prejudicially, the reform or light green approach, as a practical approach to environmental problems, can be summarized in four propositions:

Light green environmentalism

LG1   Environmental problems are identified as changes in some environment, local or global, whether brought about by human action or not, that pose a danger to human health, comfort or even survival – in short, to human well-being.

LG2   Where these changes can be controlled or reversed, any human being has reason to act in ways that will help avert the threatened harm; these will include changes in personal behaviour and supporting collectively adopted measures.

LG3 Human well-being is intimately tied up with the well-being of many other individual things, either because they are useful to us or because we care about them directly; consequently they are protected by actions designed to secure human well-being.

LG4 Since only human beings have independent moral status, the protection afforded to non-humans as a consequence of their mattering to humans is all the protection it makes sense to demand.

A note of explanation is needed of the phrase 'has reason to act' in LG2. If some change poses a danger to my well-being, then the reason I have to act is a self-interested or prudential reason. If it poses a danger to *others* but not to me then I may have a moral reason, but not a prudential reason, to act. It is possible to have both kinds of reason for the same act, for instance when some practice harms all the members of some group of which I am a member.

The four propositions define a position at one extreme end of the light green–deep green range.

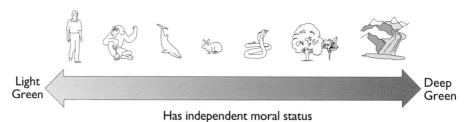

Light Green ⟵ ⟶ Deep Green

Has independent moral status

Its most fundamental feature is its restriction of independent moral status to human beings. At the opposite extreme is a position which accords independent moral status to all living things, and not merely to individual living things but to populations and species; and even to comprehensive entities that include both living and non-living elements ('rivers (watersheds), landscapes, cultures, ecosystems, "the living earth"' Naess (1989)). This deepest position may be characterized in three propositions:

Deep green environmentalism

DG1 Problems are identified as changes in some environment that pose danger to anything within this unrestricted field.

DG2 Action to prevent these dangers requires that human agents recognize duties much more extensive than those recognized by traditional moralities which accord independent moral status only to human beings.

Exponents of deep green positions – ones near the extreme – often maintain that traditional morality is inadequate as a resource for solving environmental problems. The reason they give is that LG4 of the light green position is false. In its place they propose:

> DG3   Living things and natural systems (at least those which contain living things) matter in themselves: that is, have independent moral status.

The last man

In the same year that Naess's paper was published, 1973, the Australian environmentalist and philosopher Richard Routley published a paper asking, 'Is there a need for a new, an environmental, ethic?'[2] His answer is that there is. The reason for insisting on the need for a *new* ethic is that, according to Routley, the dominant ethical tradition in the Western world holds, as a core belief, that only human beings have independent moral status, matter in themselves. This belief is often called 'anthropocentrism'[3] or – Routley's preferred expression – 'human chauvinism'.

The Routleys quote, as a representative expression of human chauvinism, and 'a core principle of Western ethics', the following:

> The liberal philosophy of the Western world holds that one should be able to do what he wishes, providing (1) that he does not harm others and (2) that he is not likely to harm himself irreparably.
>
> (Routley and Routley (1980), p.117)

This should remind you of Mill's 'one very simple principle' (see Book 1, Chapter 3). Though the Routleys' and Mill's principles are not identical it will not be misleading to use the name by which Mill's principle is known: the 'harm principle'.

The Routleys concede that this principle imposes real restrictions on the freedom of human beings to deal with the environment as they please: for example, the farmer's polluting of a community stream may be ruled immoral on the grounds that it physically interferes with others who use or would use the stream. But they argue that the restrictions it imposes are not sufficient for an environmental ethic. For those restrictions are not for the sake of any non-human object directly. The harm principle itself entails a denial of independent moral status to non-human beings. If *only* harm to human beings need limit a human agent's freedom to do as he or she pleases, then only human beings matter in themselves, and other things matter only insofar as harming them is in some way harming human beings. The following principle (call it the 'value principle'), which spells out this implication of the harm principle, is also said by the Routleys to be a core principle of Western ethics:

> Only those objects which are of use or concern to humans (or persons), or which are the product of human (or person) labour or ingenuity, are of value; thus these are all that need to be taken into account in determining best choice or best course of action, what is good, etc.
>
> (Routley and Routley (1980), p.119)

Their argument for the dominant ethical tradition of the West being insufficient for an environmental ethic consists in the presentation of counter-examples, actions which are wrong – and which are *manifestly* wrong – but are not condemned by these anthropocentric core principles. They offer several counter-examples, of which I shall quote two.

> The *last man* example. The last man (or person) surviving the collapse of the world system lays about him, eliminating, so far as he can, every living thing, animal or plant (but painlessly if you like, as at the best abattoirs). What he does is quite permissible according to basic chauvinism, but on environmental grounds is wrong. Moreover one does not have to be committed to esoteric values to regard Mr Last Man as behaving badly and destroying things of value (the reason being perhaps that radical thinking and values have shifted in an environmental direction in advance of corresponding shifts in the formulation of fundamental evaluative principles).
>
> (Ibid., p.124)

> The *vanishing species* example. Consider the blue whale, a mixed good on the economic picture. The blue whale is on the verge of extinction because of his qualities as a private good, as a source of valuable oil and meat. The catching and marketing of blue whales does not harm the whalers; it does not harm or physically interfere with others in any good sense, though it may upset them and they may be prepared to compensate the whalers if they desist; nor need whale hunting be wilful destruction... The behaviour of the whalers in eliminating this magnificent species of whale is accordingly quite permissible – at least according to basic chauvinism.
>
> (Ibid., pp.123f.)

On being presented with these examples, the Routleys expect most of us to agree that the last man and the whalers act wrongly. The method of argument used here is a common one, and one that you are familiar with from Book 2: if from a general moral principle it is possible to infer a particular moral judgement that is false, then the general principle must be false. This is a species of the **absurd consequences move**.

absurd consequences move

So the argument, if sound, refutes both principles, shows them to be false or untenable. But does it have any *positive* result, that is, establish that something is *true?* It does, by virtue of a very elementary piece of logic. If some proposition is false, then its denial or negation must be true. So if an argument demonstrates the falsity of a proposition, then it also demonstrates the truth of the negation of that proposition. Put 'It is not the case that ...' in front of each of the principles claimed to be refuted by the Routleys' argument and you have the propositions whose truth is established by the argument, if it is **sound**.   **sound argument**

What does the Routleys' argument establish if it is sound, what does it commit us to?

> That some actions are wrong even though they harm no human being (the negation of the harm principle).

> That some things are of value and must be taken into account even though they are not of use or concern to human beings (the negation of the value principle).

So we have to move beyond human chauvinism, and grant that some non-human beings have independent moral status, but how far beyond? The Routleys' examples display one of the fundamental concerns of environmentalism: the preservation of diversity of species, plants and animals. This concern for biodiversity leads them to go well beyond independent moral status for humans, and to include all living things (see p.30).

Resisting the argument

The Routleys' claim, in brief, is that Western ethics, or at least the dominant tradition of Western ethics, is human-centred, and because of that cannot provide grounds for condemning the actions of the last man. But what the last man does is wrong, so a new ethic is needed.

According to the Routleys the dominant Western ethical tradition is committed to the following arguments, the first premise of each being a core principle, expressing that ethic's human-centredness.

Argument A

Premise 1	No human action is wrong unless it harms some human being (the harm principle).
Premise 2	The last man's action harms no human being.
Conclusion	So the last man does nothing wrong.

Argument B

Premise 1   Only objects of use or concern to humans are of value (the value principle).

Premise 2   The last man destroys nothing of use or concern to humans.

Conclusion   So the last man destroys nothing of value.

Their own argument – the counter-example argument – can be summarized as follows.

Argument C

Premise 1   The last man acts wrongly.

Premise 2   The last man's action harms no human being.

Conclusion   So it is not the case that no human action is wrong unless it harms some human (the negation of the harm principle).

Argument D

Premise 1   The last man destroys something of value.

Premise 2   The last man destroys nothing of use or concern to humans.

Conclusion   So it is not the case that only objects of use or concern to humans are of value (the negation of the value principle).

EXERCISE 1

Human-centred responses to the last man argument

How might a defender of a human-centred ethics respond to the Routleys' use of the last man argument? Briefly note down as many responses as you can. Then consider the five responses below and, along with the ones you have noted, assess how effective they are as a challenge to the Routleys' claim.

1   Western ethics isn't chauvinist. One of its principles is that we should care for nature.

2   The situation of the last man is a completely fantastic hypothetical situation. No useful moral lessons can be derived from such unreal situations.

3   What the last man does is wrong, even though there are no more human beings to be harmed, but not because the plants, animals and natural systems he destroys are of value: it is an act of vandalism – wanton destructiveness – so not something that any virtuous or right-thinking person would do, even in that extreme situation.

4   The counter-example is not a counter-example. The arguments attributed
    to Western ethics are both **sound** – they are valid and have true premises
    – so their conclusions are true: the last man does not act wrongly, he
    destroys nothing of value.

sound argument

5   It is not the case that the last man harms no human being, for he harms
    himself, or that he destroys nothing of use or concern to human beings, for
    what he destroys is of use or concern to at least one human being, so it is
    not true that on a human-centred ethic he does nothing wrong.

DISCUSSION

1   This response is a rejection of a factual, historical, claim. The claim that
we need, to address environmental rights and wrongs, a 'new' ethics – new that
is in being a departure from traditional Western ethics – depends upon the
truth of the claim that at least the dominant strand of that tradition is human
centred, and supporting this claim would require historical evidence. But the
Routleys' philosophical argument can be stated in a way that is independent of
historical claims: an environmental ethics (an ethics that is adequate to guide
our behaviour towards the non-human world) cannot be based on human-
centred principles. If the philosophical argument is sound, then *if* the historical
claim is true, they are justified in saying that the ethic that is needed is new. So
this response is a weak one.

2   This response is debatable. Philosophers are divided over the relevance of
so-called 'desert island' examples – asking what it would be right or wrong to
do in some far-fetched hypothetical situation. Some hold that moral principles
are designed to guide us in the common run of situations and should not be
expected to give a definite answer to what is the right action in extraordinary
situations. Others, on the contrary, hold that moral principles, as general
principles, can be tested by asking what decisions they dictate in hypothetical
situations, and that artificially devised situations can provide good test cases.
Creating such artificial situations is often called a **thought experiment**. The

thought experiment

point of hypothetical examples is usually to isolate some factor in order to
discover whether it is relevant to a moral judgement. In the last man case, the
point is to eliminate effects on human beings in order to see whether that
removes any reason for saying that the last man does anything wrong. If it
doesn't, then there is some reason to think that in everyday cases where similar
destructiveness is judged to be wrong, its effects on human beings are not the
only reason for so judging it. Perhaps uses of artificially devised examples
should be judged on their individual merits. In this case it does seem that the
last man example concentrates the mind on the different reasons we may have
for deploring the destruction of features of the environment. If we are
perplexed by the question whether he does wrong, that may be a productive

perplexity. So I think it would be a mistake to refuse to consider the question because it is far-fetched.

3   This response needs some discussion. It may be suggested that a traditional principle of Western ethics forbids wanton destruction and condemns those who indulge in it as vandals, and that 'it is very natural to extend [this principle] to the destruction of nature as well as to works of art or forms of property. The man who cuts his name on a redwood is being a vandal, just as much as the man who scratches his initials on the portico of Wells cathedral' (Passmore (1974), p.125). The defender of human-centred ethics might then point to this principle, the no destruction principle, as one that condemns the actions of the last man without the need to introduce 'new' principles. She would be claiming that the harm principle covers only one way in which an action can be wrong – acts of vandalism, even if they do no harm to human beings, are wrong as manifestations of a vicious disposition. She thus rejects Premise 1 of Argument A, the harm principle, and she can therefore deny that the argument establishes its conclusion that the last man does nothing wrong. In response, the exponent of a 'new' ethics can ask whether the objection to vandalism is independent of the value of the things that the vandal destroys. Typically the cry of 'Vandal!' goes up when newly planted trees in a park are mutilated, when paintings in an art gallery are slashed, and similar atrocities. These are cases in which what is destroyed is undoubtedly of value to human beings. We may also deplore mindless acts of destruction when what is destroyed is of negligible value; for instance, we may discourage children from swiping the heads off buttercups, despite the fact that the damage is hardly noticeable and not lasting. But perhaps our only reason for discouraging such harmless destructiveness is that, as a habit, destructiveness is likely to be indiscriminate, and so lead to the destruction of things of value. But if so, then can we really think it matters how destructive the last man is, when there is going to be no one to regret the loss of what he has destroyed, nor to suffer the consequences of his spoiling his character? If we still condemn him, is this not on the basis of a principle whose point has lapsed in the last man's extraordinary circumstances? The exponent of a new ethics can then urge that if we persist in claiming that wanton destructiveness is still wrong in these circumstances, we must believe that the plants that the last man destroys have a kind of value that does not depend upon their being of use or concern to human beings. So it is not clear that this is an effective response.

biting the bullet

4   This response might seem to be the best for the defender of a human-centred ethic. He does best to **bite the bullet**. The last man doesn't act wrongly. He destroys nothing of value. Notice that the Routleys' argument *starts* from moral premises that contradict these two claims. The defender of

a human-centred ethic can simply refuse to accept that there is anything absurd in the conclusions drawn from the two 'core' principles. To counter this the exponents of the new ethic need to bring to bear some argument to support the unfavourable judgements they make of the last man's behaviour.

5   The final response may seem unpromising. In making this response the defender of a human-centred ethic commits herself to arguing that the last man does destroy something of value to human beings, and even that at least one human being is harmed by his action. However difficult an undertaking this may seem at first sight, it is a principal aim of this book to indicate the lines on which this position may plausibly be argued.

Getting beyond human chauvinism

If the Routleys' Arguments C and D are merely valid, but their soundness remains uncertain because the crucial second premises may be false, and hence their counter-examples are not counter-examples, then they do not establish any new moral principles. A sound argument, remember, is one which is valid *and* which has true premises. But an argument can be valid even if it has one or more false premises, and in that case the conclusion may be true, but cannot be asserted on the basis of the argument. The last man example, however, serves one useful purpose even if the second premises are not conceded. It clarifies the distinction we have been considering between human-centred and non-human-centred approaches to environmental ethics.

Let us suppose, however, that the Routleys' argument is sound, where then does it get us? The Routleys themselves note that the last man example can readily be modified to take account of the extension of moral status to sentient animals. On a deeper green environmental ethics the last man does wrong even if he harms no sentient animal, human or non-human. The next two paragraphs amplify this point.

Those who defend the moral status of animals have moved beyond a strictly human-centred view, but their position (whether it is like Singer's or Regan's or Hursthouse's – see Book 2) does not commit them to allowing that anything non-animal has independent moral status. Indeed, if either sentience (Singer) or being the subject of a life (Regan) is taken as a *necessary* condition of independent moral status, their position rules out allowing moral status to anything non-animal. On the greenness scale this position is mid-green at best, and not nearly green enough for many environmentalists.

Suppose that the two core principles of Western traditional ethics were modified to take account of the extension of moral status to sentient animals (Singer). The harm principle would be modified by interpreting 'others' to mean not 'other human beings' but 'other sentient beings'. The value principle would replace 'human (or person)' with 'sentient being'. So the hunting of blue whales would now be contrary to the harm principle, and considering only their economic value would be contrary to the value principle. So the vanishing species example would no longer be a counter-example available to the Routleys. The last man example, however, can readily be modified to sustain it as a counter-example to the modified principles. Suppose that the last man is also the last sentient creature on the planet. He sets about destroying, as far as he can, every living thing – plants and non-sentient animals. The deep green argument now is that what he does is permitted by the modified principles, but is wrong according to an environmental ethic.

The modified argument does then take us further beyond chauvinism than either Singer's or Regan's pro-animal position, and represents a radical break with both of them. For both Singer and Regan argue that the reasons we have for granting independent moral status to (most) human beings oblige us, in consistency, to grant it to (some) non-human animals also. So although in practice it may make a huge difference if we accept and act upon the conclusions of Singer's or Regan's arguments, those arguments rely upon drawing out unexpected consequences from moral ideas that we already have. Their strategy is to show that a more adequate understanding of what is valuable about human beings makes us recognize that some non-human animals are valuable in the same way. The Routleys, by contrast, do not attempt to show that principles we already have will be seen, when properly understood, to cover a new range of cases. All Singer and Regan have done, the Routleys might claim, is to tinker with, and retune, our existing moral ideas, whereas they look to new moral principles to ground our new concerns in environmental ethics.

This still leaves open the questions about the range of things that will be allowed to have independent moral status on their view. The argument, as we have seen, has only a quite general positive conclusion: that some non-human and non-animal beings must be counted as having independent moral status. We don't know yet which they are, nor on what grounds the claim to this status might be based. Besides human and non-human animals, the Routleys indicate the range as follows: 'the broader class of natural items such as trees and forests, herbs, grasslands and swamps, soils and waterways and ecosystems' (R. and V. Routley (1980), p.109). That list includes both individuals and collectives, both living things and items which are non-living (though they may contain living things). Theirs is one very deep green theory; other deep green theorists are less inclusive, as we shall see in later chapters. For the purposes of this book the most important division of the green spectrum is threefold:

1   *Light green*: the world of non-human beings, living and non-living, has no independent moral status, but only matters insofar as it matters to human beings (which do have independent moral status).

2   *Mid green*: non-human animals of some species have independent moral status, whether or not they matter to human beings.

3   *Deep green*: some or all of the broad class of natural beings have independent moral status, whether or not they matter to human beings.

The justification problem

Deeper green positions ask us to accept a radical departure from traditional moral attitudes and beliefs. So they raise in an acute form three questions: (a) How can moral principles, or systems of moral principles be validated? (b) On what grounds is a principle acceptable? (c) How can we adjudicate between rival principles or systems?

One way to answer these questions would be by appealing to our most deeply entrenched intuitions. We form general principles on the basis of particular cases and test them by seeing how appropriate they are when applied to new cases. When presented with some general principle we see what judgements it implies in particular cases. If the particular judgements are counter-intuitive we reject the principle. In some instances, however, we may be so confident about a principle that we will put up with judgements of particular cases that seem counter-intuitive: we may not like what the principle commits us to but we **bite the bullet**. The argument we have been considering, the last man argument, makes just such an appeal to intuition. The Routleys take it that their judgement of the last man's behaviour will be shared by many people, noting that 'radical thinking and values have shifted in an environmental direction in advance of corresponding shifts in the formulation of fundamental evaluative principles'. Richard Routley under the name of Richard Sylvan, in *The Greening of Ethics*, speaks of 'deep moral attitudes, drawn out ... by decisive examples, such as that of the Last Person'.[4] The assumption that the shift is in the right direction, that water from a deep well must be pure, seems too confident. As I suggested in discussing the response (4) (pp.28–9) to the Routley argument, some (perhaps many) people will not share the intuition that what the last man does is wrong, in which case there is no need to call into question the harm and value principles. Even if some are initially disposed to share the intuition, they may reject it because they regard the harm and value principles as unassailable. If their sharing that intuition is necessary to their accepting the new principles of an environmental

biting the bullet

ethic, then their failure to share the intuition means it fails to justify those new principles.

If only because of the difficulty of justifying new principles it seems wise to see how far we can get with old ones. It may be that many practical results that would be obtained by adopting new principles which recognized direct obligations to the environment could be obtained equally well by applying traditional principles, even if these are human centred, or at best sentient-animal centred.

In taking this cautious approach we need not prejudge the question whether the deep green position is correct and the only ultimately satisfactory basis for environmental ethics. It certainly seems worthwhile to consider the extent to which it is necessary for human well-being to treat the environment with care and respect because, even if there are other reasons so to treat the environment, this would remain one amongst these others.

READING The question whether a human-centred approach would yield the same practical consequences as the proposed new ethic is given different answers by the authors of the first two readings. Reading 1 is from the Routleys' paper that we have been discussing in this chapter. In this extract they move from grounding their claims on hypothetical (possible world) examples such as the last man to real world examples and argue that traditional (human-centred, instrumental) ethics and new ethics would lead to different actions and policies. The author of Reading 2, Bryan G. Norton, while not denying that a new ethics may be correct, doubts its necessity from a practical point of view because it would not lead to very different actions and policies.

These readings should reinforce your grasp of the difference between the traditional human-centred approach, and the 'new' biocentric approach. But they also look forward to questions that will be discussed in the next chapter. Norton's defence of a human-centred position here depends upon the account he gives of the human or cultural reasons that there are for preserving wildlife and natural ecosystems. As you read the Norton extract note down the varieties of human or cultural value that he distinguishes.

In both readings you will notice the phrase 'intrinsic value', and the view that natural things have intrinsic value. Norton points out that this view is 'extremely difficult to explain clearly', and mentions at least two possible things it could mean. One of them is 'that other species had value even before any conscious valuers emerged on the evolutionary scene'. Recall that the Routleys' last man example is intended to force on us the conclusion that other species would have value after any conscious valuers had *disappeared* from the evolutionary scene. Intrinsic value, understood in this way, is value that something can have even if the world in which it exists contains no beings capable of valuing it. But this is only one of the meanings than can be attached to 'intrinsic value', another sense of the expression will be is discussed in the next chapter.

Now read Readings 1 and 2, pp.163–77.

Conclusion

There is a division among the exponents of environmental ethics between those who think that traditional forms of ethical thought, if refined and critically developed, are all we need to guide our behaviour towards the natural world, and those who think that those traditional forms, at least in the West, are unsatisfactory because they are irredeemably human centred, and that, consequently, a radical departure from traditional forms – a new ethic – is required. I am proposing that in view of the problems involved in establishing new principles it is worthwhile questioning the view that a human-centred ethics is incapable of recognizing environmental values and prescribing appropriate behaviour towards natural objects.

Chapter summary

Speaking of *the* environment can disguise the fact that it is a relative term. It is better to think of an environment as someone's or something's. Several distinctions are important, in particular between a being's effect on its environment, and the effect of its environment on it, and between the environment as that on which a being depends for sustenance and its environment as its particular familiar place.

In its broadest sense environmental ethics is the study of our relations with everything that can be a part of the environment of a moral subject, someone for whom questions of right and wrong can arise. That includes other human beings and the things human beings make, such as machines and cities. A narrower sense is often adopted in which environmental ethics is concerned with only that part of the environment which is called nature – itself a problematic concept.

Philosophers have asked which beings have and which do not have a claim to be considered morally important in their own right. An ethical theory is human centred if it denies such importance – independent moral status – to any but human beings. Some philosophers maintain that no ethical theory can be satisfactory as an account of our moral relations with nature if it restricts independent moral status to human beings.

How green an ethical theory is depends on how far it extends independent moral status beyond the human. The ethics of animal concern escapes human centredness because it accords that status to at least some non-human animals, but deeper green theories extend it to living things in general, or even to collective entities such as species, forests and rivers.

The last man argument, introduced by Richard and Val Routley, is intended to demonstrate the need for new ethical principles: the judgement that the last man's destruction of natural things is wrong would be endorsed by a large number of people nowadays, but what he does seems not to be wrong according to traditional principles of Western ethics. There is however more than one possible response to this argument, including stubborn refusal to agree that there is anything wrong in what the last man does.

In view of the difficulty of justifying wholly new principles it is reasonable to reserve judgement on new, deep green ethical principles until there has been an assessment of the resources of traditional ethical thinking.

Further reading

David E. Cooper is very good on changing ideas of what an environment is in 'The idea of an environment', one of the essays in *The Environment in Question,* edited by David E. Cooper and Joy A. Palmer, Routledge, 1992. Mary Midgley's essay, referred to in this chapter, is included in *Environmental Ethics,* edited by Robert Elliot, Oxford University Press, 1995. The classic work exploring the resources of traditional ethics in approaching environmental issues is John Passmore's *Man's Responsibility for Nature,* Duckworth, 1980 (2nd edn). Richard Routley's essay in which the last man makes his entrance (and destructive exit), 'Is there a need for a new, an environmental, ethic?' is included in *Environmental Philosophy,* edited by Michael E. Zimmerman, Prentice Hall, 1993.

Notes

[1] Midgley's categories suggest a distinction between 'animal' and 'inanimate', and include both living things (plants) and non-living things in the inanimate category. This agrees with one common use of 'inanimate', but there is another use in which the pair animate/inanimate corresponds to the pair living/non-living. According to this use plants would be classed with other living things, not with rocks.

[2] I cite this paper, which was delivered to an international philosophical congress, for the historical record. In what follows I refer to and quote from a much expanded version: Richard and Val Routley, 'Human Chauvinism and Environmental Ethics' (Routley and Routley (1980)).

[3] 'Anthropos' is Greek for a human being, 'human centred' is a precise equivalent of 'anthropocentric'. 'Chauvinism' may be regarded as equivalent to either 'anthropocentrism' or 'human centredness', except that it has a pejorative flavour that is absent from either of the other terms. The pejorative flavour has been transferred from male chauvinism, which inherited it from the original chauvinism, an extreme nationalistic fervour.

[4] Sylvan and Bennett (1994), p.34. Richard Sylvan is the same author, under a different name, as the Richard Routley whose work in collaboration with Val Routley we have been discussing. Val Routley has also changed her name; work by her, written under the name Val Plumwood, will be discussed in Chapter 7.

CHAPTER 2

Environmental Goods and Human Well-being

OBJECTIVES

When you have worked through this chapter you should:

- Have a good grasp of the distinction between instrumental and non-instrumental value and of the relation of each to well-being.

- Understand the argument for saying that environmental goods are not only instrumental goods but in many cases valued for themselves.

- Understand why the pure mental-state account of well-being is inadequate.

- Understand some of the arguments for and against cost benefit analysis as a method of assessing environmental values.

Introduction

This chapter begins the enquiry, to be continued in Chapters 3 and 4, into the question whether a human-centred account of value and morality is a sufficient foundation for environmental ethics. In pursuit of this it expounds a distinction between instrumental and non-instrumental value, and explains the case against the view that well-being consists in agreeable states of consciousness. Some features of their environment are valued by human beings as constituents of their well-being,[1] not only as external means to it. But then the question arises whether this account of environmental values is compatible with cost benefit analysis, a much used method of assessing the overall consequences for their well-being of decisions affecting the environment of numbers of people.

Human centredness – how severely does it restrict our concern for the non-human?

Western ethics is found wanting by the Routleys because, at least in its dominant form, it is human centred. Western ethics is a protean animal, about which it is difficult to generalize. We can probably agree that there have been, and still are, quite widespread moral beliefs that are damaging in their effects on the global environment, and on local environments. The traditional belief that other living things exist for our use, and have no value except their instrumental value to us, and the belief that one can do what one pleases with one's own land are examples. Such beliefs are not uncontested in the history even of Western thought about our relationship with the non-human world, but it remains true that they have been used, and still are, to justify many harmful actions and equally harmful failures to act.

Caution is needed in laying these harmful actions at the door of human-centred ethics. It might be said with equal justice that there are widespread beliefs that are hostile to humanity, or to large portions of it, such as the belief in the superiority of men to women, of one's own race, one's own country, one's own religion. The human centredness that is criticized by many environmentalists is not an ethics of impartial concern for human beings as such, regardless of culture, creed, gender and generation. Advocates of environmentally friendly policies and ways of living sometimes castigate human beings *en masse* as selfish, as though we look after our own at the expense of other species. But it is far from true that we look after our own, if by our own we mean human beings at large. We use up the resources and poison the atmosphere that will be needed by future human beings. The inhabitants of one country export their pollutants to damage the environment of the inhabitants of other countries. Speaking of human beings collectively harming *the* environment can obscure the fact that much environmental damage is a consequence of one group of human beings disregarding the interests of other human beings.

There is an important difference between the propositions, 'All human beings matter' and 'Only human beings matter'. Neither implies the other. Many wrong actions – including ones that damage environments – result from failing to heed the first. The use of the word 'chauvinism' might remind us of what it originally stood for: a virulent form of nationalism, which is hardly compatible with a properly developed ethic of human concern. One of the features of a moral tradition within a culture is that it subjects particular beliefs that are prevalent within the culture to an internal critique. For instance the critique of racist or sexist prejudice can appeal to notions of justice that already exist in traditional moral discourse, but that are in need of interpretation and reformulation. One of the tasks of moral philosophy is to contribute to the process of interpretation.

The application of this line of thought to the present subject is to ask whether human centredness has been too narrowly understood. Are the traditional beliefs about our relation to nature that lead to excessive exploitation, pollution and other evils really justified by an ethics that is centred on human beings?

So the question to ask is, 'Would *a properly developed*, human-centred ethic be an adequate environmental ethic?' (The story is told that when a Western visitor asked Ghandi what he thought of Western civilization, Ghandi replied, 'It would be a good idea'. One might say the same about human-centred ethics.)

Let us look first at the aspect of morality that is concerned with the promotion of human (and animal) well-being. The Routleys' challenge to human chauvinism is that it fails to account for judgements about how we ought to treat non-human things. They consider the possibility that the practical results of traditional (human-centred) and new ethics would be the same.

EXERCISE 2   Re-read Example 2 in Reading 1 (pp.164–5), the one about being noisy in the forest.

1   What is the behavioural difference between the two sorts of people?

2   What does it mean to regard the forest and its inhabitants as a conventional utility?

3   Still looking through human chauvinist eyes, can you see a reason, beyond those given by the authors, for not making a noise?

DISCUSSION   1   The difference is between how the two will behave in the absence of other human beings: respectful silence on the one part and unnecessary noisiness on the other. The absence of other human beings provides the test for the difference in attitude.

2   By 'conventional utility' the Routleys mean something whose value is normally thought of as its usefulness to human beings. The question is whether being useful is the only way in which something can be of value to a human being, which leads to the third question.

3   We might think that by being noisy the walker in the forest is *missing* something, that by keeping his eyes and ears open, by being receptive, rather than imposing himself, he would enjoy a more rewarding experience. Just from the point of view of human well-being there is something to be said for silence.

And from this same point of view there may even be some reason for the last man to find some better way of spending his final hours. Suppose him to be in a woodland glade. The sun is slanting through birches just coming into leaf and there are clumps of native daffodils. There is no birdsong – the birds have all been killed – but there is a breeze stirring the trees. These are things that the last man has always loved, and many before him. Will he want to expire amid the wreck of this scene, having done his worst with a flame-thrower?

These remarks are hardly conclusive; they are intended to hint at a possibility to be explored. The possibility is that from the standpoint of human well-being there is a kind of value to be recognized that is not the same as usefulness. Nature may be necessary to our well-being in ways other than providing things we can use.

Ways nature is necessary to our well-being

There are many ways in which natural things and processes matter to us, and correspondingly many ways in which changes to them, including those we bring about ourselves, affect our well-being for good or ill. One of the most fundamental areas of concern to environmentalists is the diversity of species of organisms on earth (biodiversity). The extinction of species is a process that has been going on for many millennia, quite independent of human activity; but it is greatly accelerated by human activity, for example, by the destruction of rain forest. The increased pace of species extinction is believed by many environmentalists to threaten human interests, and in more than one way. The biologist Edward O. Wilson in the final chapter of *The Diversity of Life* asks why we should care about preservation of biodiversity, and finds that the reasons are not all of the same kind.

Now read the whole of Reading 3, E.O. Wilson's 'The Environmental Ethic' (pp.178–86). Then read it again, more carefully, from the paragraph beginning 'Why should we care?' (p.181). When you have completed the reading, do the following exercise.

READING

Make notes of the different kinds of reason Wilson believes we have to care about the preservation of biodiversity.

EXERCISE 3
'The environmental ethic'

DISCUSSION

One reason is that particular species of animal and plant provide us with medicines, food and raw materials, and loss of biodiversity will almost certainly deprive us of undiscovered sources of these.

A second reason is that it is impossible to predict which organisms will prove to be critically important to the maintenance of the ecosystems which sustain human life.

Wilson does not believe that these are the only reasons, nor does he think that recognizing the importance of nature's 'services' is enough for an enduring environmental ethic. For that leaves open the possibility, or encourages the illusion, that human beings could find substitutes for them, even to the point of constructing artificial environments. Even if that were possible, and Wilson does not commit himself on the feasibility of a 'prosthetic environment', it would ignore the significance of the fact that human beings have evolved alongside diverse other species and that our nature, especially our emotional nature, owes much to our origins and to the history of interaction between our species and others. From the final paragraphs of the reading, in which Wilson gives his examples of *biophilia* (from Greek *bios* = life and *philia* = love/affection/friendship), I venture to elicit two further reasons. But I am aware that other readings may be possible.

The third reason is that to understand ourselves we need the full diversity of the natural world in which the secret of our origins lies.

The fourth reason is that from our evolutionary past we bring emotional needs that can be satisfied only by contact with the natural world (compare 'the connections that human beings subconsciously seek with the rest of life'). Note especially the last of the examples, which reminds us that most of us, if we have the means and leisure, backpack, hunt, fish, birdwatch and garden (though not necessarily all of them).

Instrumental and non-instrumental value

The differences between these reasons are best understood in terms of a distinction that philosophers habitually use, namely between *instrumental* and *non-instrumental value*.

READING

Now read Jane Howarth on instrumental and non-instrumental value and replaceability, Reading 9, pp.229–32.

Consider each of the four reasons above in the light of Howarth's discussion. In each case decide whether Wilson is talking about instrumental or non-instrumental value.

Particular bugs and weeds, as Wilson elegantly puts it, are instrumental in enabling us to fulfil particular purposes that we have. Particular species, as sources of medicine, food or raw material, are things we use, are valued for their causal properties and therefore are in principle replaceable by other species (or synthetic products) that have the same causal properties. So the first reason concerns a straightforward case of instrumental valuing.

More fundamentally, ecosystems are instrumental in sustaining the health or even survival of the human species. We may not be aware that we are part of an ecosystem; it is not like a tool or a material that we consciously use, but all the same we benefit from its existence, and if we come to value it for that reason it is for its causal properties – what it can do for us – that we are valuing it. As for replaceability, it is not as easy to replace an ecosystem as it is to replace a tool. But we can at least *imagine* an artificial environment in which we could live as well as in our present natural one. Insofar as we value the present one *only* instrumentally we have no reason to refuse an artificial substitute.

The third reason also, on the face of it, involves instrumental value. One way of expressing the distinction between the two kinds of value is by use of the phrase 'for the sake of': if one desires/values x for the sake of y then one values x instrumentally. So if one values the diversity of the natural world for the sake of understanding human nature, one is valuing it instrumentally. This is a puzzling case, however, because it does not seem possible even to imagine what a substitute for the actual world would be like for this purpose. The replaceability criterion seems not to apply.

It is only the fourth reason that clearly involves non-instrumental value. The activities that Wilson mentions are engaged in because we want to experience nature for the specific properties it has, not for what we can use it for; we enjoy having it around, or being around it; we contemplate it; we value it for itself. Howarth's observation that the distinction is between kinds of valuing rather than between kinds of object applies here. A thing or an activity may be valued for the sake of some further purpose and also for its own sake, either at different times or by different persons, or simultaneously and by the same person. Hunting may be engaged in for the sake of getting edible prey, but if it is merely that, then a visit to the supermarket will do equally well.

Having introduced this distinction between two kinds of value, or valuing, it is necessary to return briefly to a point of terminology mentioned in Chapter 1 (pp.32–3). The distinction is between valuing things for their usefulness and valuing them for their own sake. Howarth uses the terms 'instrumental' and 'non-instrumental'. I follow this, using 'non-instrumental value' for things insofar as they are valued for their own sake. The term 'intrinsic value' is often used in this sense, but we saw that it is also used in a different sense, that of something having value entirely independently of the existence of anyone who evaluates. The term is frequently used in writings on environmental ethics, often in a way that runs the two senses together. But the two senses are quite different, and to avoid confusion between them it is best not to use the term 'intrinsic value' at all. More will be said about the sense which implies independence of evaluation in an Afterword to the book.

Well-being: conditions and constituents

As part of the discussion of instrumental and non-instrumental value, it is useful to distinguish between things that are necessary conditions of, or conducive to, well-being, and constituents of well-being. Having food to eat, or a roof over one's head, are necessary to one's well-being, but if the food is unappetizing and the roof waterproof but without any other merit, then they are of merely instrumental value; one's well-being depends on, but does not consist in, having such food and such shelter. Among the things that make life good (a value in itself) are having friends and spending time with them, having worthwhile work and getting a kick out of its going well, having an interest, for instance, in the geology of the Lake District or the life cycle of some bug, playing golf or messing about in boats. Hardly a complete list, just some samples. The question is whether these are merely of instrumental value. It seems to me inaccurate to say so. These things, or some similar set, are what a person's life consists in, are its substance, and are what make it go well. They are not instrumental to some further transcending end. They contribute to having a good life by being part of it. And crucially, they are not replaceable. That is to say, for any particular person, the things that he or she values as contributing to a good life are not readily replaceable by other things. Different people value different activities. Golf and tennis, say, may be regarded as alternative recreations, but that is not to say that the golfer can see her favourite sport as replaceable, for her, by tennis, or vice versa. Sometimes one may have to forgo some important constituent of well-being (for example, giving up tennis because of infirmity), and try to make up for its loss or inaccessibility by investing more in something else. This may seem to be accepting the second as a replacement or substitute for the first, but this is not at all the same as the ready intersubstitutivity of instruments, all of which are equivalent as means to an end. You may have to sacrifice personal relationships in order to carry the responsibilities of public office, or vice versa (resigning office in order to spend more time with the family); it is true that the one may come to fill one's life in place of the other, but this is not to say that they are equivalent ways of achieving some further aim – well-being – for personal well-being would just be fulfilling the responsibilities of public office or of engaging fully in family relationships.

For many people, probably for most, some would say for anyone, contact of some kind with the natural world is a *constituent* of the good life. Swimming with dolphins, studying ferns, walking the fells, seeing the cherry trees in bloom; these are among the enormous variety of forms of experiences of the natural world that are valued for their own sake. It is as good in themselves, not as instrumentally good that they contribute to well-being. To these may be added some of Wilson's examples of biophilia. Some of his examples, however, seem to be of spontaneous *reactions* to organisms or natural features, rather than specifically affectionate or favourable responses. Norton's account of how he might get the girl to see a value in sand dollars apart from their commercial value is an attempt to show how they are constituents of the good life (note in particular the impoverishment of experience involved in having a purely consumer relationship to nature – 'the greatest losers will be children who have lost the ability to wonder at wild, living nature' (Reading 2, p.172)).

An objection may be made here to the attempt to construct a human-centred environmental ethic. Let us grant that these are non-instrumentally valuable forms of *experience*. But what about nature itself? The discussion so far, it may be said, goes no way to show that dolphins, ferns, fells and cherry trees have anything more than instrumental value. Enjoying experiences of these things, the objection goes on, is just one more use we make of the natural world to satisfy our desires. We might seem to have confirmed the deep green view that a human-centred ethic cannot properly value environmental goods: we can show that natural features are necessary to our having valuable experiences, and therefore necessary to well-being in a more direct way than clean air; but that does not show that those features themselves are good in themselves, and surely that is what an adequate environmental ethic has to do?

To see whether the deep green position can be avoided we need to press on a little further with the investigation of well-being. One view of well-being is that it consists of having agreeable conscious states. The view known as 'classical' utilitarianism, as propounded, for instance, by Jeremy Bentham (1748–1832) and John Stuart Mill (1806–73), identified well-being with happiness and happiness with pleasure and the absence of pain. Pleasure and pain seem to be paradigms of conscious states of a subject. If I am in pain, or having a pleasant sensation, I am having an experience of a particular sort. The painful or pleasant sensation may be caused by some physical event (e.g. having an injection, eating an ice-cream), but what matters to me is how it feels. Not all their successors have agreed that all desirable experiences can be brought under the headings of pleasure and pain, but it may still seem inevitable that it is the felt quality of conscious life that matters to whether one's life goes well or not. Events and objects outside consciousness are important for well-being only as causes of the experiences within consciousness.

Why might this seem inevitable? Suppose I enjoy looking at a beautiful picture; for instance, one of Constable's cloudscapes. What I enjoy is the aesthetic experience that I get from looking at the painting. It seems that I can separate the experience from its object. True, without the painting I would not have the enjoyable experience, but still the painting is only a condition, not a constituent of the experience. Its value is instrumental only.

In the same way it can be argued that, although we may have experiences that depend on our relationship with the natural world and in some of these nature is the immediate object of the experience, the separation can still be made between the experience and its object; it is the experience that is valuable in itself, the object only instrumentally so.

A consequence of this separability would be that the painting, or the natural object, is only contingently the source of the valued experience. Some device that could simulate the painting, or create the illusion of looking at a natural object, if it produced an experience the subject found indistinguishable from the experience produced by the real thing, would be a satisfactory substitute for it. The substitution would not remove anything of non-instrumental value.

Can this conclusion be resisted? It can. The way to test it is to develop the technology, if not for real, then at least in imagination. The development of virtual reality technology has almost overtaken the 'experience machine', a **thought experiment** conceived by the American philosopher Robert Nozick a quarter of a century ago.

thought
experiment

> Suppose there were an experience machine that would give you any experience you desired. Superduper neuropsychologists could stimulate your brain so that you would think and feel you were writing a great novel, or making a friend, or reading an interesting book. All the time you would be floating in a tank, with electrodes attached to your brain. Should you plug into this machine for life, pre-programming your life's experiences? If you are worried about missing out on desirable experiences, we can suppose that business enterprises have researched thoroughly the lives of many others. You can pick and choose from their large library or smorgasbord of such experiences, selecting your life's experiences for, say, the next two years. After two years have passed, you will

have ten minutes or ten hours out of the tank, to select the experiences of your next two years. Of course, while in the tank you won't know that you're there; you'll think it's all actually happening. Others can also plug in to have the experiences they want, so there's no need to stay unplugged to serve them. (Ignore problems such as who will service the machines if everyone plugs in.) Would you plug in? *What else can matter to us, other than how our lives feel from the inside?*

(Nozick (1974), pp.42f.)

To cater for the special tastes of environmentalists, one of the programs available provides the experience of a journey through a wilderness, devoid of (other) human beings as the best wildernesses are, but otherwise rich in vegetation and a great variety of animal species. All the sensations and emotions that would be experienced in a real wilderness are faithfully replicated. If one were plugged in without knowing it, one would believe oneself to be having a genuine experience of a wilderness.

Well, would you plug in? If not, what would your reasons be for not doing so?

EXERCISE 5

The 'experience machine'

Nozick would not plug in, and he takes his refusal to show something about people generally, since he confidently uses the first person plural.

DISCUSSION

> What does matter to us in addition to our experiences? First, we want to *do* certain things, and not just have the experience of doing them. In the case of certain experiences, it is only because first we want to do the actions that we want the experiences of doing them or thinking we've done them ... A second reason for not plugging in is that we want to *be* a certain way, to be a certain sort of person. Someone floating in a tank is an indeterminate blob. There is no answer to the question of what a person is like who has been long in the tank. Is he courageous, kind, intelligent, witty, loving? It's not merely that it's difficult to tell; there's no way he is. Plugging into the machine is a kind of suicide ...
>
> Thirdly, plugging into an experience machine limits us to a man-made reality, to a world no deeper or more important than that which people can construct. There is no *actual* contact with any deeper reality, though the experience of it can be simulated. Many persons desire to leave themselves open to such contact and to a plumbing of deeper significance.
>
> (Ibid., p.43)

If we agree with Nozick then we have to say that the world being as it is matters to us, not just as a contingent, but in principle replaceable, condition of our having certain valuable experiences, but for itself. Things other than states of mind can be valuable non-instrumentally; objects in the world need not have only instrumental value.

So the result of the thought experiment is that a pure mental state account of well-being is inadequate. If seeing cherry trees in bloom is a constituent of my well-being, then there must be real cherry trees for me to see. Nozick gets to this conclusion by asking what, over and above how something feels from the inside, we want, and says that what we want is to do certain things, to be a certain way, and to be in contact with reality. In each case what is wanted is not a state of mind but a state of the world. This suggests an alternative account of well-being. If well-being is not a succession of blissful mental states, or a succession of mental states at all, then it may be better thought of as *the fulfilment of desire* or, equivalently, as *the satisfaction of preferences*. An account of well-being in terms of fulfilled desire or satisfied preferences is now widely accepted by many philosophers and economists.[2] One advantage of such an account over a mental-state account is that it allows us to acknowledge that states of the world are often essential constituents of well-being. What is required to satisfy the preference for wilderness experience is to experience a real wilderness. If that is one of my settled preferences then the experience machine cannot satisfy it, because it can provide only the illusion not the reality.

If the argument set out in this section is sound then the conclusion is that one of the constituents of well-being for many people – it has not been argued that it must be a constituent for everyone – is experience of nature, where experience is not simply a conscious state but one that corresponds with reality.

EXERCISE 6
Nozick's argument

Lay out as premises and conclusion Nozick's argument for denying that only how our lives feel from the inside matters to us.

Check your answer against the one at the back of the book before reading on.

Weighing goods

Environmental goods are not the only goods, and non-instrumental values in nature not the only constituents of well-being, so conflicts are almost inevitable. The preservation of tropical rain forest competes with the demand for the income that is yielded by its conversion into timber. A cause célèbre of conservation versus development was the Tellico Dam versus the snaildarter in the United States. The Tennessee Valley Authority had almost completed the dam of the Little Tennessee River when conservationists were able to demonstrate that it would have destroyed the only known habitat of a variety of perch. The US Supreme Court stopped the dam under the terms of the Endangered Species Act of 1973, only for the decision to be circumvented by executive action. In north-west England a conflict has arisen over a proposal to impose a 10 mph speed limit on Windermere, a lake which lies within a National Park, a designated area of peace and tranquillity, but which is much used by power-boat enthusiasts and water skiers, whose activities contribute substantially to the economy of the area, and of course to their own enjoyment, but detract from the peace and tranquillity of the lake.

When decisions are made in such cases as these, there are losses and gains, and the losers and gainers may be (but are not necessarily) different people, or species. Decisions have to be made, and that involves somehow weighing the goods lost and gained. The goods that have to be compared are of quite diverse sorts: how does one compare the value of biodiversity with the wealth provided by development, the value of clean energy from the harnessed river with the preservation of a small fish, or the pleasure of power boating with that of quiet contemplation of a beautiful land-and-waterscape?

How can a method be devised by which decisions can be made that will secure the greatest possible good to all those concerned? One of the prime aims of the nineteenth-century utilitarians was to develop a procedure by which alternative social policies could be assessed. Bentham worked out in detail a procedure that consisted in finding out, for each alternative, how much pleasure or pain would be experienced by each person affected, adding together the amounts of pleasure, adding together the amounts of pain, subtracting the latter total from the former, and opting for the policy with the best balance of pleasure over pain. Translating this schematic procedure into a method that can be implemented presents great difficulties. The assumption that pleasure is a uniform feature of different kinds of experience, varying simply in how much of it there is, is questionable. It is unlikely that anyone now could be found to defend it. But the aim of developing a method by which the choice of best policy becomes a matter of calculation, given empirical data about the consequences for those affected, remains very much alive. One important attempt to carry out this aim is cost benefit analysis (CBA), the method developed by economists and often used in environmental decision making.

Like some modern utilitarians, economists regard well-being as desire or preference satisfaction, and they solve the difficulty of comparing different goods by considering them all alike as the objects of desires, whose value to a person is measured by the strength of his or her desire for it. It can plausibly be suggested that the strength of the desire for an object is indicated by how much one would be prepared to spend in time, effort, or other goods, to get it, or, if one has the object already, what one would accept to part with it. Since money represents the exchange value of different goods it provides a universal substitute for expenditure of real goods, as a measure of how much people desire things. The measure of the strength of a person's preference for some good, which in turn is the measure of the contribution the good would make to the person's well-being is *willingness to pay*.

That is the essential basis of the branch of economics which is concerned with planning the use of resources that maximizes desire satisfaction and thus well-being (or welfare, the term most favoured by economists). The environment presents a special problem for economics because environmental goods have economic value, in that they contribute to well-being, but are often not bought and sold, and so do not have a monetary value placed on them by the operation of the market. In consequence environmental goods are often undervalued, and the aim of environmental economics is to remedy that situation by showing how it is possible to place monetary values on the environment.

The need to do this, and the way to do it, were set out in *Blueprint for a Green Economy* (1989), a report commissioned by the Department of the Environment in the UK, prepared by the economist David Pearce and two collaborators. This is what they say in their introduction about valuing the environment:

> One of the central themes of environmental economics, and central to sustainable development thinking also, is the need to place proper values on the services provided by natural environments. The central problem is that many of these services are provided 'free'. They have a zero price simply because no market place exists in which their true values can be revealed through the acts of buying and selling. Examples might be a fine view, the water purification and storm protection functions of coastal wetlands, or the biological diversity within a tropical forest. The elementary theory of supply and demand tells us that if something is provided at a zero price, more of it will be demanded than if there were a positive price. Very simply, the cheaper it is the more will be demanded. The danger is that the greater level of demand will be unrelated to the capacity of the relevant natural environments to meet the demand. For example, by treating the ozone layer as a resource with a zero price there never was any incentive to protect it. Its value to human populations and to the global environment in general did not show up anywhere in a balance sheet of profit and loss or of costs and benefits.

The important principle is that resources and environments serve economic functions and have positive economic value. To treat them as if they had zero value is seriously to risk overusing the resource. An 'economic function' in this context is any service that contributes to human well-being, to the 'standard of living', or 'development'. *This simple logic underlines the importance of valuing the environment correctly and integrating those correct values into economic policy.*

(Pearce, et al. (1989), pp.5–7)

How does this simple logic apply to the Windermere example? It is easy in principle to assess the economic value of some of the elements in this complex situation: powerboating brings money into the area. How can the value of peace and tranquillity be assessed, so that the benefit of jobs can be compared with the cost of lost environmental goods? Environmental economics insists, first, that environmental goods have *economic value.* This is simply a consequence of the way economic value is defined: an item has economic value if it contributes to human well-being. It insists, secondly, that the economic value of an item, including peace and tranquillity, is determined by the strength of preferences for it. And it insists, thirdly, that it is possible to apply the measuring rod of money to discover the relative strength of preferences. If the costs and benefits of imposing the speed limit, however different in character, are commensurable, then it becomes possible to decide whether the costs outweigh the benefits or vice versa.

Various methods are used to assign monetary values in the absence of an actual market. We don't need to consider them all here,[3] but one should be mentioned because it has been the focus of much controversy: the *contingent valuation method* (CVM), which consists in asking people directly how much they would be willing to pay – for example in taxes – to prevent the development of an area of natural beauty, or to help preserve some endangered species; or, alternatively, how much they would be willing to accept in compensation for the loss of the environmental good. This method is explained in Reading 4, in an extract from *Blueprint for a Green Economy.*

Philosophers and economists are still engaged in vigorous, and sometimes quite heated, controversy over the appropriateness of CBA as a way of estimating environmental values. Not all economists line up in defence of it, nor do all philosophers line up in opposition to it. That needs to be said because the objections to it that we are about to consider are ones that are more likely to come from a philosopher.

There are three objections to be considered to the method of CBA as developed by environmental economists. Each objection fixes on a different assumption of the approach to valuing the environment. The assumptions are:

Assumption 1   Money is an appropriate measure of the value of environmental goods.

Assumption 2   The preferences people actually have accurately reflect what is good for them.

Assumption 3   The value of environmental goods is contingent on their being desired.

EXERCISE 7
Objections to CBA

What objections might be made to each of the three assumptions? Earlier discussions in this book should help in finding possible objections to the first and third assumptions. In looking for an objection to the second do not overlook the obvious. You may of course *agree* with one or more of the assumptions. It can be difficult to think of possible objections to a statement if you don't personally disagree with it; but even if you agree with one or more of these assumptions try to think how it *could* be attacked – in that way you test the reasonableness of your belief.

DISCUSSION

Objection 1 The measuring rod of money implies that goods to which it applies are tradeable. The money one is willing to pay or accept in compensation represents an alternative bundle of goods that is equivalent in value. So the assumption amounts to saying that goods, including environmental goods, are intersubstitutable. But many non-instrumental goods are not substitutable: to value them appropriately implies unwillingness to buy or sell them. They are not tradeable.

Objection 2 People often make mistakes about what is good for them.

Objection 3 Environmental goods have value independent of being desired. The survival of natural beings should not be at the mercy of human likings and dislikings.

Let us consider each of these objections.

Are all goods tradeable?

Many people, when presented with questionnaires in contingent evaluation surveys, respond in a way that rejects the tradeability assumption, refusing to say how much they would pay to preserve some natural feature, or putting an infinite price on it. These responses tell one little about the reasons for rejecting the questions. Light is thrown on this by a study undertaken in New Zealand in which residents of an East Auckland suburb were asked their views on the value of Rangitoto Island, 'a notable landmark in the Auckland Region'

(Vadnjal and O'Connor (1994)). A majority of respondents who answered WTP (willingness to pay) questions, when asked 'Do you think the money amount you finally agreed to pay is an accurate measure of the value to you of continuing protection of [the island]', said 'no'.

They were then asked to explain why they did not think so. Their answers were varied. Points mentioned included: the island as an essential part of the identity of the place; its familiarity from childhood to long-time residents; its not being owned, but being for everybody; its being an asset to be handed down to future generations unspoilt; just the fact of its being there, a part of nature. In these various ways the island has a meaning for these people that makes them resist treating it as a commodity, something that could be exchanged for other goods which were its equivalent in value. That many of the respondents did say what they would be willing to pay turned out not to mean that they thought of themselves as putting an economic value on the island. Rather they thought of themselves as making a gesture of protest, or making a contribution to a campaign to oppose the development.

Does well-being consist in the fulfilment of the desires people actually have?

People make mistakes about what will make their lives better or worse. Actually winning the lottery may ruin one's life, though one intensely desires to win it. If one desires something one generally believes that it will be good to have it, but that belief can be mistaken. For this reason philosophers who prefer a desire-fulfilment account of well-being insist that what count are not any desires agents may happen to have, but the desires they would have if they were fully informed about their objects. Suppose, for example that you are asked what you think about a building development that would involve draining a marshy bit of land that has no obvious attractions. You may prefer the development to the marsh because you do not know that the marsh supports an unusual community of plants and animals. If you were fully informed, your preference might be different, and if you discover too late the nature of what has been destroyed, you may have a sense of loss. So CBA will not give reliable results, will not accurately assess the impact on human well-being of such developments unless a serious effort is made to give full information to the people who are to be canvassed.

The problem with this apparently straightforward suggestion is that it is not only full information that is needed but minds equipped to make use of the information. What can be put on a sheet or two of A4 paper, or explained at a public meeting, may be better than nothing, but cannot be a substitute for an education in the relevant areas of knowledge, or the development of aesthetic sensibility. If people have no knowledge of ecology of what significance are their preferences concerning wetland? If they have assimilated nothing in sculpture after Henry Moore, why should their preferences about the siting of windfarms be worth consulting?

Should the fate of the environment be dependent on human preferences?

This objection overlaps with the previous one – whether an at first sight unremarkable wetland is preserved should not depend on uninformed preferences – but goes beyond it. The objection would stand, in the opinion of deep green environmentalists, even if preferences were fully informed. It might be conceded – at least by some deep green environmentalists – that a fully informed person would place the correct value on the environment, but it would still be contended that it gets things the wrong way round to think that what makes it the correct value is that it is preferred by those who are fully informed. According to this objection the fundamental trouble with CBA is that it recognizes value only in the sense of utility – the contribution that environmental goods make to human well-being.

How effective are the objections to CBA?

What is the effect of these objections, if we accept them? The most radical objection is the third. It does not object that CBA is the wrong way to assess the impact on human well-being of environmental policies, but dismisses it for its assumption that assessment in terms of human well-being is the appropriate kind of assessment of environmental goods.

The second objection is less radical. It questions the accuracy of CBA, making use of CVM, in assessing the real impact on human well-being, in view of the ignorance and ill-formed desires of potential respondents. So far as this goes, the more reasonable it is to assume an informed and educated response, the more adequate the method of assessment.

It is the first objection that, if sustained, is fatal to the claim of CBA to provide a way of assessing overall impact on human well-being, since it undermines the feasibility of providing a measuring rod. The different interests of different people cannot now be aggregated.

Despite these criticisms CBA has its defenders. David Pearce has answered some of its critics in an article (Reading 5).

EXERCISE 8
*Pearce's
defence of CBA*

1 Read the extracts from *Blueprint for a Green Economy*, 'Economic valuation of environmental goods' (Reading 4), and from Pearce's article 'A reply to some criticisms' (Reading 5). How successfully do you consider Pearce defends the use of CBA?

2 Supposing that CBA is not a satisfactory method of assessing environmental goods, what alternative method for resolving such questions as the Windermere speed limit can you think of?

DISCUSSION

1 Pearce's most powerful argument is the one he illustrates with the example of the British government's failure to cost the environment when making the decision about whether to take the M3 motorway over Twyford Down or through a tunnel. The argument is that if a decision is going to be made on the basis of economic value as measured by a monetary yardstick, then refusal to apply that yardstick, that is, refusal to assign a monetary value to environmental goods, means that their value is not taken into account at all. This has considerable pragmatic force, but it is evident that it does not demonstrate that the monetary yardstick is an appropriate measure of environmental goods, that it gives a true representation of the *kind* of value they have.

2 It is doubtful that anything like a decision procedure of the kind envisaged by utilitarianism is available, that is, a routine that can be applied to a set of data (about, say, people's preferences) to yield a definite answer, and that does not need judgement or imagination but could be carried out by a machine. What is the alternative? The only possible alternative seems to be the exercise of practical judgement, an approach which may involve the use of rules of thumb, but cannot be exhaustively specified in terms of rules; it is an art, not an exact science. In the Windermere case it might involve asking whether there exist other, less sensitive, places where people could take their speed boats; whether the aesthetic and ecological values of the lake are uniquely to be found there, and are therefore irreplaceable; whether the opportunities for employment in the area are necessarily dependent on this particular way of using the lake, or could be replaced by other forms of economic development in the region. One of the advantages of this approach is that it can involve debate, exchange of information and argument, by which initial preferences of the various parties may become modified and their arguments scrutinized. CBA, like the utilitarian calculus which it replaces, is a machine that needs only a single operator. The parties affected by the decision are involved only as the source of the data that the operator feeds into the decision-making machine. As one of its recent critics puts it, 'Cost benefit analysis yields policy without debate' (O'Neill (1993), p.78).

Conclusion

An adequate account of well-being recognizes the non-instrumental value of natural features, and so can meet the objection to human-centred views that they treat nature as having instrumental value only. But this account of well-being creates difficulties for the attempt to aggregate preference satisfactions.

Chapter summary

Features of the natural environment contribute to human well-being in two ways. They have instrumental value in providing the resources necessary for the satisfaction of vital needs. They also have non-instrumental value as constituents of well-being. An adequate conception of well-being must recognize the importance of these non-instrumentally valuable features, not assimilating them to instrumental status by treating them as causes of valuable experiences.

A philosophically influential view of well-being as consisting of conscious states, often known as 'the mental state account', implies that non-mental objects have value only as causes of agreeable conscious mental states, and so only instrumental value. Nozick's thought experiment (the 'experience machine') refutes the mental state account of well-being.

Whereas things that are merely of instrumental value are replaceable, things of non-instrumental value often are not. This creates a difficulty for the use of cost benefit analysis as a tool for assessing the value of environmental goods. That method involves assigning monetary values to everything that is to be assessed, but that implies that everything is tradeable (i.e. replaceable by anything of equivalent monetary value).

The failure of CBA does not mean that decisions cannot be made about the effects of some action on the well-being of many people, but it does mean that they cannot be made by a mechanical decision procedure.

Further reading

Edward O. Wilson's *The Diversity of Life*, Penguin Books, 1994 (first published 1992), from which Reading 3 is taken, gives a great deal of information about the 'service' aspect of the value of biodiversity. It also vividly conveys by example a sense of nature's diversity as a source of wonder. Pearce, et al., in *Blueprint for a Green Economy*, give a persuasive presentation of the case for the environmental economist's approach to the valuation of environmental goods. R.M. Hare makes a case for some form of CBA as part of the valuation process in the essay 'Moral Reasoning about the Environment', in his collected *Essays on Political Morality*, Oxford University Press, 1989. John O'Neill, in *Ecology, Policy and Politics: Human Well-being and the Natural World*, Routledge, 1993, gives a detailed critique of CBA in the course of a defence of a human-centred approach.

Notes

[1] The terms 'well-being' and 'welfare' seem in most contexts to be interchangeable. To be concerned about the welfare of one's children is the same thing as to be concerned about their well-being. I use 'well-being', but some philosophers prefer 'welfare' or use both terms without distinction.

[2] Among philosophers, two contemporary utilitarians, Peter Singer and Richard Hare, hold this view.

[3] Pearce, et al. give a clear description of the various methods (op.cit., Chapter 3).

CHAPTER 3

Environmental Goods and the Problem of Cooperation

OBJECTIVES

When you have worked through this chapter you should:

- Understand the view that narrow, basic morality has the function of counteracting limited sympathies.

- Have a grasp of the prisoners' and cooperators' dilemmas.

- Have an increased awareness of some of the factors that can impede or facilitate cooperation in the production of environmental goods.

- Be able to distinguish between prudential reasons and moral reasons.

- Be able to identify the different senses of 'self-interest'.

Introduction

Many, indeed most, of the things that are necessary to our having a good, or even a tolerable, human life depend upon cooperation. That is certainly true of environmental goods. It needs a group of people working together to maintain footpaths so that an area of natural beauty can be visited by many people without damage to what they have come to enjoy. The danger of global warming can be averted only if there is cooperation internationally to restrict emissions of greenhouse gases. This chapter is concerned with the aspect of moral thinking that considers the question how human beings can achieve the cooperation that is needed to secure the essentials of their well-being. In this respect it is a continuation of the topic of the previous chapter: the extent to which an intelligent and informed concern for human well-being can support a morality that values and protects the environment.

READING
'The tragedy of the commons'

Reading 6 consists of extracts from a much-discussed essay by the American biologist Garrett Hardin. His story of the herdsmen, their cows, and the common that is destroyed by their collectively disastrous behaviour may be taken as a model of many environmental problems which have analogous features. Some of these are mentioned by Hardin, and you should make a note of these and of any others that occur to you that have a similar pattern.

Read Garrett Hardin's 'The tragedy of the commons' (Reading 6, pp.201–15) now.

The object of morality

How do we get into difficulties of the kind described by Hardin? Is it inevitable that we should? If not, how might we avoid them? A useful way to approach this question is to consider an account of morality given by two recent philosophers, G.J. Warnock (1923–95) and J.L. Mackie (1917–81). Their approach is to ask, 'What is morality for? What is its object or function?' Mackie says that it is of 'morality in the narrow sense' that this question is raised. What does he mean by this phrase?

> A morality in the broad sense would be a general, all-inclusive theory of conduct: the morality to which someone subscribed would be whatever body of principles he allowed ultimately to guide or determine his choices of action. In the narrow sense, a morality is a system of a particular sort of constraints on conduct – ones whose central task is to protect the interests of persons other than the agent and which present themselves to an agent as checks on his natural inclinations or spontaneous tendencies to act.
>
> (Mackie (1977), p.106)

Mackie does not say what the particular constraints in the narrow morality would be, but they would, fairly obviously, include constraints on injuring others, on unfair competition, on theft, on failing to honour agreements and so on. A narrow, basic morality of this sort would seem to be required of any member of a society. A morality in the broad sense is a more personal matter, and will include the ideals and commitments that one individual may subscribe to without thinking that everyone else should do so as well.

So what is morality in this narrow sense for? It is needed to make what Warnock calls 'the human predicament' somewhat better than it would otherwise be.

> It seems reasonable, and in the present context is highly relevant, to say, without necessarily going quite so far as Hobbes did, that the human predicament is inherently such that things are liable to go badly. This seems to be inherently so, but not completely hopelessly so; that is, there are

circumstances, not in the least likely to change significantly or to be changed by our own efforts, which cannot but tend to make things go badly, but also something at least can be done, many different things in fact, to make them go at least somewhat better than they would do, if no such things were done at all.

(Warnock (1971), p.17)

What are these circumstances that tend to make things go badly? Warnock lists five things that are in short supply: resources, information, intelligence, rationality and sympathy. It is the lack of these that leads to the frustration of human needs and desires. Limited resources, and lack of the information and intelligence that would make their optimum exploitation possible, ensure that 'there is no practical possibility of everyone's having everything that he wants, or would be the better for having, or even perhaps everything that he needs' (ibid., p.20). But even if resources and the technical capacity to exploit them were adequate to supply the desires and needs of all the earth's inhabitants, things would still be liable to go badly.

> We have already mentioned, as limiting factors, limited resources, limited information, limited intelligence. What we need now to bring in might be called limited rationality, and limited sympathies. In the first place it may be said – certainly with extreme vagueness, but still with pretty evident truth – that human beings in general are not just naturally disposed always to do what it would be best that they should do, even if they see, or are perfectly in a position to see, what that is. Even if they are not positively neurotic or otherwise maladjusted, people are naturally somewhat prone to be moved by short-run rather than long-run considerations, and often by the pursuit of more blatant, intense, and obtrusive satisfactions rather than those cooler ones that on balance would really be better. While mostly 'rational' in the minimal sense – able in at least some degree to envisage practical alternatives, to deliberate, and to decide – they are not all just naturally, or indeed in any other way, rational in the more exacting sense of being regularly disposed to deliberate well and to act accordingly. And this is so, of course, even where a person has to consider no interests, wants, or needs but his own.

> Next, limited sympathies. This may even be too mild a term for some of the things that I have in mind. One may say for a start, mildly, that most human beings have some natural tendency to be more concerned about the satisfaction of their own wants etc., than those of others. A man who does not like being hungry, and who is naturally inclined to take such steps as he can to satisfy his hunger, may very well care less, even not at all, about the hunger of others, and may not care at all whether anything is done to satisfy them. Even if he does care to some extent about others, it is quite likely to be only about *some* others – family, friends, class, tribe, country, or 'race'. There is also, besides complete or comparative indifference, such a thing as active malevolence, perhaps even

purely disinterested malevolence; a man will sometimes be not only unconcerned about, but actively malevolent towards, others whom he may see as somehow in competition with himself, and sometimes perhaps even towards some whose frustrations or sufferings are not even supposed to be for the advancement of any interest of his own. There are two obvious ways in which, consequentially, things in the human predicament are liable to go badly. For people are not simply confronted, whether as individuals or groups, with the problems of getting along satisfactorily in material conditions that may in varying degrees be ungenial or hostile. They are also highly vulnerable to other people; and they often need the help of other people. But, given 'limited sympathies', it cannot be assumed that needed help will naturally be forthcoming; and it cannot even be assumed that active malevolence will *not* be forthcoming. And perhaps above all, there may be the impossibility of trust. Whether, in pursuit of some end of my own, I need your help, or merely your non-interference, I may well be unable to trust you either to co-operate or to keep out of it, if I think that you are not only much less concerned about my ends and interests than your own, but possibly even actively hostile to my attainment of my ends. If so, then it may be impossible for either of us to do, either separately or together, things that would be advantageous to us both; and it may be necessary for us individually to do things, for instance in self-protection, the doing of which may be exceedingly laborious, wasteful, and disagreeable. It will be obvious that this applies as fully to relations between groups as between individuals; and indeed that distrust and active hostility between groups has been, in the human predicament, as frequent and constant as between individuals, and vastly more damaging.

(Ibid., pp.21f.)

Warnock asks which limitation is more important in making things go badly, limited rationality or limited sympathy. Though conceding that goodwill may often be frustrated by failure to think, and that much ill will is the consequence of unreason (as in the case of racism), he none the less decides that lack of sympathy is the more fundamental limitation.

Rationality in fact seems, like intelligence and skill and resources, to be something that can be used to do harm (at least to some) as well as good; what is ultimately crucial is how it is used. Nothing in the end, then, seems to be more important, in the inherent liability to badness of the human predicament, than that limitation which I have called, vaguely enough, 'limited sympathies'.

(Ibid., pp.25f.)

Warnock suggests, and Mackie concurs, that the object of narrow or basic morality is 'to contribute to betterment – or non-deterioration – of the human predicament, primarily and essentially by seeking to countervail 'limited sympathies' and their potentially most damaging effects' (ibid., p.26).

EXERCISE 9

The tragedy of the commons

1 Assuming that the herdsmen in Hardin's parable are clear sighted about their own interests, despite having limited sympathies, do you think that they could avoid the degradation of the common if, as individuals, they were to deliberate more rationally?

2 Why does Hardin think that 'mutual coercion mutually agreed upon' is the best way to avert tragedy?

3 What alternative way(s) can you think of?

Note down your answers before reading on, for you will be asked to reconsider them at the end of the chapter.

Prisoners' and related dilemmas

Warnock's discussion dwells on the difficulty of cooperation that is one of the effects of limited sympathies. Mackie brings into much sharper focus one aspect of this difficulty. He is able to do so because he brings to it a formal analysis, derived from Games Theory, of situations in which two or more individuals must make choices, each knowing that the outcome depends on the choices made by the other(s). Games Theory has been widely applied in the social and biological sciences, and in the last twenty years or so some philosophers have explored its relevance to ethics. Such explorations usually begin with the situation known as the 'prisoners' dilemma', so-called because the original story that exemplified the situation was about two prisoners under arrest for an alleged crime. But the situation can be exemplified by many different concrete situations. The important thing is the form of the dilemma, thus Mackie's story of two characters, Tom and Dan, is a perfectly good example, and has the advantage of being tolerably realistic.

READING   Now read Mackie's 'Game theory analysis' (Reading 7).

Although I think that Mackie's exposition is very clear, and needs little explanation, it may be helpful to set out the dilemma in a more formal way, using a diagrammatic device that is often used known as a matrix.

There are four sets of combined choices, each with a pay-off for the two soldiers. Each soldier has an order of preference, determined by how favourable to his own interests the outcome is.

Tom's order is:

1 Tom runs, Dan stays.

2 Tom stays, Dan stays.

3 Tom runs, Dan runs.

4 Tom stays, Dan runs.

Dan's order can be seen by reversing the names. Their first and fourth preferences are opposite to one another – what is best for either is worst for the other; but they have identical second and third preferences. In the diagram, read across horizontally to see Tom's preference ranking of each outcome, represented by the solid figure; read down vertically to see Dan's ranking, represented by the white figure.

		Dan		
		runs		stays
Tom	runs	3/3		4/1
	stays	1/4		2/2

EXERCISE 10

The prisoners' dilemma

1 Explain why, on the stated assumptions, Tom and Dan cannot reach the 2/2 solution?

2 What are the assumptions that make this outcome impossible to reach?

3 Why does their having made an agreement not make any difference to the outcome?

4 Why would it be in their interest to be tied to their posts?

5 What alternatives are suggested that would have the same effect as their being tied to their posts?

6 Why does it make a difference if Tom and Dan know that they will have to play the game again in future?

Check your answers against those at the back of the book before reading on.

DISCUSSION

The most obvious lesson of the prisoners' dilemma is that there are situations in which prudent (i.e. self-interested) agents, making rational choices, cannot achieve the outcome that is best for both of them. It is obvious what we should do, if we were jointly making a decision that would be mutually acceptable, but, making decisions independently, it is not rational for either of us to do it.

Mackie's discussion puts into sharper perspective two aspects of Warnock's account. First it makes precise the nature of the difficulty of achieving cooperation, and thus throws light on the human predicament: we see exactly why things are liable to go badly for Tom and Dan. Secondly, the sharper definition of the problem makes it clearer what problem narrow or basic morality is called in to solve, and what form it must take if it is to be a solution.

The problem is that our limited sympathies can land us in situations in which we cannot secure the advantages of cooperation. People who always put their own interests first do less well than they would if they could restrain themselves. The solution is in two parts. The first is to agree the terms of cooperation: what actions we are to do, what rules we are to accept as binding on us, or what policies we are to adopt. But we have seen that agreement is not enough. Self-interest will lead to the breaking of agreements when it is advantageous to break them. So the second part of the solution must be some form of *assurance* that if I abide by the agreement the other player(s) will do so as well. Coercion is one solution to the assurance problem: the institution of a system of penalties for defection, but that is not a *moral* solution. The moral solution is the development of 'psychological substitutes' for external penalties, which Mackie also calls 'psychological fetters' and 'invisible chains'. These metaphors are intended to draw attention to the way that internal constraints can perform the same function as external coercion. They are misleading insofar as they also suggest restraints to which one submits unwillingly. This could obscure the importance of the fact that they are *internal* not *external* constraints. They modify the individual's motivation in such a way that, without the fear of penalties, she is not inevitably moved on every occasion to act according to pure self-interest. Once such moral dispositions have developed, either by natural selection or cultural trans-mission (e.g. education), they reinforce both the individual's motive to cooperate and her confidence that others will do so too.

To be able to reap the rewards of cooperation, what we need is a disposition to resist the temptation to gain an advantage at the expense of others. But this does not mean that we have to be prepared to go on cooperating when we know that the other is going to exploit us. Work carried out by an American political scientist, Robert Axelrod, shows that the best strategy to adopt in repeated or continuous prisoners' dilemma situations is to cooperate on the first occasion, and on subsequent occasions to do whatever the other did on the previous occasion, cooperating if the other player does, defecting if he defects. Axelrod calls this strategy tit for tat (Axelrod (1990)). In this way one conveys one's willingness to cooperate, reinforces any willingness on the part of the other, and signals one's unwillingness to be taken advantage of. So if one wants to design the ideal disposition for the members of a group who stand to gain from having the ability to cooperate, one will choose a flexible disposition that makes a person a reliable cooperator with other cooperators, and a reliable punisher of non-cooperators.

Cooperation and public benefits

There are many situations in which something that benefits everyone requires the cooperative efforts of many people, yet rational self-interest does not clearly dictate cooperative action to the individual. These situations share a form that is a variation of the prisoners' dilemma, in which there are more than two players. It is sometimes called the 'cooperators' dilemma', and we began the chapter with an example of it, Garrett Hardin's 'herdsmen's dilemma'. Many environmental issues are concerned with situations of this sort. Here are two examples.

First, a relatively small-scale example. In an area of natural beauty much used by walkers, all walkers have an interest in the maintenance of the features of the area that make it an attractive one to walk in. Free access makes the area vulnerable to damage; for example, erosion caused by the passage of many booted feet. If all walkers refrained from walking except on suitably constructed paths, and voluntarily rationed their use of the most vulnerable routes, erosion would be kept within acceptable limits. Does that give an individual walker a good enough reason to act accordingly? Suppose that whatever she did erosion damage would continue to be inflicted by all the other boots. Then she would impose a loss upon herself without her sacrifice doing any good.

To take a global example: the 166 nations taking part in the 1997 conference in Kyoto on climate change have a common interest in climatic stability. Geoffrey Lean, a journalist, wrote:

> If the world decides at Kyoto to take strong action against the pollution that causes global warming, climate change may well be kept at a manageable level. If they do not, the world's top scientists warn, our descendants will suffer the consequences for centuries, even for millennia, to come.
>
> (*Independent on Sunday*, 30 November 1997)

Part of the difficulty of securing an agreement is that not all countries are equally threatened, so do not have an equally strong self-interested reason to agree to limit the emission of 'greenhouse gases'. (You may have noticed that Mackie draws attention to this possibility, which can result in agreements that disadvantage some parties relative to others (Reading 7, p.219). Moreover, the cost of reducing emissions may be greater for some nations than for others. But the overriding problem is the general one we have already encountered. Each nation, if it is to take the necessary measures, needs an assurance that the others will meet the reduction targets that are agreed. Promises made by the rich countries at the Earth Summit in Rio in 1992 were not kept, while developing countries, it is claimed, have kept theirs. This is not likely to encourage adherence to future agreements on the part of those who have been deceived in the past.[1]

Resources which are common benefits, such as unspoiled natural country-side and the earth's atmosphere, have the characteristics of what economists term 'public goods'. These are:

1   to produce the good requires the coordinated action of some, but not all, members of the group to which the good is available;

2   once the good is produced its benefits are available to all, including those who did not contribute to its production;

3   it is impracticable to exclude non-contributors from the benefits;

4   contributors to the production of the good incur a cost;

5   The cost to each contributor is less than the benefit.

It can be seen that the members of a group who wish to have the benefits of an environmental good that has these characteristics are in a situation that can usefully be analysed as a many-person prisoners' dilemma, or a variant of it – the variant in which the 'players' are involved not just once, but repeatedly. We will call this the cooperators' dilemma.[2]

In a pure (once for all) many-person dilemma, any given agent has the choice of cooperating or not cooperating in producing (or maintaining) the good, and is aiming to maximize his own interests whatever other agents may choose to do. The diagram below shows the outcomes of the four possible combined choices in the same way as the earlier diagram of the two-person dilemma, except that the outcomes shown are in terms of the benefits of the good (G) and costs for the individual agent.

EXERCISE 11
The cooperators' dilemma

What must the self-interested individual's preference ranking of these outcomes be, and why?

		Others		
		cooperate		doesn't cooperate
Individual	cooperate	benefits of G cost of cooperation		no benefits G cost of cooperation
	doesn't cooperate	benefits of G no cost		no benefits G no cost

Obviously the most preferred outcome is that which provides the benefits at no cost to the individual, and the least preferred that in which she has to pay the cost with no compensating benefit. Since we have assumed that the benefits outweigh the cost of contributing, the outcome of cooperating when others do is preferable to the outcome of neither the individual nor others cooperating.

As in the two-person case, the non-cooperative option is forced on the self-interested individual. Either sufficient others are going to cooperate, so that the good will be produced, or insufficient others are going to cooperate, so that (unless the individual's contribution would tip the balance), it will not be produced whatever she does. In either case self-interest prescribes non-cooperation. The exception clause, in brackets, may be relevant in a few cases where the group is small. For example, if a car with four occupants has broken down and has to be pushed off the road, it may be that every occupant has to push if the car is to be moved. In any case, however, where the relevant group is large, as in the case of walkers and erosion, it is unlikely that any one person's action is going to be critical.

DISCUSSION

Conditions of cooperation

The general form of the solution is clear from Mackie's discussion of the prisoners' dilemma. Just as Tom and Dan needed both an agreement to cooperate *and* some device, coercive or moral, to provide mutual assurance, so in the many-person case; so we need to seek agreements among the members of the relevant group, and we need also to see what possible devices are available already, or can be constructed, that will motivate the participants to honour the agreements (to meet the assurance problem).

Making agreements

First we need to clarify what constitutes an agreement. Agreements can be more or less formal, more or less explicit. A contract is a form of agreement that is highly formal and explicit. The parties must be known to one another, aware that entering into a contract is a solemn and binding undertaking, imposing clearly specified rights and obligations. Such agreements imply communication (either direct or indirect) between the parties. But agreements may consist, not of exchanges in which each party makes an explicit undertaking, but of mutual expectations which are mutually understood and accepted. The behaviour of two people can fall into a cooperative pattern without their having exchanged words. That an agreement exists can be revealed when one fails to perform as expected and receives reproaches. Implicit agreements of this sort in larger groups most readily develop in face-to-face communities in which most members interact at some time with a large proportion of others. But there are examples of much larger groups in which any one person is likely to encounter only a small proportion of the others, and then most probably only briefly, but between whose members there are agreements on proper behaviour. Lorry drivers seem to be such a group. 'Serious' walkers are another. Fell-walkers invariably exchange greetings with fellow walkers who are complete strangers who may never be met again, and there are well-understood rules of acceptable and unacceptable behaviour, which, even if now enshrined in official codes, certainly predate them. I suspect that the explanation of this is twofold. First, a natural sympathy grows up among people who share the same passion, especially when their activities are, at least traditionally, non-competitive. Secondly, the mutual awareness of potential need for help in dangerous situations forms a bond. But even much looser associations can give rise to implicit agreements. The example of queuing among bus users is one case, where what people have in common is hardly a shared passion. It seems undeniable that the larger, the more amorphous the group, and the less communication between its members, the less likely it is that agreements, either explicit or implicit, can be formed. The largest and most amorphous group is that which comprises all human beings. It seems unlikely that, even though human beings have some interests in common, there can be agreements of any kind between all human beings as individuals. Whether that is so or not, for practical purposes agreements to secure the common interests of human beings have to be made by governments. That has an obvious advantage. Representatives of nations can meet and hammer out explicit agreements. But there are familiar disadvantages as well, stemming mostly from the fact that governments are usually under enormous pressure to push the interests of their own public, or, what is worse, the interests of powerful sections of their public. This limits their freedom to commit their nations to measures that serve common interests.

Another important factor is the strength of the interests that have to be sacrificed by the participants in cooperation. The higher the cost of cooperating to some or all of the individuals concerned, the less likely it is that agreement can be reached. This is especially so where the cost to some is much higher than to others, so that those who have a great deal to lose, although they would share in the common benefits, will stand out against the agreement unless the costs can be more equitably distributed.

Yet another factor is variable vulnerability to the loss of, or failure to produce, the public good or common benefit. For example, if, as has been predicted, global warming is causing a rise in sea-levels, low-lying countries, such as the Maldive Islands, are much more at risk than others. The more a member of the group stands to lose if the good is not produced, the greater the pressure on that member, even on unfavourable terms, to agree to cooperate, and to try to secure the agreement of others. The Deputy Prime Minister, John Prestcott, on behalf of the British Government exerted himself mightily to bring about an agreement at the Kyoto conference. It would be unduly cynical to suppose that the government's motivation was entirely selfish, in the sense of concern for national interest alone, but it is not irrelevant to point out that the effects of global warming could include a catastrophic change in Britain's climate.

The logic of the prisoners' dilemma is that however conditionally willing to cooperate an individual may be – that is, to cooperate if enough others do – unilateral action involves the cost without the benefit, and so is ruled out on prudential grounds, and does not even make sense on utilitarian grounds, because if not everyone, or nearly everyone, cooperates, no benefits are produced for anyone.

The assurance problem

We suppose that agreement has been reached. What means exist or can be created to assure those who are willing to keep the agreement that others will do so too? The answer depends very much on the character of the group concerned, how big, how scattered, how communicative, whether it consists of individuals or representatives of groups, e.g. nations. Earlier we distinguished two main types of device that could help with the assurance problem: coercion and what Mackie terms 'psychological fetters': dispositional tendencies to keep agreements, a sense of obligation to others, traditions of loyalty and honourable behaviour, virtues, etc. We noticed the strategy called tit for tat, which Axelrod's research revealed as the most effective in securing cooperative outcomes in the repeated or continuous prisoners' dilemma game. That strategy, on reflection, combines features of both main types of control device. It is coercive in that it involves punishing non-cooperators by depriving them of the fruits of cooperation. The other side of this coin is what behavioural psychologists term 'positive reinforcement' – it rewards cooperation. But to operate the strategy one has to have a disposition to cooperate oneself, not to take advantage of others who show a similar willingness; in short to trust and be trustworthy.

The coercive effect of tit for tat, as a strategy employed by individuals, is somewhat limited. It depends upon one's being able to identify defaulters and withholding from them the fruits of cooperation. In a face-to-face community it can be effective, and it is also in such communities that trust and loyalty are most likely to operate as psychological controls on non-cooperative behaviour. But in large, dispersed and anonymous groups non-cooperation is likely to escape detection and go unpunished. In this way those who are unwilling to cooperate, who lack the appropriate dispositions, have no motive to change, and therefore those who do have the dispositions find their cooperative actions of no avail, so for them too there is no motive to persist. The last point needs qualification. If an individual is strongly inclined to cooperate, two thoughts may motivate irrational efforts. One is the thought that one does not know how many potential cooperators there are out there. Perhaps there are enough to make a difference. Although it will make no difference to the atmosphere if I am alone in using 'green' petrol, or, more drastically, giving up my car, I do not know how alone I would be. Even a few people can do something towards raising consciousness of an issue, especially if they take part in social movements dedicated to spreading the word and advocating measures to save energy. The other thought is a last resort, the thought of many a pacifist: my stand may be completely ineffective, but I will not contribute to destruction. In many cases, and car use is one, voluntary and uncoordinated abstention is not enough. The cost of restricting the use of private cars, in the absence of a transport system that can replace them, would be just too high for many. Only government has the resources and the legislative powers to bring about the changes in collective behaviour that would save the environmental good. This is the sort of case which it is in everyone's interest to set up a coercive mechanism which operates directly by giving the unwilling a motive to cooperate, and indirectly by giving the willing the assurance they need to be able to cooperate.

The walking case is one in which tit for tat can hardly be effective as a coercive device, and in which coercive measures introduced by central or local government bodies are problematic in that they are difficult to enforce, and, if enforced, tend to be destructive of the good which it is sought to preserve (i.e. not only unspoilt country, but freedom of access to unspoilt country). This is one case, and there must be many others, in which there is no substitute for goodwill towards others who want to enjoy the good.

Finally, to consider cases in which international agreements to protect the environment are concerned, such as the currently hoped for agreement on the emission of greenhouse gases, what hope is there for a solution to the assurance problem? There is some scope for tit for tat. A country that defects can be punished by being denied economic assistance, or by trade or cultural boycotts. But this is only when it is a case of the powerful punishing the weak. A powerful country can defect with impunity. An international body such as the United Nations may have coercive powers which are in theory supranational, but in practice their employment tends to be influenced by the national interests of powerful players. In these cases it is hard to estimate the effectiveness of moral (internal) restraints. All governments use moral rhetoric, and most dislike being branded with epithets implying moral turpitude, such as 'the dirty man of Europe'; but unfortunately a bad reputation may be combated by image manipulation rather than by changing behaviour. The fundamental problem is that governments do not have unlimited power to act in the interests of humanity, given the necessity they are under, and not only democratically elected ones, to be seen to protect their national interest.

Prudence, morality and rationality

Three terms have been used in this chapter, and in the readings, without explicit explanation: 'prudence', 'morality', and 'rationality'. Of course they are all terms in common use, and we all have a rough idea of their meaning, but the relations between them are not unproblematic. In particular, consider the case argued in the Reading by Mackie: if people lack the moral disposition to keep agreements and act solely by calculating long-term self-interest (i.e. prudently), they will fail to secure the benefits of cooperation. The conclusion to be drawn from this can be put in a way that sounds paradoxical: it is not prudent to be prudent. To see how paradox can be avoided we must say something more about these three terms.

Consider prudence first, and the associated notion of self-interest. There is a narrow conception of prudence/self-interest, according to which it consists in the pursuit of one's own pleasure, comfort, security, health and profit. To be prudent or self-interested in this narrow sense is not necessarily to be selfish.

To say that a person is selfish is to say that he pursues such goods for himself with little or no consideration for the similar interests of others. Self-interest in the narrow sense simply refers to a limited class of reasons for action.

There is a wider conception of prudence/self-interest. According to the account of well-being adopted in Chapter 2, it consists in the satisfaction of desires. A prudent person may be said to be one who acts in such a way as to achieve or maintain her own well-being. But now, a person may have desires not only for good things for herself, but also for good things for others, these are altruistic desires. If one has altruistic desires, then prudence will dictate actions designed to benefit others. In the wide sense of prudence/self-interest there is no absolute contrast between prudence and altruism.

The definition of 'moral' and 'morality' is something that philosophers disagree about, but most would agree that morality is not the same things as prudence. A prudent person who has altruistic desires will take into consideration the effect of her actions on others, those at least who are within the range of her limited sympathies, but will not necessarily give priority to the good of those others when it competes with her own good, nor even give it equal consideration with her own. Morality may require one to put oneself second. It may require one to set aside the pursuit of one's own well-being when that is necessary to honour an agreement that one has entered into, even when the others with whom one has entered into the agreement mean nothing to one in any personal way – they may be outside the range of one's sympathies.

Many people with whom we have to get on are outside the limits of our sympathies. It is in our relations with these that we get into cooperators' dilemmas. It is in our interest to be able to cooperate with them, but to do so we have to be capable of non-self-interested action. If what makes cooperation possible is external coercion, then the motivation involved is still purely self-interested, even though the actions performed are not – they benefit others as well. But if cooperation is made possible by dispositions such as the disposition to keep agreements, to honour obligations, to act loyally, then the motive is a moral one. The point of the approach we have been considering is that the person who has these moral dispositions has the best prospect of benefiting from cooperation with others. If one has them, one will not ask on particular occasions when one is called on to play one's part in the joint endeavour, 'What is most in my interest?'; that may lead one to defect. Prudence comes in when one asks, 'What sort of person is it in my interest to be', to which the answer, according to this theory, is, 'The sort of person who has moral dispositions that override the temptation to defect from cooperative endeavours'.

Finally, a necessarily brief word about the terms 'rational' and 'rationality'. A minimal sense is that in which a rational person is one who adopts the means necessary to achieve whatever ends he may have; who, for example, takes an umbrella if he wishes not to get rained on. Since people have many desired ends, which frequently compete, and are not all of equal importance, this minimal sense may be expanded so that a rational person is one who acts in such a way as to satisfy as many of his desires as possible, giving due priority to those which are most important to his overall well-being over the course of his life. It is self-interest which is rational in this sense that argues for the advantageousness, from the individual's point of view as well as from the group's point of view, of having moral dispositions.

Free-riding and sensible knavery

There will be some who find the approach we have been discussing in this chapter objectionable because it appears to recommend morality on the ground that to be moral is in one's interest. A specific objection is that the approach leaves open the possibility of free-riding. A free-rider is someone who enjoys the benefits made possible by cooperation among the members of a group without playing her part. The problem is whether it is possible to show that the free-rider is irrational from the standpoint of self-interest. If not, then self-interest does not unequivocally support morality. It recommends morality to those who cannot get the benefits of cooperation without doing their share.

This is how the problem is introduced by David Hume:

> Treating vice with the greatest candour, and making it all possible concessions, we must acknowledge that there is not in any instance, the smallest pretext for giving it the preference above virtue, with a view to self-interest; except, perhaps, in the case of justice [by which he means roughly the same as Mackie's morality in the narrow sense], where a man, taking things in a certain light, may often seem to be a loser by his integrity. And though it is allowed that, without a regard to property, no society could subsist; yet according to the imperfect way in which human affairs are conducted, a sensible knave, in certain incidents, may think that an act of iniquity or infidelity will make a considerable addition to his fortune, without causing any considerable breach in the social union and confederacy. That *honesty is the best policy,* may be a good general rule, but is liable to many exceptions; and he, it may perhaps be thought, conducts himself with most wisdom, who observes the general rule, and takes advantage of all the exceptions.
>
> (Hume (1975 edn), section 232, pp.282–3)

This problem is implicit in the cooperator's dilemma. The best outcome for the cooperator is to secure the benefits of cooperation without the cost. That is achieved by agreeing to share the cost and then defecting. It is the cooperative efforts of others that one has an interest in promoting, not one's own, unless playing one's part is necessary to being allowed access to the benefits. The situation changes when we consider repeated or continuous variations of the dilemma. There is now good reason for the individual to cooperate in order to be accepted by other cooperators. She needs to be accepted as trustworthy and the best way of being accepted as trustworthy is actually to be trustworthy. But it may not be the *only* way. Circumstances and personality might still conspire to favour the circumspect defector. There could be, and no doubt are, some individuals who are sufficiently cunning, and others who are sufficiently trusting, for free-riding to be good policy. The cunning free-rider impersonates a cooperator; he is a wolf in sheep's clothing. He risks being caught out, but the risk may be worth taking. The free-rider is not necessarily, from the point of view of self-interest, irrational.

It has to be conceded, I think, that the free-rider cannot be condemned, on the approach we are considering, as irrational. But the free-rider acts immorally. It follows therefore that immorality is not necessarily, from the standpoint of self-interest, irrational.

There are considerations, however, that somewhat mitigate the force of this conclusion. Consider first that people are not always rational in their behaviour, and this applies to free-riders as much as to the rest of us. Some free-riders may be quite wrong to believe that they can defect with impunity, over-estimating the effectiveness of their disguise or the gullibility of their victims. Experience of the consequences of being caught out, or even persuasion, may convince them that knavery is not, for them, sensible. Others, however, may be right to think that free-riding is on balance advantageous to them. There is no way in which we can convince them by argument that free-riding is against their own interests. But we are not committed to dealing with free-riders in practice by argument alone. The interests of cooperators dictate that free-riders, whether rational or irrational, should be deterred by other means, namely, whatever coercive measures they have at their disposal. Society, or those it entrusts with the education of the young, have the responsibility of passing on to the young the traditions of agreement keeping which restrain the tendency to take free rides, and we all have the responsibility to encourage our politicians and planners to create social conditions in which free-riding is less likely to pay.

The return of the herdsmen

Before you did Exercise 9 you read extracts from Warnock on limited rationality and limited sympathies. You were asked to think about the tragedy of the commons and to note your answers to three questions about Hardin's essay.

Look back at Exercise 9 (p.60) and, in the light of what you know, answer questions (1)–(3) once more.

EXERCISE 12
The tragedy of the commons – a second look

DISCUSSION

1   In answering the first question it is tempting to think that if something is very clearly in the interest of each individual, then the prudent thing to do is whatever will help to realize that state of affairs. But the herdsmen are in a cooperators' dilemma. Rational self-interest leads to the very outcome that it is in their interest to avoid.

2   An agreement to set up coercive machinery is in the interest of every herdsman. It is not oppressive because voluntarily accepted. Although Hardin considers the possibility that the inculcation of conscience might do the same job, he objects to the attempt to solve the problem in this way because he considers a coercive system more effective and morally more acceptable.

3   Because of his view about conscience, Hardin would no doubt be little impressed by Mackie's account of psychological substitutes for coercion. But many of Hardin's critics have pointed out that, traditionally, common land has been sustainably used by communities of pastoral people with a firm sense of customary limits and a common concern for the use of the common by their descendants. Oddly (see (2) above), his favoured paradigm is a good example of how implicit agreements can be maintained with non-coercive solutions to the assurance problem.

Conclusion

The ability to make and keep agreements is necessary if people are to escape cooperators' dilemmas and avoid the loss of environmental goods. It is in an individual's interest to have a disposition to be ready to cooperate with others who are similarly ready, and to have a reliable agreement-keeping disposition. Mutually agreed coercion is an alternative, and in some cases a necessary supplement, to the moral solution to the assurance problem.

Chapter summary

Basic, or narrow morality may be viewed as a remedy for the limited nature of our sympathies and one of the consequences of that, namely, our difficulty in achieving cooperation with people outside the range of our sympathy. The prisoners' and cooperators' dilemmas demonstrate precisely the nature of the difficulty: the inability of rational self-interested individuals to produce the best outcome for all. The remedy consists in willingness by the members of the group to make agreements committing them to cooperation in producing or maintaining the desired good, coupled with some device by which all the members are assured that each will keep the agreement. This device does not have to be a form of coercion. There are psychological substitutes: moral dispositions. Examples of cases in which cooperation is needed to preserve some environmental good reveal various factors that affect the possibility of agreement and some variations in the effectiveness of moral constraints in maintaining them.

Further reading

The book by G.J. Warnock, *The Object of Morality*, Methuen, 1971 and that by J.L. Mackie, *Ethics: inventing right and wrong*, Penguin, 1977 are both interesting introductions to ethics. Neither is a neutral account of alternative theories; each argues for a particular view. Warnock's is probably the easier read. On the prisoners' dilemma and the problem of cooperation, Axelrod's *The Evolution of Co-operation*, Penguin,1990 is full of interesting information and argument. Axelrod's main results are explained with great enthusiasm by Peter Singer in *How are We to Live?*, Oxford University Press, 1997.

Notes

[1] In the article quoted, Lean reports the claim of '2000 economists' that cutting pollution actually brings economic advantages to a country. Of course, if this is true it alters the character of the problem completely, for now all countries have a self-interested reason to act that does not depend on what others do, and the combined result of their self-interested choices would produce the benefit in which all would share.

[2] The cooperators' dilemma is discussed in Miller and Sartorius (1979) to which this discussion is indebted.

CHAPTER 4

Environmental Virtues

OBJECTIVES

When you have worked through this chapter you should have:

- Understood the distinction between virtues of character and virtues of intellect.
- Considered how some virtues relating to the senses and emotions operate in our dealings with nature.
- Considered virtues of character and intellect associated with the disinterested contemplation of nature.

Introduction

Traditionally moralists have been mainly concerned with the question 'What virtues must one have to be a good human being in relation to others?' Environmental ethics is concerned with human beings in a wider context, so it asks 'What are the dispositions a good human being must have in relation to the natural world?' It may be that in answering this question one will find oneself recognizing some *new* virtues, so in that sense environmental ethics could be said to be new. But the enquiry is human centred in the sense that it asks the question, 'What dispositions must a good *human being* have?'

If we want to decide what dispositions a good person needs to have in this area of life, we have to think about the various ways in which we relate to the environment in our thoughts, actions and feelings. That looks like an endless task, but a simplifying distinction suggests itself.

1 Where our actions, through the effects on their environment, affect human/sentient beings, then obviously the virtues that come into play are those that are appropriate in our dealings with those beings – humans and other animals. If I dump my litter in your backyard or smoke in your sitting room (say you don't smoke), I pollute your environment and that is inconsiderate and selfish. If, in order to protect our common environment, it is necessary for many of us to cooperate,

we have to have the virtues that make such cooperation possible: trust, reliability, self-denial, trustworthiness.

2   More problematic is the gamut of our dealings with natural things and phenomena directly, where we are not simply concerned with their effects on other human/sentient beings. It is with the virtues needed in these dealings that this chapter is concerned.

Character virtues and virtues of intellect

You read in Book 2, Chapter 6, quite a full account of what it is to have a virtue of character, so I shall not go over that ground again. There are, however, some additional points that will be helpful in considering environmental virtues.

Virtues of character are those most obviously relevant to morality. Traditionally, virtue ethics was concerned not just with living a moral life, but with living a good life, and it was supposed – for example by Aristotle, who is the real founder of this tradition – that to live a good human life involves more than developing a good character, having the right character traits. It involves also developing and using the powers of the mind. So Aristotle divides the virtues into virtues of character (or, as they are often termed, moral virtues) and virtues of intellect.

The concept of a virtue, in the account given by Aristotle, is much broader than the one the word is likely to suggest to a modern reader. In fact, it is even broader than I have so far suggested. When, in Plato's *Republic,* Socrates explains what he means by speaking of a virtue, he uses the example of a pruning knife. The knife has a function, something that it is specially adapted to do – to prune vines – and it has a property that enables it to do its work well – it has to be sharp. Sharpness is its virtue.

So a thing's virtue is that which enables it to do its work well. That notion can be applied to the powers and capacities that we have. Take the capacity to experience fear. Fear has a function in our lives. It makes us avoid danger. But it can also make us avoid things wrongly perceived as dangerous, such as spiders, or things that need to be endured, such as a visit to the dentist; so there are right and wrong ways to feel fear. Courage is the virtue that enables us to fear what we should and when we should; it is a character trait and therefore a moral virtue.

To take a different capacity, we have the capacity to construct and appraise arguments, to draw conclusions, give reasons and so on. To think straight we need to see what follows from what, recognize inconsistencies and so on, for which we need the intellectual virtue of logical acumen. That is just one example of an intellectual virtue. It is obviously not the only one, for there are many kinds of thinking, and so many ways in which one can think well or badly, correctly or incorrectly. So people are described as observant, perceptive, of good understanding, quick on the uptake, rational, judicious, thoughtful, imaginative, inventive, and so on. Are these qualities ones that a person needs in order to be good? When someone is said to be good, period, what is usually meant is that he or she is kind, fair and so on, in short that he or she has a good character. But the intellectual virtues are ones for which people are admired, and in which they take pride; and to have some share of them is necessary to having a good life.

An important division among intellectual virtues, which we owe to Aristotle, is between those we need in theoretical and those we need in practical thinking. Theoretical thinking aims at truth in belief, practical thinking at correctness in action. So if I am thinking about whether it is true that fox-hunting causes suffering to foxes, that is theoretical thinking. If I am thinking about whether to take part in an anti-fox-hunting demonstration, that is practical thinking.

One very important intellectual virtue is the good judgement needed if one is to make correct moral decisions. A person may have a good character, having the virtues of, for example, justice and compassion. In particular situations it may be difficult to decide what action is the just or compassionate action. Decision is especially difficult in situations where justice seems to require one action, but compassion suggests a different action. Some people are better at making such decisions than others; they are said to be wiser, or to have better judgement. The ability they have is the ability to assess the situation, to grasp which features of it are morally significant, and judge which are of most importance, in general or in the particular case. This ability is not itself a character trait, but it is an ability that is indispensable to the effective exercise of such virtues as justice and compassion: it's not much use being compassionate if you have no judgement about the sorts of thing that upset people. The Aristotelian word for this intellectual virtue is usually translated as 'practical wisdom', which sounds rather grand; more manageable, though still quite rare, varieties of it are implied by such terms as 'judicious', 'having good judgement', 'prudent', or even the modest 'sensible'.

Both character virtues and both kinds of intellectual virtue are involved in our dealings with the natural world.

Virtues involve actions and responses appropriate to the objects of those actions and responses. The emphasis of virtue ethics is on the question, 'What qualities of character and intellect must one have to have a good life?' But (for most of the virtues) what makes a quality a virtue is that it enables the person who has it to do the right things and have the right feelings towards other people and things. As noted at the beginning of the chapter, traditional accounts have focused almost exclusively on our relations with other human beings; but what we have to do now is to try to figure out what virtues enable us to act and respond appropriately to *nature*. Are these quite different virtues from the ones that make us good neighbours, or can we hope to find among the list of familiar virtues some that will turn out, suitably developed, to cover our relations with nature? I think it's going to turn out that some, at least, of the virtues needed are analogues of those needed in relations with other people. This is not an accident. We have desires and emotions which connect us in related ways both to other human beings and to natural forces. The objects of fear include both human beings who threaten us and natural phenomena: one can be brave in a battle or a storm at sea. One can be grateful to someone who feeds us and also to, or at least for, the shower that refreshes a wilting row of lettuces in the garden.

Some environmental virtues

Virtues related to pleasures of the senses

The traditional word for the virtue exercised in this sphere is temperance, which is unfortunate in suggesting abstinence, or restraint, whereas one really wants a word that indicates a correct indulgence. Classical and Christian treatments of this virtue have largely attended to bodily appetites, and while it has been allowed that in moderation it is not bad, and may even be good, to gratify these appetites, the appropriate virtue tends to be seen as a disposition not to go to excess. Aristotle acknowledges that to be insensible to physical pleasures is a fault, but one that no one is likely to fall into. The emphasis on excess is not out of place when one considers the way in which habits of consumption in rich countries have largely ignored their environmental impact. In poor countries, where few people can over-consume, necessity takes the place of virtue. In rich countries, on the other hand, excessive consumption can be restrained only by the cultivation of temperance.

But temperance is not the only virtue in this sphere. Aristotle draws attention to the fact that the enjoyment of sights and sounds, and even of tastes and smells, can be a kind of sensuous pleasure that is distinct from gratifying appetites, and he thinks that the notion of going to excess does not apply to indulging in the sounds of music or the smell of new-mown hay or the look of the greens of a wood. With regard to these sources of sensory enjoyment it may be suggested that it is a virtue to have a developed capacity for responding with enjoyment to the enormous variety of forms, colours, sounds, textures and smells that nature presents to our senses. Unlike the appetite-related pleasures, these are more likely to need cultivation than restraint. It is easy not to look, listen, etc., or to look and listen with only pragmatic eyes and ears. There does not seem to be a name of general currency for this virtue, but the terms 'sensitivity' and 'sensibility', in context, serve to point to it.

Virtues related to emotions

As already noted, fear is an emotion that relates to natural phenomena just as much as to human ones. Courage is not being immune from fear, or disregarding danger – that would be to have the vice of rashness – but making a correct assessment of the danger and not allowing fear to prevent one from taking appropriate action, whether that is avoidance or resistance. Nature is formidable, and to have a realistic awareness of its destructive powers is rational; to be over-confident about one's ability to contain those powers is a common form of foolishness. On the other hand, there are irrational fears, fears of what is not truly fearful, which need to be dispelled by learning what is truly dangerous and what is not.

Awe is an emotion related to, but not the same as, fear. Fear is inspired by danger, that is, by the threat of harm to oneself or to those for whom one cares. Awe is a response to what is in some way great; for example, in magnitude or power. What is awesome may be dangerous, but it need not be. Awe may involve a recognition that one is puny in comparison to the object that evokes it. In that way, it is a humbling experience. But it can also be an elevating and exhilarating experience in which consciousness of self is overwhelmed by what is outside self. To awesome things we apply such terms as grandeur, magnificence, sublimity, majesty; terms which acknowledge values in the object. In fear, what is valued is my safety, not the object feared. Is it a virtue to cultivate the capacity for awe? Do we think of indifference to the power and magnitude of nature, refraining from any response but a dispassionate acknowledgement that there is a lot of it, as inadequate? Refusing to be impressed by what is grand or magnificent may indicate such undesirable qualities as meanness, conceit and self-absorption. It seems reasonable then to regard a proper sense of the grandeur of nature as a virtue, and indifference as a vice.

Awe is a transient emotion, and an overwhelming one – it would seem odd to say that one was slightly awed by a tremendous thunderstorm, or by the immensity of the universe. Wonder is a related notion, but further removed from fear and the concern for self implicit in fear, and it is unlike awe because it is not confined to transient intense emotional experiences, nor evoked only by nature in its more tremendous manifestations. Wonder is a form of experience that has been thought by a number of philosophers to be important in several areas of life – in the scientific, the religious and the aesthetic spheres. In all these spheres, wonder is a response to the natural world or to particular aspects of it. In the scientific and aesthetic spheres the response is to natural phenomena in and for themselves; in the religious sphere it is a response to the natural as revealing more than natural powers. If the capacity for wonder can be exercised well or badly – too much or too little, to appropriate or to inappropriate objects – then there is a virtue, or virtues, and a vice, or vices, associated with it. What they might be is to be explored next.

Wonder and associated virtues

The nature and value of wonder has been discussed by the philosopher Ronald Hepburn; in his essay 'Wonder' (in Hepburn (1984)), he suggests that wonder has affinities with several virtues that are relevant to our attitudes and behaviour towards the non-human. But first we need to get clear about what wonder is, and how it differs from such related experiences as amazement, astonishment and curiosity. To begin with there is wonder in the sense of wondering why – the kind of wondering that leads someone to find something out.

> Undeniably wonder can stimulate a person to enquiry: it may be intensified when the enquiry succeeds and the enigmatic in nature becomes intelligible. But it may thereafter dwindle, as its object becomes assimilated and commonplace knowledge. The question then arises: Must it always be so? Often the displacement of wonder is of no great moment to us. Yet, equally undeniably, wonder can also be highly valued as a form of human experience, overlapping with both the aesthetic and the religious; and we may wish it did possess stability and were invulnerable to undermining ...We do not wish to be found in the posture of foolish wonder – wonder that is purely the function of our ignorance. Yet many of us are no more happy with the thought of the universal displaceability (even if only in principle) of wonder: 'the odds is gone, And there is nothing left remarkable Beneath the visiting moon'.
>
> Consider then the question of what I called the displacement and stabilising of wonder. Some philosophers have indicated, in different idioms, a distinction between an ephemeral emotional response to some baffling phenomenon or disturbing discontinuity in experience, and a steadier, perhaps permanently available, response to what is apprehended as worthy of wonder.

Kant's usage is striking and suggestive. He certainly distinguishes between astonishment (*Verwunderung*) which fades as a sense of novelty diminishes, and wonderment that is steady and unthreatened (*Bewunderung*). We apply the expressions 'sublime' and 'noble' to certain objects, 'provided they do not so much excite astonishment', which is directed at 'novelty exceeding expectation', as admiration (or wonder) – 'an astonishment that does not cease when the novelty wears off'. And there is no reason to omit the best known of all Kant's remarks on wonder:

> Two things fill the mind with ever new and increasing admiration (*Bewunderung*) and awe, the oftener and the more steadily we reflect on them: *the starry heavens above and the moral law within.*
>
> [Kant (1873 edn), p.260]

The oftener and more steadily... Kant, that is, is untroubled by worries about instability in this occasion of wonder. Its objects are 'connected directly with the consciousness of my existence', i.e. they reveal to me how things stand. In the transient shock of astonishment one may suspect illusion – 'doubt in one's own eyesight'; but wonder endures, where no doubt about eyesight remains. We read rather of an 'expansion of the mind'.

We could then, tentatively, bring wonder in some of its manifestations into close relation with the concept of *truth* and concern to attain the truth. It would be unsurprising if a person attached more importance to experience of wonder at an object which he sees himself as having truly apprehended, than to wonder or 'astonishment' that may well have a misperceived object. Foolish or stupid wonder may be wonder arising only from failure to grasp or realize what is before one.

[...]

I want to revert to the contrast, picked out in Kant, between the proper objects of wonder, and astonishment at 'mere' novelty. Although wonder itself has a questioning and questing aspect, it rests in its objects, once they are judged in some way *worthy* of wonder. This is an attitude quite different from the thrust of curiosity or the itch after the novel. Heidegger touches on such contrasts in *Being and Time.* Mere curiosity is given an inferior place in Heidegger's scheme. He speaks of curiosity as 'leaping from novelty to novelty... not tarrying'. 'Curiosity has nothing to do with observing entities and marvelling at them. To be amazed to the point of not understanding is something in which it has no interest. Rather it concerns itself with a kind of knowing, but just in order to have known'. When curiosity 'obtains sight of anything, it already looks away to what is coming next', it never 'dwells anywhere'.

This rings true: curiosity–knowledge is seen as a kind of possession, a tick on the tourist's place-list. Wonder does not see its objects possessively: they remain 'other' and unmastered. Wonder does dwell in its objects with rapt attentiveness. There seems, too, a variable relation between the element of curiosity or interrogation in wonder and a contemplative–appreciative aspect ('dwelling'), in which it is furthest from mere curiosity. I think, however, that even where enquiry has reached some terminus – perhaps the mystery of the sheer existence of the world – that interrogative element, no longer expecting any further answers, may still persist in a muted and generalized form within wonderment. With it also may persist an odd sense of the *gratuitousness* of the object and its qualities. Its existence strikes us as a gift, undeserved. A sense of *unlikelihood* pervades the experience. But these aspects are highly elusive, and their description can hardly avoid metaphor.

(Hepburn (1984), pp.132–5)

To be appropriate objects of wonder, then, phenomena must not be surprising simply because we are unfamiliar with them, nor improbable only to someone who is ignorant of the explanation of their happening. But despite these conditions they do seem to leave us with quite a variety of things that are appropriate objects of wonder. Of these, some disclose themselves only to the systematically observant eye or to the reflective mind; others make an immediate impact on the senses. In what follows I give a number of examples (drawing upon Hepburn's paper, but treating his account with some freedom).

There are attention-grabbing natural phenomena of an extravagantly spectacular kind –rainbows, sunsets, suddenly revealed vistas as one reaches a special viewpoint, great waterfalls; but also equally breathtaking miniatures – a tiny delicate fern in a rock crevice, a pattern of different lichens, rust and lime-green, on a stone. These are just accepted as gifts, not things to be subjected to scrutiny.

But there are less obvious objects of wonder; in nature, for instance, there is the astonishing variety of living things, the intricacy of their structures and complexity of their behaviour. Such things used to be taken as evidence of design in nature. Now people are more likely to believe that natural selection can explain them. That might seem to reduce the sense of wonder, but does it? The fact of the matter, that things are like this, is a source of wonder; and it is an additional source of wonder that apparent design should be the result of processes that operate without intention.

The last point introduces a third source of wonder, the fact that the world is intelligible, that it is possible to explain the vast variety of goings on in the world in a systematic way, that there are laws of nature. Moreover, those laws have produced beings capable of discovering them. As Hepburn says,

Wonder may be elicited not only by the bare notion of intelligible structure. For the particular set of laws progressively uncovered are laws which have produced life, consciousness, freedom, moral and aesthetic awareness. Certainly, had they not done so ('had it in them' to do so), we could not make this observation or do any wondering. Yet that does not rule out the appropriateness of wonder at the fulfilment of enormous numbers of conditions, successive and simultaneous, for the emergence of sentient and rational beings.

(Ibid., p.141)

And it seems that the more we know about those conditions the more there is to wonder at.

That the world is the way it is is a source of wonder, but that it exists at all is perhaps the greatest source of wonder. There might have been nothing. It does not seem necessary that there should be a world rather than no world. That a world exists is a contingent fact. The possibility that the world might not have existed, but does, has seemed and still seems to many people, to deserve, and possibly to demand, an explanation. God has been suggested as an explanation by some. Others prefer to resign themselves to the belief that no explanation is to be had. But whichever of these opposed stances is adopted, that the world exists is a source of wonder.

Having considered what makes something an appropriate object of wonder it is timely to reflect on how the experience of wonder relates to the virtues that may be exercised in our dealings with natural things. The key to this lies in the *quality of attention* that is characteristic of the wondering attitude.

Below is a further extract from Hepburn's essay. Read it with the following questions in mind, and note down your answers. Compare answers (1)–(3) with those at the back of the book before reading my discussion that follows.

EXERCISE 13
Wonder

1   What considerations does Hepburn offer in support of the claim that wonder is a reasonable attitude to the world?

2   What are the virtues that are explicitly said to have an affinity with wonder?

3   There is another, not mentioned in the following extract but suggested in the final paragraph of the previous extract (p.82); what is it?

4   Which of these virtues are ones that you think might be exercised in our dealings with the non-human?

The ethical affinities of wonder. No ... argument seems feasible to show that wonder is rationally demanded towards the world ... I see no way of decisively excluding a wide range of alternative responses to the basic cosmic situation in relation to man: sardonic or ironical or depressive (at the disproportion between our capacities and aspirations and the limitations and 'chanciness' of human life and fulfilment). 'Nausea' and dread are others. Yet this is not to say that there is nothing for reason to do in discriminating between the alternatives.

83

Temperamentally, individuals find certain of the options specially compelling: but the responses are also modifiable by reflection. For instance it can be argued that ironical and sardonic attitudes, when they predominate, tend regrettably to shield or mask a person from experiences of certain types of value, including high values which (once acknowledged) would evoke awe or humility. Again, a response of dread at the human predicament keeps the prospect of our individual death before us, anticipates it, as it were, and so gives the 'dreadful' a gratuitously debilitating hold over life as a whole.

Considerations of the same order can be brought in favour of fostering the attitude and experience of wonder. They arise from the life-enhancing character of wonder, appreciative and open, opposed to the self-protective and consolatory. Particularly relevant is a set of liaisons or affinities that connect wonder with moral attitudes. They concern dispositions which, if they are given place in an integrated human life, form a consistent, harmonious set.

The attitude of wonder is notably and essentially *other-acknowledging*.[1] It is not shut up in self-concern or quasi-solipsistic[2] withdrawal. Some philosophers have thought that moral solidarity with others was best promoted by a metaphysic which denied the ultimate separation of individual selves (Schopenhauer was one). I should want to argue on the contrary that the task and distinctive point of view of morality are obscure until the *otherness* of one's neighbour is realized, and realized with it is the possibility of action purely and simply on another's behalf.

Admittedly, it is easy to exaggerate the reliability of carrying over attitudes and emotional responses from one domain to another, from the non-moral to the moral. Few people can have taken more seriously than Wordsworth both the fostering of wonder and exploring the affinities between attitudes to non-human nature and to persons in moral relationship. Yet 'even in his own case', John Beer has recently written, Wordsworth 'could not be sure that the experiences of wonder had always led to the love of humanity: there was some evidence that, in his youth, cultivation of the wonderful in nature led to an isolating aestheticism'.

There is, even so, a close affinity between the attitude of wonder itself – non-exploitative, non-utilitarian – and attitudes that seek to affirm and respect other-being. Unlike some religio-ethical attitudes, for instance the Puritanical, wonder does not deflect attention and concern away from the phenomenal world [the physical world as presented to experience], but on the contrary values and enjoys its diversity. Respect for nature as such, and in particular for living beings, is not Kant's *Achtung* [respect for persons as ends in themselves], though it does rule out acts of vandalism and thoughtless manipulation. The nearer the object comes to having the life, sentience, and rational powers proper to moral person-hood, the more the element of respect in wonder takes on the

Kantian quality. The more intense a person's wonder at the human brain, so inadequately modelled by any of our favoured mechanical analogies, the less bearable becomes the thought, for instance, of wantonly putting a bullet through it or crushing it with a rifle-butt.

A close affinity between wonder and *compassion* has been acknowledged by various writers. Where a human life is the object of wonder, there can be a poignant realization of both potentiality and fragility. From that view of humanity compassion can readily flow.

To respect and compassion, as moral correlates to wonder, we could add *gentleness* – a concern not to blunder into a damaging manipulation of another. The agent realizes the blinding effects of self-absorption, the mis-perception of others and others' needs that can stem from it.

From a wondering recognition of forms of value proper to other beings, and a refusal to see them in terms of one's own utility purposes, there is only a short step to *humility*. Humility, like wonder, involves openness to new forms of value: both are opposed to the attitude of 'We've seen it all!'

The latter attitude is even more hostile to wonder than the attitude of 'taking for granted', for behind it stands an implicit false picture of the world. It sees us as standing *vis-à-vis* nature as a spoiled child stands to his home – arranged for his sole convenience and support, and when it fails so to function, the proper object of his rage, resentment or sullen boredom.

(Ibid., pp.144–6)

DISCUSSION

This discussion includes, but goes well beyond, what you could have been expected to answer to Questions 1–3.

In the first paragraph of this extract, Hepburn acknowledges that the appropriateness of wonder is not amenable to proof; it is not 'rationally demanded'. But he also claims that reasons can be given for preferring it to alternative responses to the world. His main claim is that wonder is 'life-enhancing', 'appreciative and open, opposed to the self-protective and consolatory'. The terms 'appreciative' and 'open' are further elucidated in what follows. Wonder is 'other-acknowledging', an attitude towards objects – which may be human or non-human – which are recognized as being separate from the wondering self, and worth attending to for what they are. Wonder is open in the sense that it is an attitude that lets others into consciousness, prompting us to look at them as they are, not projecting on to them our own fantasies and desires. In the case of other human beings this involves heeding one of George Bernard Shaw's epigrammatic dicta: 'Do not treat others as you would like to be treated. They may have different tastes'. What may be called a disinterested or impersonal attention (terms often used by philosophers but not actually by Hepburn) may be paid to the non-human too. Disinterested or impersonal attention is to attend to what things are in themselves, to refrain from looking at them as useful to us. That wonder involves disinterested attention implies that, as Hepburn puts it, it is non-exploitative, non-utilitarian.[3] It looks past their instrumental value to what is there of non-instrumental value. That there is value other than instrumental value to be appreciated is a **necessary condition** of the appropriateness of wonder. Wonder, to be appropriate, must involve the valuing of what is worthy of being valued. But what things have in them worth valuing is only apparent to those who know how to look at them disinterestedly.

necessary and sufficient conditions

Hepburn is careful not just to lump together the respect for non-human nature and respect for rational and sentient beings. These, he implies, are different kinds of respect. The kind that is associated with Kant is restricted to beings who have a conception of themselves, and are in Tom Regan's sense 'subjects of a life' (see Book 2, pp.222–32). But equally, Hepburn clearly believes that both forms of respect are appropriate, and that both are fostered by wonder. Leaving aside the Kantian respect, Hepburn gives us a complex description of a virtue which seems to have both intellectual and moral components. Openness includes the disinterested attention to things that allows a correct apprehension of them, and the appreciative attention that allows a recognition of their value, which is not merely an intellectual matter but involves enjoyment, absorption, delight, fascination, all the feelings with which we respond to the endless variety of the natural world.

To respect, Hepburn adds three other virtues that, as he puts it, have an affinity with wonder: compassion, gentleness and humility. Compassion is a virtue that regards the feelings, and in particular the sufferings of others, so the others to whom it is extended can include only those who have feelings (cf. Hepburn's claim that morality's task is to realize 'the *otherness* of one's neighbour'). Compassion for trees is ruled out as incompatible with a correct apprehension of their nature. Gentleness has wider scope: 'concern not to blunder into a damaging manipulation of another' can encompass restraint in dealings with nature at large. Humility calls for rather more comment.

Humility is conventionally contrasted with pride. In the Christian tradition humility is a virtue and pride, if not a vice, is at any rate a dangerous thing. In contrast to this, in the ethics of the classical pagan tradition pride is a virtue. If humility means simply not over-estimating one's own merit and importance, not denying one's dependence, not thinking that everything is owed to one and one owes nothing to others, then it may not be at bottom incompatible with what the ancients called pride, because what they meant by pride was a correct estimate of those things. There is still a difference. For the Christian moralist the greater danger is to claim too much, for the pagan moralist the greater danger is to claim too little. Both are, no doubt, to be avoided. We should discriminate between different sorts of claim too. To see nature as 'arranged for [our] sole convenience and support' is to have a picture of the world which is false, as Hepburn points out, and also conceited. But the view of some radical environmentalists that we should attach no special value to the possession of rational capacities, regarding all nature, of which we are but a part, as of equal value, may involve species denigration, an excessive and false humility.

In the final paragraph of the first Hepburn extract (p.82) he speaks of certain aspects of the world, or of the existence of the world as a whole, as gratuitous – 'a gift, undeserved'. Such a view is grounded on the virtue of gratitude – a virtue that has an affinity with wonder. We think that gratitude is due to those who have conferred benefits on us – that it is owed to persons. So it may be thought that this is an appropriate attitude to nature only if nature is the work of a benign personal being. There's no doubt that one can feel thankful for a shower of rain, for the beauty of a spring morning and for many other things. There is something right about the feeling, but perhaps thankfulness is not its appropriate name. The reason why it is natural to call it thankfulness or gratitude may be that the feeling is closely analogous to the one we have when we receive good from some person. That this is one of the feelings that finds expression in religious language addressed to a creator need not mean that it presupposes the existence of such a being. But if we wish to sterilize our language of religious associations – a difficult thing even for the most secular minded – we can simply speak of being glad. Voltaire said that if God did not exist it would be necessary to invent him, and perhaps this is one of the better reasons for inventing him. (A test: read Hopkins's poem 'Pied Beauty' (Reading 16) and ask yourself whether the feeling expressed would still make sense if there were not, contrary to Hopkins's belief, anyone to praise.)

Religious and secular attitudes

There is a virtue not discussed by Hepburn, but which appears to be related to wonder and which is held by some to be exercised in relation to the non-human world. That virtue is piety. Roger Scruton, in *Animal Rights and Wrongs,* characterizes it in such a way that it has some similarities to Hepburn's wonder:

> Put in simple terms, piety means the deep down recognition of our frailty and dependence, the acknowledgement that the burden we inherit cannot be sustained unaided, the disposition to give thanks for our existence and reverence to the world on which we depend, and the sense of the unfathomable mystery which surrounds our coming to be and our passing away. All these feelings come together in our humility before the works of nature ...
>
> (Scruton (1996), pp.55–6)

To someone committed to some form of theism this will seem entirely acceptable, but, unlike Hepburn's wonder, it is questionable whether it can be given a secular interpretation. In this discussion I have not wanted to deny the truth of theistic views of nature, but rather to identify some virtues that remain appropriate even if religious beliefs and attitudes are left aside. If Scruton implies that sustaining 'the burden we inherit' – whatever burden that is supposed to be – requires *supernatural* aid; that we have a disposition to give thanks to and feel reverence for something above and beyond the natural world itself, then piety understood as he intends it cannot be a secular virtue, because it necessarily presupposes a religious point of view of the world. There is no such presupposition with respect to wonder.

It is important to the secular environmentalist to escape the charge that her valuing of nature depends on an implicit appeal to religious beliefs that she officially rejects. Her defence is that nature, just viewed as itself, is wonderful. It is not wonderful because a god created it, and we do not need to think a god created it to think it is wonderful. That gets things the wrong way round: if we think a god created the natural world and deserves our thanks for it, that must be because it is worth giving thanks for – this is not a case where it is just the thought that counts. Any argument for the existence of a god based on the goodness of the world must presuppose that it is good. Thus the secular and religious conservationists share a common basis for their concerns, and if anything it is the religious who must borrow from the secular, rather than the other way round.

EXERCISE 14

Two problems with wonder

Consider the following two problems in the light of the Hepburn extracts. Write your own brief answers to the questions posed.

1   Wonder is said to imply an attitude to others (remember that 'others' here is meant to include any natural object, not just other human beings) that is non-instrumental and non-exploitative. But human beings necessarily exploit nature, manipulating it in their agriculture and their production of articles of use. Does an ethic of respect for nature rule out all such activity? Must we, to be virtuous, avoid any kind of modification of nature?

2   Although not claiming that wonder is rationally demanded – that it can be proved to be the only attitude to the world that a rational person could have – Hepburn does claim that it gives us the possibility of becoming aware of 'high values' which some other attitudes make unavailable. Do you think these values are indispensable to human well-being? *yes*

---

1   *Must we, to be virtuous, avoid any kind of modification of nature?* The problem is whether the virtues that involve a non-instrumental and non-exploitative concern for nature preclude any exploitation of nature's resources. If so, we would have an absurd result which would undermine the case for these virtues, for a policy of no exploitation, no digging, no cultivation, no building, would make human life impossible. Recognizing these virtues does not in fact have this **absurd consequence** because virtues do not imply absolute rules. That is to say that acting in accordance with the virtues cannot be reduced to a set of rules which say never do this or always do that. A virtuous agent will often be confronted by a choice between actions that involve competing values. Conservation values and human needs frequently compete, for instance, when decisions have to be made about the preservation or exploitation of old-established forest. What the environmental virtues ensure, if they genuinely operate in the agent's choices, is that instrumental values do not automatically decide the issue. But since values compete, and the agent's virtues do not automatically point to one choice as the correct one, something else is needed to make choice possible. This is the intellectual virtue of judgement or practical wisdom – the ability to identify the relevant features of the situation, assess the consequences of alternative choices, weigh the different values at stake, and finally decide on the best practicable solution. This is a description that will fall far short of satisfying the demand for a surefire method of making decisions about environmental issues, or indeed any other kind. But it is doubtful whether any ethical theory can actually satisfy this demand. Utilitarianism claims to satisfy it, as does the utilitarian-inspired method of cost benefit analysis (pp.47–53), but we have seen that there are strong reasons for doubting that either succeeds. Rights theory requires some way of resolving conflicts between competing rights, and it is far from obvious that any simple rule exists for doing this. Contractarian ethics gives a general description of the *method* of making moral rules, but leaves open which rules in particular the contracting parties will arrive at. A possible explanation of this general failure is that providing surefire decision procedures is no part of the business of theoretical ethics; indeed, that a proper understanding of the limits of theory involves the recognition that ultimate

DISCUSSION

absurd
consequences
move

choices of action or policy are necessarily a matter of intelligent practice, not theory.

2   *Are Hepburn's 'high values' indispensable to human well-being?* The problem is whether the virtues attendant on the capacity for wonder, or those involved in the activities of scientific and aesthetic appreciation of nature, prove to be indispensable for human well-being? There are other objects of wonder than the works of nature. One may wonder at the stupendous creations of human culture – cities, great works of art, masterpieces of engineering, religions, philosophical systems, computers, music, chess. There are capacities for enjoying and participating in the production and continuance of these, and virtues required for proper participation. Many people enjoy worthwhile lives largely, or even entirely, through cultural activities, not only including those mentioned, but also such things as pubbing, discoing, playing or watching football (on artificial grass pitches). Who needs nature when the full tide of human existence flows at Charing Cross, as Dr Johnson remarked? (Over-pious sentiments about nature can find an antidote in some stanzas from Auden's 'Letter to Lord Byron' (Reading 16).)

Any reply to this must concede that it is probably true that for many individuals direct contact with nature is not a prime necessity, and a strong argument would be needed to show that they must be living less than fully human lives. But this conceded, it remains to be said that the life of culture depends for its very existence on the life of nature, and that to be unaware of that shows an inadequate sense of reality. Humility, a recognition of the dependence of our created forms of life on a nature that we do not create, is a virtue that even the complete urbanite does well to cultivate.

The value of scientific enquiry

For Hepburn wonder is a feeling that is involved in quite various kinds of experience and activity, scientific enquiry being but one. Some readers, including some with green sympathies, may be surprised to find science included at all. There is a widely held view that science, as practised since the seventeenth century, regards the natural world instrumentally, as something to be understood in order that it can be controlled and exploited. Many green writers believe that science has a malign influence and is the cause, not the cure of environmental ills. We now consider an examination of the value of scientific enquiry which opposes this view. It emphasizes a way of perceiving things that is, in Hepburn's terms, non-exploitative and other-acknowledging.

Now read the extract by John O'Neill (Reading 8) and then answer the questions below.

EXERCISE 15
Science and wonder

1   Set out the argument of the first section, 'Science, value and human well-being', as premises and conclusion(s).

When doing this sort of analysis of an argument remember that the first thing to do is to identify the conclusion or conclusions that the writer is arguing for. This may not be immediately apparent: the conclusion may not be flagged as such, and may not even be stated in so many words. Remember too that arguments often have **unstated premises**; this argument has an important one, which you should try to identify. The argument may give you a bit of trouble – it did me – and you would be well advised not to get stuck on it: give it a go, but allot a limited time to it.

enthymeme

2   How would you explain the phrase 'the humanization of the senses' (p.222)?

3   Why, according to O'Neill, is the humanization of the senses conducive to human well-being?

4   What are the virtues, moral and intellectual, that can be developed by a scientific education?

5   What are the vices of the form of scientific enquiry criticized in the second section of the Reading?

DISCUSSION

1   The argument aims to establish that there is, or can be, a connection between the practice of science and human well-being. The connection is made by the idea of the disinterested (non-instrumental) use of the senses. This is the capacity that allows responsiveness to the particular qualities of natural objects, and so to what is wonderful and beautiful in them. The connection with well-being is that this capacity is characteristically human and its exercise therefore 'part of a life in which human capacities are developed. It is a component of human well-being'. The connection with science is that, practised in a certain way, it realizes the capacity for the disinterested use of the senses. So the main conclusion, I suggest, may be stated as follows:

   Conclusion   Science, practised in a certain way, is a component of human well-being.

Here is one way – there may be others – to lay out the argument for that conclusion:

   Premise 1   Contemplation of the wonderful and beautiful in nature exercises the capacity for disinterested perception.

Premise 2	The capacity for disinterested perception is a characteristically human capacity.
Conclusion 1	Contemplation of the wonderful and beautiful in nature exercises a characteristically human capacity.
Premise 3	An activity that exercises a characteristically human activity is a component of human well-being.
Conclusion 2	Contemplation of the wonderful and beautiful in nature is a component of human well-being.
Premise 4	Science, practised in a certain way, is the contemplation of the wonderful and beautiful in nature.
Conclusion 3	Science, practised in a certain way, is a component of human well-being.

The important unstated premise is Premise 3.

2   The idea of the humanization of the senses depends on the same distinction that Hepburn also uses between the disinterested way of viewing things and the instrumental way of viewing them. O'Neill suggests, following Aristotle and Marx, that the former is characteristic of human beings, and its development necessary if a person is to enjoy a distinctively human kind of life.

3   The connection between the humanization of the senses and human well-being depends on the view of well-being developed by Aristotle, that, for human beings, well-being consists in the exercise of specifically human capacities. There are capacities that we share with other animals: we enjoy eating, just as pigs do; but a life that satisfies a pig cannot satisfy a human being, because it does not exercise the capacities that we have but pigs do not. This is a particular case of the unstated premise, Premise 3, of the argument.

4   O'Neill does not pretend to offer a systematic account of the intellectual virtues exercised in scientific work, but he probably says enough: highly developed powers of observation, critical ability in appraising arguments, openness to the criticism of others. The principal moral virtue seems to be similar to the respect that Hepburn also identifies, which is associated with the recognition, arising from the disinterested view, that things have non-instrumental value (see Chapter 2, pp.40ff. above). It is their possessing this sensitivity to non-instrumental value that he thinks justifies listening to ecologists on questions of what is worth preserving.

5   O'Neill, elsewhere in his book (O'Neill (1993), pp.148–52), deplores the tendency of some environmentalists to attack science as encouraging an

instrumental view of nature; Reading 8 goes some way to explaining why he thinks that attack to be misguided. But an important reservation is implied when he says 'A scientific education *can* allow the observer to see what is there and to respond to it in a disinterested way'(p.223). 'Can' is not 'must'. There is, he contends, a corrupt form of science in which the investigator is motivated by 'the itch of curiosity'. What vices are exemplified in scientific work pursued in this way? I don't think he wants to suggest that the curiosity-driven investigator lacks the intellectual virtues mentioned in the answer to Question 4, although the discussion of the cases of Bernard and Fowles in terms of failure to *see* (or in Bernard's case, to see or hear), might suggest otherwise. In one sense they see and hear perfectly well. It is not that their observation is inaccurate, but that it is not disinterested. The first passage from Fowles makes it clear that he must have observed the orchid with care in order to identify it. What he has not done is to let his attention dwell on it for its own sake, for what qualities it has in itself, not considered as a rarity, a collector's 'scalp'.

One of the vices O'Neill thinks is exemplified in science pursued in this way is intemperance – the excessive pursuit of pleasure, or of one kind of pleasure – to the exclusion of other goods. Curiosity, the 'appetite to know' as described by Augustine, is presented as analogous to the bodily appetites, so may be described, metaphorically, as lust or greed. Heidegger's strictures on curiosity, quoted by Hepburn (p.81), are on similar lines. But it might well be objected that just as one need not pursue bodily pleasures to excess or to the exclusion of other goods, and so not intemperately, so one may avoid excessive curiosity. This objection seems to me well taken, and prompts the question whether there is anything vicious about curiosity in moderation. It might be replied, however, that this is to overlook the fundamental objection to curiosity: that it reduces natural things to a means to the end of satisfying the desire to know. This involves a failure of practical wisdom (pp.225–6), O'Neill believes. The nature of the mistake is brought out in the paragraph about friendship (p.225). The analogy may be summed up in this way: just as one misses out on the pleasures of friendship if one seeks friendship for the sake of pleasure, so one misses out on the pleasures of knowledge if one seeks knowledge for the sake of pleasure. These are particular instances of the general principle that to achieve one's own well-being one must have some objects of disinterested concern, that one cares about but not for one's own sake.

Consider the following problem in the light of the discussions in the Hepburn extracts and the O'Neill Reading. Write your own brief answer to the question posed.

EXERCISE 16
Wonder: a third problem

There appears to be a third problem with wonder. Two aspects of Hepburn's view need to be looked at together, because their combination may seem perplexing. On the one hand, he rests the case for wonder on its life-enhancing character, connecting it with 'dispositions which, if they are given place in an integrated human life, form a consistent, harmonious set' (p.84). This puts the emphasis on the benefit to the individual of having a disposition to view the world with wonder. On the other hand, 'the attitude of wonder is notably and essentially *other-acknowledging*. It is not shut up in self-concern or quasi-solipsistic withdrawal' (ibid.). It is often thought that to be truly altruistic, to be concerned with others for their own sake, is incompatible with the agent's having any concern with his own interests, or standing to gain any benefit of his own. In other words, does it involve a contradiction to say that to view others in a disinterested and impersonal way is in the interest of the agent?

The O'Neill Reading suggests a way in which this problem can be answered.

DISCUSSION

Does it involve a contradiction to say that to view others in a disinterested and impersonal way is in the interest of the agent? There seems to be a paradox in saying that a disinterested concern for natural objects can be in a person's own interest. I hope that the air of paradox will have been dissipated by the discussion of the Reading from O'Neill, especially the paragraph towards the end (p.226) where he draws an analogy between friendship and knowledge. The point is if well-being depends on the development of one's human capacities, and if the development of certain of my capacities requires disinterested concern for others (human or non-human), then such disinterested concern will contribute to my well-being. What creates the seeming paradox is the idea that one cultivates one's powers of observation, for example, for the sake of pleasure, or satisfaction, so that this state of oneself, rather than an understanding of the object, is the aim of one's activity. That is to make pleasure (satisfaction, well-being) the motive rather than – as it should be – the consequence of the activity.

READING
Care

Read now the remainder of the Reading by Jane Howarth (Reading 9, pp.232 onwards) in which she gives an account of cherishing and draws a comparison between it and care, the term that the phenomenologist Heidegger uses to denote a fundamental relationship between human beings and nature. The philosophical approach is different from those of Hepburn and O'Neill, but there are interesting similarities. Two things to take particular note of are: the account of contemplation, and the description of 'contemplating well'; the connection between contemplating well and 'taking care of'.

Conclusion

The results of this chapter complement Chapter 2 in developing further the distinction between instrumental and non-instrumental attitudes to, and ways of seeing, nature. Although this account of some of the virtues is human centred in the sense that the virtues are all obviously human qualities, none the less they involve attitudes to nature that transcend a merely instrumental interest. This is a central contention of both Hepburn and O'Neill. Both emphasize the possibility of seeing things as they are, of disinterested awareness, which yields an appreciation of the non-instrumental values in natural features and objects, and connects with satisfactions of contemplation, rather than consumption, and conduct that is conservative rather than exploitative and protective rather than destructive.

Chapter summary

An account of virtues as qualities that enable us to use our capacities well involves the recognition of virtues of intellect as well as virtues of character, both of which can be exercised in our dealing with nature. Among the latter are sensitivity to the pleasures of seeing, hearing and the other senses, and susceptibility to the grandeur of nature. Other virtues, both of character and of intellect, come into view when the experience of wonder is examined. Wonder is characterized by its disinterestedness: it is a mode of attention to an object which is concerned not with its instrumental properties but with what it is, and opens the mind to the appreciation of the particular qualities of the object. Science is one activity in which the experience of wonder, and its associated virtues, can be (but not inevitably) found, though the activity is not unique in this respect.

Disinterested openness to the world, and the exercise of the human capacities required to observe and understand it, contribute to human well-being. This claim implies that caring disinterestedly for something outside oneself contributes to a person's well-being. That may seem paradoxical at first sight, but there is reason to think that it is true. Caution is needed, however, in claiming that any person needs their life, if it is to be a good life, to contain a large element of first-hand experience of nature. Life-enhancing experiences come in many forms, and it may be that none is absolutely indispensable.

Further reading

Because so little has been written on the virtues in relation to environmental ethics, I would only suggest John O'Neill's *Ecology, Policy and Politics*, Routledge, 1993 (from which Reading 8 was taken). It is the most thorough example that I know of an Aristotle-inspired approach to environmental ethics.

Notes

[1] [Others here includes any natural object, not just other human beings.]

[2] [Solipsism is the belief that only I exist.]

[3] This use of the word 'utilitarian' is a non-technical one, unconnected with the ethical theory utilitarianism. In this non-technical use it characterizes an attitude which considers things under their instrumental aspect, as useful to human beings (what the thing is for).

CHAPTER 5

What Entities have Independent Moral Status?

OBJECTIVES

When you have worked through this chapter you should have:

■ Understood the view that any living thing has a good of its own in virtue of which it has independent moral status.

■ Have considered a criticism based on a distinction between two senses of 'the good of a being': its well-being and its perfection.

Introduction

This chapter returns to an issue that was raised in Chapter 1. Which beings have independent moral status? We considered the division between those who think that a human-centred ethics can, and those who think that it cannot, provide an adequate foundation for an ethics of care for local environments and the global environment. I suggested that the first thing to do in trying to resolve this issue was to consider what implications for our treatment of our environments a properly developed human-centred ethics would have. The last three chapters have followed up that suggestion. What I believe emerges from this enquiry is that many human goods – things that contribute to our well-being – depend on the existence of an unspoiled natural environment, not only in ways that make natural features and systems instrumentally valuable, but in ways that make them non-instrumentally valuable.

Is that enough? Should it satisfy the exponents of deep positions? I think it should make them more careful in painting the evils of the human-centred standpoint, which has often been caricatured as narrowly instrumental, concerned with the natural world only as a set of resources to be exploited. That is not an adequate representation of the way nature matters to us. Even so, the deep green environmentalist will protest that the enriched account of the human-centred approach still leaves the case for conservation of nature dependent on the human interest in it. However non-instrumental our concern for nature, in view of its value as a constituent of human well-being, it is still as an object of our concern that nature has value on this approach. That is not the same, the protest continues, as acknowledging that nature has value in its own right, that it has independent moral status.

Independent moral status and its extension

To ascribe independent moral status is different from ascribing either instrumental or non-instrumental value. To understand how, consider the difference between the ways in which human beings can matter. First, it is quite proper to value others for their usefulness. The celebrated Kantian principle (the 'categorical imperative'), 'Act in such a way that you always treat humanity, whether in your own person or in the person of any other, never simply as a means, but always at the same time as an end' (Kant (1948 edn), p.91) does not forbid treating people as means, but treating them *merely* as means. Secondly, there are many people whom one regards, unless one is a complete misanthrope, with varying degrees of friendship; one values them for their own sake. These are the people who are within the range of one's limited sympathies (pp.58–9). But the majority of human beings are beyond that range; they are not my friends and I do not value them in the way I value my friends. But they still matter. I have to consider them, taking their interests or rights into account as making claims upon me independent of my own interests, or attitudes, or feelings. They are objects of respect in the sense indicated by the Kantian principle.

To have independent moral status is to be, in this sense, a source of claims that others must take into account independent of their own interests, attitudes, or feelings. It is this status that nature is denied, even by the enriched version of the human-centred approach.

In this chapter we shall consider an attempt to extend independent moral status, in this sense, beyond human beings, beyond sentient beings, to all living things.

The whole of Book 2 was about the reasons that can be offered for believing that animals matter, either all species of animal or some species. Two of the theories that were discussed, though opposed in one way, have an important feature in common. Singer's utilitarian defence of animals and Regan's rights-based defence give different basic reasons for bringing them into the circle of moral concern. Singer holds that it is the fact that (most) animals have interests, because they are sentient. Regan holds that (some) animals have inherent value, because they are experiencing subjects of a life. What the two theories have in common is that both justify attributing independent moral status to animals on the basis of their possessing a single characteristic which is claimed to be the passport to that moral status. Two points about this approach are noteworthy:

1. The validity of the passport is assured by the fact that it is because human beings possess that single characteristic they are already admitted. It can only be arbitrary to exclude other passport holders. The argument for extending independent moral status to animals has the form:

   Premise 1   Human beings have independent moral status because they possess feature *F*.

   Premise 2   Animals also possess *F*.

   Conclusion   Therefore animals have independent moral status.

2. Passports are designed to keep people out as well as let them in. To cash the metaphor, both sentience and being the subject of a life are principles of exclusion as well as inclusion. If a being is not sentient, it can have no interests, so in its case there is nothing to consider. If a being is not a subject of a life, it lacks inherent value, so in its case there is no question of its having rights. Each principle identifies a favoured class of beings and marks a boundary around them.

The advance of animal liberation as a movement was regarded with marked reserve by environmentalists because the philosophical rationale provided for it, by Singer in particular, extended moral status to animals by establishing a criterion that excluded most of the natural world as surely as the most narrowly human speciesism.[1] One of them, in a paper whose title deliberately echoes that of Singer's original review article (Singer (1973)) and of his book (Singer (1975)), declared:

> I need only to stand in the midst of a clear-cut forest, a strip-mined hillside, a defoliated jungle, or a dammed canyon to feel uneasy with assumptions that could yield the conclusion that no human action can make any difference to the welfare of anything but sentient animals.
>
> (Rodman (1977), p.89)

The view being challenged here is that only sentient beings – those that can experience pleasure and pain – can sensibly be said to fare well or badly, that the notion of welfare (well-being) simply does not apply to non-sentient beings, such as a tree, a forest, or a river.

To many people it has seemed obvious that at least all living things, whether sentient or not, are worthy of respect. That is an important principle in some cultures. In the Western tradition it is perhaps thought of by most people as a kind of rather admirable eccentricity – rather like celibacy, all right as an ideal but seriously practised by few. In recent environmental philosophy a serious attempt has been made by some philosophers to provide a rational defence of the principle. One philosopher who has done so, and whose view we shall consider here, is Paul W. Taylor. He calls the principle 'respect for nature', but 'respect for life' might be a better name, because, as we shall shortly see, it is individual living things that are the primary objects of respect, and such entities as rivers or collective entities such as species only insofar as they contain or consist of individual living things.

A brief review of Taylor's theory

We are going to examine one aspect in particular of Taylor's theory, but to see how that aspect fits into his overall argument, we need to begin with a survey.

The attitude of respect for nature

For Taylor, respect for nature is more than a principle, it is a whole way of thinking, feeling and acting – he calls it 'the attitude of respect for nature'. To have the attitude is to consider the flourishing of wild (undomesticated) living things to be a good thing, good not instrumentally because their flourishing in various ways promotes our own flourishing, as human beings, but good in itself. It is also to refrain from harming and to promote the good of wild living things, and to feel pleased when they flourish and displeased when they are harmed. So to have the attitude is not just to make a value judgement, but to adopt certain purposes and feel certain emotions. The value judgement is, however, central to the attitude, and we must look at Taylor's careful and somewhat technical account of it, which involves understanding two concepts. One is the concept of *inherent worth*:

> To have the attitude of respect for nature is to regard the wild plants and animals of the Earth's natural ecosystems as possessing inherent worth. That such creatures have inherent worth may be considered the fundamental value presupposition of the attitude of respect.
>
> (Taylor (1986), p.71)

The other concept is that of a being having *a good of its own*, which is necessary for it to have inherent worth:

> To say that an entity has a good of its own is simply to say that, without reference to any other entity, it can be benefited or harmed ... We can think of the good of an individual non-human organism as consisting in the full

development of its biological powers. Its good is realized to the extent that it is strong and healthy. It possesses whatever capacities it needs for successfully coping with its environment and so preserving its existence throughout the various stages of the normal lifecycle of its species.

(Taylor (1981), p.199)

That a being has a good of its own is not the same as its having inherent worth. That a being has a good of its own is a fact about it, the fact that it possesses certain biological powers by the exercise of which it flourishes. To attribute inherent worth to it, however, is to commit oneself to more than the fact that it can or does flourish. It is to say that its flourishing is *a good thing*. And Taylor takes that to involve a practical commitment:

> The assertion that an entity has inherent worth is here to be understood as entailing two moral judgements (1) that the entity is deserving of moral concern and consideration, or, in other words that it is a moral subject, and (2) that all moral agents have a prima facie[2] duty to promote or preserve the entity's good as an end in itself and for the sake of the entity whose good it is.
>
> (Ibid., p.75)

You may wonder how much Taylor's concept of inherent worth has in common with the similar sounding concept *inherent value* employed by Tom Regan and discussed in Book 2, Chapter 4. Rosalind Hursthouse suggests that to have inherent value, as Regan understands the term, 'is to have the right not to be treated merely as a means'. Compare that with Taylor's statement that to assert that an entity has inherent worth entails (judgement (2) above) 'a ... duty to promote or preserve the entity's good *as an end in itself* ...'. In fact both philosophers are making conscious use of the Kantian principle quoted earlier (p.98). Further confirmation of their similarity is provided by Taylor, who refers to Regan's concept, saying, 'his concept of 'inherent value' and my concept of 'inherent worth' are essentially identical' (ibid., p.75n.). There is, however, a very important difference between the extension of the concept according to Regan and according to Taylor, and that is the range of entities to which each is prepared to apply it. Regan thinks that it applies to human beings and to members of other species who share the feature of being 'experiencing subjects of a life'. Taylor thinks it applies to everything that has a good of its own, and that is to every living organism. That is a huge difference. That there can be such a difference of opinion underlines very clearly the need for an argument to justify its application to one rather than another range of entities.

Taylor does not overlook this need. The relationship between Taylor's concept of inherent worth and his concept of a good of one's own is that having a good of its own is a **necessary condition** of a being's having inherent

necessary and
sufficient
conditions
worth, but not a **sufficient** one. If there is nothing that counts as some being's flourishing then one cannot think that it is good that it flourishes. If there is something that counts as its flourishing, however, it does not immediately follow that its flourishing is a good thing. Some further reason must be forthcoming. If we ask for a justification of the attitude of respect for nature – some line of reasoning that could support the conclusion that we ought to adopt it – we might ask: 'Why should the fact that a being has a good of its own be a reason for respecting it?' or, more pithily, 'This plant, for example, may flourish or it may wilt and die – why should one care which?'

How is the attitude of respect for nature to be justified?

The attitude of respect for nature is supported by a set of beliefs – a 'belief system' – about the nature of the world and our place in it. This belief system Taylor calls 'The biocentric outlook on nature'. In his book, he describes it in detail (ibid., pp.95–161), but here we must make do with a summary, at least it is Taylor's own. In it he describes the beliefs that make up the biocentric outlook, and the way in which they support the attitude of respect. He recognizes that a further question arises about the justification of the biocentric outlook itself, but does not attempt to answer it here.

READING Now read the first section of Reading 10, Taylor's 'The biocentric outlook on nature' (pp.241–3).

There are four beliefs at the core of the biocentric outlook.

1   The belief that humans are members of Earth's Community of Life in the same sense as, and on the same terms that, other living things are members of that community.

2   The belief that the human species, along with all other species, are integral elements in a system of interdependence such that the survival of each living thing, as well as its chances of faring well or poorly, is determined not only by the physical conditions of its environment but also by its relations to other living things.

3   The belief that all organisms are teleological centres of life in the sense that each is a unique individual pursuing its own good in its own way.

4   The belief that humans are not inherently superior to other living things (Taylor (1986), pp.99f.).

How do these observations support the conclusion that we ought to adopt the attitude of respect for nature? They draw attention to respects in which members of the human species are similar to all other living things. If we recognize our 'common bond' with other organisms, our common dependence on the whole system of life, our common nature as goal-directed entities, and the absence of a hierarchy – of 'higher' and 'lower' forms of life – then we will see that it is reasonable to accord respect to all alike. That is the claim.

The claim is a very strong one, since it requires equal respect for all living things. If, however, we set aside the fourth belief – the absence of a hierarchy of value – it seems that the first three beliefs alone could support a weaker but still significant claim: that all living things are deserving of (some degree of) respect. Here we shall only be concerned with this weaker claim. If it cannot be sustained, then the stronger claim must fail.

Taylor offers his argument as an informal one; that is, one that does not pretend to be deductively valid. The premises do not give logically conclusive support to the conclusion, but support it with more or less strength.[3] Consequently the premises may be true, and yet the conclusion false. The criticism of Taylor's position in this chapter is one that does not question the premises, but denies the conclusion. It fastens on the concept of the good of a being, and says: living things may all have a good of their own, but they are not for that reason appropriate objects of respect. The conclusion is then that the weaker claim fails and therefore neither can the stronger claim be sustained.

The concept of the good of a being

The concept of the good of a being plays a role in Taylor's theory similar to the role of the concept of sentience in Singer's theory (Book 2, Chapter 1), or to the concept of an experiencing subject of a life in Regan's theory (Book 2, Chapter 4). Each of them denotes the characteristic in virtue of which independent moral status is attributed to a being: the status-conferring characteristic. Each, in other words, is intended to answer the question: '*What* is it about a being that makes it an appropriate object of respect or concern?' Because it plays such a pivotal role in Taylor's theory we will need to examine in more detail his exposition of the concept of the good of a being, and try to assess its success.

Now read the remaining two sections of Reading 10, 'The concept of the good of a being' and 'The concept of inherent worth' (pp.243–50), and then do the exercise below.

READING

EXERCISE 17	Answer in one or two sentences the following questions.
Taylor on the good of a being	1 How does Taylor distinguish between (a) 'X has an interest in being well nourished' and (b) 'It is in the interest of X to be well nourished'?

2 In which of the sentences (a) and (b) above can 'X' be replaced by 'a dandelion', 'a mouse', 'a human being'?

3 How does Taylor distinguish between 'objective' and 'subjective' value concepts?

4 In what way is that distinction important to Taylor's view that non-sentient living beings have a good of their own?

Check your answers against those at the back of the book before reading on.

DISCUSSION

You may think that, from the point of view of ordinary conversational usage, he is splitting hairs in claiming that there is an important distinction between having an interest in something and something's being in one's interest. But his substantive point does not depend on the niceties of usage. The point is that something can be in one's interest just because it is good for one. If you need more vitamin C in your diet in order not to get scurvy, that is true whether you have heard of vitamin C or not, and therefore irrespective of whether or not you desire more of it. If having interests implies having desires, then beings who lack consciousness have no interests. Taylor wants to circumvent a possible objection to his view, namely, that since non-sentient things *have* no interests they have no good of their own to be considered – nothing is *in* their interest. That is no objection if having a good does not depend on having interests, but depends rather on being susceptible of being benefited or harmed.

As Taylor uses the phrases 'X has an interest' and 'It is in X's interest', it benefits a dandelion to be well nourished, so to be well nourished is in its interest; but it *has* no interest in that, or anything else, being devoid of consciousness. A mouse does not have the concept of being well nourished, but at least it can feel hungry, so perhaps it isn't stretching the sense too far to say that it has an interest in being, as well as its being *in* its interest to be, well nourished. There is no problem about both applying to human beings, but the distinction is still important in the human case, because one can fail to have a (conscious) interest in something that is none the less good for one, as I will now explain.

The distinction between objective and subjective value concepts can be understood in terms of the distinction between what is actually for a being's good ('objective value') and what the being thinks is for its good ('subjective value'). In Chapter 2 I drew the distinction between these in making the related distinction between what would be desired by a being if it were fully informed about the object of desire, and the actual desires or preferences of the being. Taylor wants to defend this distinction because he believes that if there is an objective concept of what is in a being's interest or for its good, that is, one that holds independent of the subject's own judgement, then this supports the idea that we can speak of the good of a being that does not have the capacity to make judgements about what is good for it, because it is not the sort of being that can make judgements of any kind at all.

Taylor makes it clear, in his explanation of the distinction between objective and subjective values, that what a being desires or consciously pursues is irrelevant to what is good for it. If properly informed, a being capable of acting on conscious desires will go for what is in fact good for it, but the object is desired because it is good, not good because it is desired. What is good for it would be good for it whatever its desires, and even if it had no capacity for desiring anything. So we are free to detach the concept of the good of a being from desires and preferences, indeed from any form of conscious life. The way we can apply it to beings who lack conscious life is well exemplified by the butterfly, and that case can easily be generalized to plants, and, as Taylor indicates, to even the simplest life forms. All that is needed is to understand, for the species in question, what is required for the being to survive in a healthy condition and perform the functions that are characteristic of the species.

Suppose we concede the non-sentient, non-conscious, living things have a good of their own. What is the significance of that? Taylor's reply is that it shows that there is something to be concerned about, something to take into consideration in our actions. If individual living things did not have a good of their own there would be nothing to respect, so if Taylor is successful in arguing that they do, he has established a necessary condition of respect being the appropriate attitude to take towards them. But only a necessary condition: that there is something to be concerned about does not immediately demonstrate that we must be concerned about it: 'X has inherent worth' is not deducible from 'X has a good of its own'. Taylor is himself insistent that there is no such demonstration. The reason for that is that the statement that a being has a good of its own is a factual statement, whereas respect for nature is a moral attitude which commits one to caring that living things achieve their good. (This distinction between factual statements and moral attitudes or judgements will be discussed further in the next chapter.) But he contends that, from the standpoint of the biocentric outlook, respect for nature, though not demonstrable, is appropriate and reasonable. For one who accepts that outlook, the fact that a being has a good of its own is a sufficient reason to care whether it fares well or ill.

'Teleological centres of life'

One of the component beliefs of the biocentric outlook has special relevance to the concept of the good of a being. It is as 'teleological centres of life'[4] that organisms have goods of their own:

> We conceive of the organism as a teleological centre of life, striving to preserve itself and realize its good in its own unique way. To say it is a teleological centre of life is to say that its internal functioning as well as its external activities are all goal-oriented, having the constant tendency to maintain the organism's existence through time and to enable it successfully to perform those biological operations whereby it reproduces its kind and continually adapts to changing environmental events and conditions. It is the coherence and unity of these functions of an organism, all directed toward the realization of its good, that makes it one teleological centre of activity. Physically and chemically it is in the molecules of its cells that this activity occurs, but the organism as a whole is the unit that responds to its environment and so accomplishes (or tends to accomplish) the end of sustaining its life.

> Understanding individual organisms as teleological centres of life does not mean that we are falsely anthropomorphizing. It does not involve 'reading into' them human characteristics. We need not, for example, consider them to have consciousness. That a particular tree is a teleological centre of life does not entail that it is intentionally aiming at preserving its existence, that it is exerting efforts to avoid death, or that it even cares whether it lives or dies. All organisms, whether conscious or not, are teleological centres of life in the sense that each is a unified, coherently organized system of goal-oriented activities that has a constant tendency to protect and maintain the organism's existence.

> Under this conception of individual living things, each is seen to have a single unique point of view…

> This mode of understanding a particular individual is not possible with regard to inanimate objects. Although no two stones are exactly alike in their physical characteristics, stones do not have points of view… This is not due to the fact that [they lack] consciousness. As we have noted, plants and simple animal organisms also lack consciousness, but have points of view none the less. What makes our awareness of an individual stone fundamentally different from our awareness of a plant or animal is that the stone is not a teleological centre of life, while the plant or animal is. The stone has no good of its own. We cannot

benefit it by furthering its well-being or harm it by acting contrary to its well-being, since the concept of well-being simply does not apply to it.

(Taylor (1986), pp.121ff.)

Criticism of Taylor's theory

The main objection to an ethic of respect for nature or life is well expressed by the philosopher W.K. Frankena, commenting on Albert Schweitzer's declaration that the 'truly ethical' man 'tears no leaf from a tree, plucks no flower, and takes care to crush no insect' (Schweitzer (1949), pp.384f.): 'Why, if leaves and trees have no capacity to feel pleasure or to suffer, should I tear no leaf from a tree?' (Frankena (1979), p.11). The question is rhetorical, but Taylor has offered an answer and if it is to be rejected he is owed an argument.

One philosopher who has offered what purports to be an argument is R.M. Hare. The argument appeals to a form of moral reasoning in which the moral agent considers the interests of all those affected by a proposed action by placing herself in turn in the position of each being affected and asking how she wishes to be treated on the supposition that she is in that position. Hare calls this form of reasoning a generalization of the Golden Rule: treat others as you would wish to be treated.

Suppose – to adapt an example of Hare's – that I propose to cut down a tree in a field in which cows graze. If I put myself in the position of a human neighbour who enjoys the tree as part of her view, I prefer that it should not be cut down. If I put myself in the position of one of the cows who shelter from the rain under the tree, I prefer to be dry rather than wet. But if I put myself in the position of the tree I couldn't care less what happens to me. Hare considers the suggestion that we should take account of the interests of trees:[5]

> We do, perhaps, speak of the good of trees. Trees have a nature, and grow in accordance with it, even if they are not conscious. The interest of the acorn is to become a full-grown oak, for example. That is what it would be for the tree to realize its own good ...

> But the question is whether such interests, desires, and tryings have moral relevance, in that they constitute moral reasons for treating trees in one way rather than another. For it is possible to agree that we do speak of the good of trees without admitting that this has any moral relevance for environmental policy. If the basis of morality is the Golden Rule to do to others as we wish that they should do to us, then if, as I have said, I could not care less what happens to me if I am a tree, I shall not care in particular whether, if I am the tree, it realizes its peculiar good or not. I no more care what happens to me if I am the tree than I do what happens to me if I am the bicycle that I knock over. The bicycle too

has a good; one can harm it by knocking it over. But that does not entail that the bicycle has interests of the sort that could generate moral rights or duties.

(Hare (1989), p.244)

EXERCISE 18

Hare's criticism of teleological theory

Is Hare's criticism of the teleological theory sound? If you think that it is unsound, explain why you think it fails.

DISCUSSION

Hare's Golden Rule method of reasoning, since it consists in asking *what one would wish* in the position of each being affected, presupposes that only the interests of those beings that are capable of having wishes (or desires or preferences) can be taken into account as morally relevant. But it is precisely this view that Taylor is arguing against. Hare's argument then presupposes the very matter that is in dispute, and so appears to **beg the question**.

begging the question

refutation

If it is correct that Hare's objection begs the question, then it amounts simply to a **repudiation**, not **refutation** of Taylor's position. We may still feel that more needs to be done before that position is compelling. Golden-rule thinking may strike us as having an obvious cogency that is lacking in the more extended consideration that Taylor recommends. His distinction between beings who *mind* what is done to them, and beings who lack the capacity to mind anything at all, is clearly neither arbitrary nor unimportant. Is it important enough to mark the cut off point between beings that have moral status and beings that lack it?

Bernard Williams is another philosopher who criticizes the supposition that beings who have no experiences do none the less have morally relevant interests:

> To say that a thing has interests will help in these cases only if its interests make a claim on us: we may have to allow in some cases that the claim can be outweighed by other claims, but it will have to be agreed that the interests of these things make some claim on us, if the notion of 'interests' is to do the required work. But we cannot plausibly suppose that all the interests which, on this approach, would exist do make a claim upon us. If a tree has any interests at all then it must have an interest in getting better if it is sick; but a sick tree, just as such, makes no claim on us. Moreover, even if individual members of a species had interests, and they made some claims on us, it would remain quite unclear how a species could have interests: but the species is what is standardly the concern of conservation. Yet again, even if it were agreed that a species or kind of thing could have interests, those interests would certainly often make no claims on us: the interests of the HIV virus make no claim on us, and we offend against nothing if our attitude to it is that we take no prisoners.

> (Williams (1995), pp.236f.)

Is Williams's criticism of the teleological theory effective? If you think it fails, explain why.

Although he avoids saying that non-conscious organisms have interests, as opposed to things being in their interest, Taylor's view is surely of the kind of which Williams is thinking. Substitute 'has a good of its own' for 'has interests' and no difference would be made to the point he is making. The only argument that Williams offers is to give examples: it is a form of the **absurd consequences** argument. But it does not seem a very strong argument. Many people would say that a sick tree does make a claim on us. Granted we cannot minister to every sick tree, but then we cannot minister to every sick human being, but that does not show that sick people make no claim on us. Even the HIV virus example is not impressive: examples of organisms that pose a deadly threat to human beings do not show that in general the interests of non-conscious organisms make no claim on us.

absurd consequences move

So it seems to me that so far we have no decisive argument against Taylor's view.

Sumner on Taylor

In his recent book, *Welfare, Happiness and Ethics*, L.W. Sumner has an argument that may take us a bit further. Sumner believes that Taylor's theory exploits an ambiguity in the concept of *the good of a being*. 'The good of a being' can refer either to its well-being or to its being good of its kind. The former involves what he terms 'prudential value', while the latter involves 'perfectionist value'. We need to see how Sumner explains these two concepts.

> Welfare assessments concern what we may call the prudential value of a life, namely how well it is going for *the individual whose life it is*. This relativization of prudential evaluation to the proprietor of the life in question is one of the deepest features of the language of welfare: however valuable something may be in itself, it can promote my well-being only if it is good or beneficial *for me*.
> (Sumner (1996), p.20)

This is further explained by being contrasted with perfectionist value, aesthetic value and ethical value. Here is the contrast with perfectionist value:

> To say that something has this sort of value is to say that it is a good instance or specimen of its kind, or that it exemplifies the excellences characteristic of its

particular nature. The scope of perfectionist evaluation is therefore at least as broad as that of aesthetic evaluation, since it extends to any object, natural or artificial, which can be located in an appropriate species or kind. Although the two modes of value are often near kin (we commonly find excellence appealing and praise it in aesthetic terms), the perfection of a thing is clearly a different matter from its beauty or nobility: a slug or a piece of kitsch may be a paragon of its kind despite being ugly or vulgar.

As in the aesthetic case, however, what is to count as a virtue or excellence in a thing will be determined by the kind of thing it is. A perfectionist assessment of a life is therefore likely to employ standards derived from the species to which the subject of that life belongs. The derivation might take something like the following form. We begin by seeking the essential characteristics of creatures of the species in question – what it is that identifies them as the particular kind of creature they are. These will then be the characteristics whose possession at an exemplary level makes an individual member of the species a particularly good specimen of that kind. The traits or abilities so selected will count as personal excellencies, conferring perfectionist value on their bearers. In our own case we might imagine that certain cognitive abilities would be included among the essential characteristics of humankind, in which case having a well-developed capacity for abstract thought or computation would score high on the perfectionist scale.

Like prudential (and aesthetic) value, perfectionist value needs a theory... However, even in the absence of such a theory the distinction between prudential and perfectionist value is clear enough. Once again, you can easily imagine yourself, at the end of your life, taking pride in your high level of self-development, but none the less wishing that you had got more out of your life, that it had been more rewarding or fulfilling, and thinking that it might have gone better for you had you devoted less energy to perfecting your talents and more to just hanging out or diversifying your interests. Whatever we are to count as excellencies for creatures of our nature, they will raise the perfectionist value of our lives regardless of the extent of their payoff for us. There is therefore no logical guarantee that the best human specimens will also be the best off, or that their undeveloped rivals will not be faring better. Like aesthetic value, the perfectionist value of a life is conceptually independent of how well it is going for its owner.

(Ibid., pp.23f.)

Although the phrase 'a good of its own' is in this way ambiguous, according to Sumner, it can apply to non-sentient organisms in only one of its two senses, the perfectionist sense. The prudential sense, the one we use when we speak of life going well *for the subject,* requires that the subject have a point of view, from which it can make its own assessment, or have its own sense, of how well its life is going. Many organisms do not in this sense have a point of view. At the same time Sumner thinks that only beings who have a point of view, who are conscious that their lives are going well or not, can sensibly be thought to have moral status:

> Our ethical sensibilities seem to have much to do with our ability to see things from the point of view of potential victims and beneficiaries. I am prepared to think that mountains and stars can fare better or worse on some objective scale of perfection, but this fact does not give them a point of view on whose behalf I can marshal my services. Having a point of view in this sense seems to require being a subject, but perfectionist value is not confined to subjects.
>
> (Ibid., p.211)

An important clue to the difference between Taylor and Sumner can be found by comparing Taylor on the concept of the good of a being, and Sumner on prudential and perfectionist value. Taylor clearly holds a different view from Sumner of what makes one's life go well. For Taylor it is an objective matter, and the objective value of one's life is independent of one's own assessment of it. If that is true of the life of a being capable of experience and judgement, then it makes little difference whether we are dealing with a being that has, or one that lacks, such capacities. In both cases the good of a being consists in the perfection of its natural capacities, whatever those are. There is for Taylor no important sense of the good of a being that depends upon the being's experiencing its life *as* good, so Taylor is, in Sumner's terms, employing only the concept of perfectionist value. When the two writers use the notion of a being's point of view there is a parallel difference. For Taylor considering a being from its point of view means no more than considering what is good or bad for it without reference to any other being. For Sumner it means understanding the view that the being takes of things.

Sumner's two criticisms of Taylor

The first criticism of Taylor's theory is that it uses the ambiguous notion of a being's having a good to slide from perfectionist value to prudential value. 'It is a fallacy to slip from saying that something can be good or bad of its kind to saying that it therefore has a welfare.'

The fallacy is an instance of the fallacy of **equivocation**. How exactly does the argument go?

equivocation

Premise 1   If any being has a good of its own then we ought to promote that good.

Premise 2   Every living thing has a good of its own.

Conclusion   So we ought to promote the good of every living thing.

Sumner's view is that if we take 'has a good of its own' in the prudential sense then Premise 1 may be true, but Premise 2 is certainly false (the reason is given on pp.110–11); while, if we take it in the perfectionist sense, then Premise 2 may be true, but the first is certainly false. In neither case is the conclusion established. The only way to make both premises true is to take 'has a good of its own' in Premise 1 in the prudential sense, and in Premise 2 in the perfectionist sense. But then the conclusion cannot be validly inferred.

Sumner's second criticism of Taylor's view is the following: a being's welfare may make a moral claim upon us – in that sense to promote its good is to make its experienced life better; but non-sentient organisms do not have a welfare, for they only have a good in a perfectionist sense – in that sense to promote their good is to make them better examples of their kind – but, as Sumner says, 'What is unclear to me is why we should think we have a moral reason to make things better examples of their kind' (ibid.). This criticism does not rely upon the suggestion that Taylor slides from one sense of 'the good of a being' to another. It simply claims that he has overlooked the fact that in a perfectionist sense there is no moral claim upon us to care whether non-sentient living things realize their good or not. Sumner's argument may be summarized as follows.

Premise 1	We have no moral reason to make things better of their kind.
Premise 2	Furthering the realization of a being's good (in Taylor's objective sense) is making it better of its kind.
Conclusion	So we have no moral reason to further the realization of a being's good.

EXERCISE 20   How sound are Sumner's two criticisms? Make your own brief notes before *Sumner's criticisms* reading the discussion below.
of Taylor

DISCUSSION   With respect to Sumner's first criticism, it seems plain to me that Taylor does not equivocate. I say this with confidence because I think it is plain, from a reading of his exposition of the concept of a being's good, that he entertains only the perfectionist sense of the concept. In his terms it is unambiguously an objective value concept. So also are three terms that in Sumner's terminology are prudential concepts: well-being, welfare and happiness. Taylor does not often use these terms, but when he does it is clearly in a perfectionist (objective) sense. Sumner may be right, as against Taylor, in thinking that when we ascribe well-being to some being – even more certainly when we call it happy – we do not just mean that it is a good specimen of its kind. But however implausible a perfectionist account of well-being may be, Taylor sticks to it consistently.

The argument summarizing the second criticism is valid, and Premise 2 is true. The question is whether Premise 1 is true. The only argument Sumner gives in support of it is in the passage quoted earlier (p.111), from which we may extract this argument.

Premise 1   Only beings from whose point of view we can see things can engage our ethical sensibilities.

Premise 2   Beings which have a good only in a perfectionist sense have no point of view.

Conclusion   So beings which have a good only in a perfectionist sense cannot engage our ethical sensibilities.

But, we might ask, is Premise 1 of *this* argument true? After all we might claim on Taylor's behalf that his account of the biocentric outlook is precisely what is needed to engage our moral sensibilities with all nature's denizens, whether they have a point of view or not. Taylor's argument from the biocentric outlook to respect for nature is not claimed to be conclusive. It is an informal argument, not one in which, if one accepts the premises, one must accept the conclusion. Informal arguments are difficult to assess: just how strongly do the premises, if we accept them, support the conclusion? There is at least one doubt that may be raised: about the notion of the *point of view* of beings that lack sentience. Earlier, I suggested that when Taylor speaks of viewing things from such a being's point of view he should not be interpreted in a literal sense. We may wonder none the less whether his argument is less convincing if we studiously avoid terms, such as 'point of view', that can be used in their strict sense only of sentient beings.

Does Sumner's argument, in the end, take us further than Hare's? He gives no conclusive reason for saying that we do not have any moral reason to make things better of their kind. On the other hand, the distinction between the two kinds of value and the two senses of 'a good of its own' makes clearer the difference between considering the good of sentient beings and considering the good of non-sentient beings. If we agree with Sumner that the good of which Taylor speaks, which he thinks can be ascribed to non-sentient beings as well as to sentient ones, is not the good of well-being, but perfectionist good, then we may be much less willing to go along with Taylor in adopting the attitude of respect for nature, at least in the ambitious terms in which he characterizes it.

The moral status of rivers, ecosystems, species...

From the conservationist point of view there is a line of criticism of Taylor's position that has not been considered in this chapter, although its target has been hinted at. Taylor is concerned to argue that moral status belongs to a wider range of entities than are recognized by 'animal liberation' positions. It extends to all beings who have a good of their own. His exposition of that concept seems to limit its application to individual organisms, and he himself is quite content that it should be so limited. Collections of individuals, or natural features that contain individuals, do not have moral status as such, but only derivatively: their moral importance is just the moral importance of their individual living constituents. From a conservationist point of view this, in one way, does not go far enough: the focus of conservationist concern is not individuals but species, ecosystems, areas of special scenic or scientific or historical significance. Suppose that the few remaining members of a rare plant species die without reproducing. On Taylor's view it does not seem to be wrong if those who could prevent this fail to do so: no individual living thing has been harmed. In another way Taylor's position goes too far, again from a conservationist standpoint, because conservation of an ecosystem may require control of a particular member species, or of an alien species (e.g. 'liberated' mink). Similarly, species conservation may require the control of a population that has increased beyond the capacity of its habitat. 'Control' is here a nice word for killing, which does nothing for the good of the individuals who are controlled.

With respect to the complaint that Taylor goes too far: there are already conflicts between conservationists and animal liberationists, and this is independent of the extension of moral status to all living things. Taylor's extension would greatly add to the conflicts between concern for the individual and concern for collective entities. Of course, if he is right, then it just has to be accepted as a fact that principles sometimes conflict, and we have to look for ways of resolving conflicts in practice as they arise.

With respect to the complaint that he does not go far enough: on the face of it we do value species and ecosystems, not only their members, and we value mountains, for instance, irrespective of whether they support lives of value; but to attribute a good of their own to such things is difficult. As objects of care, concern, interest and love, however – that is, as things people value, either instrumentally or non-instrumentally – such things present no great puzzle. There is no reason to think that these valuing attitudes can take only living things and only individual entities as objects. This is an additional reason to that given by Sumner (p.112) to adopt an alternative approach to Taylor's on valuing nature.

Conclusion

The attempt to assign moral status to all living things by arguing that each has a good of its own is seriously challenged by the suggestion that the sense in which sentient beings have a good is different from the sense in which non-sentient beings have a good. Even if a being's having a good in the sense of well-being makes a moral claim on us, it does not follow that a being's having a good in the sense of perfection makes a claim on us. Another difficulty for this theory is that it does not fit well with conservation values. Neither objection is conclusive, but together they suggest that an alternative approach may be preferable, even if it is human centred.

Chapter summary

The human-centred approach to the valuing of nature seems unsatisfactory to greens of a deeper persuasion because it leaves nature's value apparently dependent on human interest and concern. So the question whether non-human, natural things have independent moral status has to be addressed. One well worked out positive answer to the question is Paul Taylor's. The basis of his account is the concept of the good of a being. As teleological centres of life all living organisms have a good of their own, and it is this that confers moral status on them. The attitude of respect for nature incorporates a commitment to take into consideration and where possible to foster the realization of the good of living beings. Hare criticizes this position on the ground that only beings who have interests in the sense which entails being aware of, and having preferences concerning, the effects that actions have upon them, need to be taken into account in our moral decisions. This criticism seems to beg the question against Taylor, since it makes the assumption that Taylor questions – that it is having (conscious) interests, rather than having a good of one's own, that confers moral status. A second criticism (Sumner's), however, may have more force. It is that Taylor fails to distinguish two senses in which something can be for a being's good: by contributing to its well-being, or by contributing to its perfection. Beings which lack conscious life have a good only in the second sense, but moral status requires that they have a good in the first sense. A criticism that is made from a conservationist point of view is that Taylor's view is too individualistic and cannot account for the value of species, ecosystems, etc. Neither this nor Sumner's criticism conclusively refutes

Taylor's view, but together they are serious enough to suggest that we might do better with an alternative approach.

Further reading

Taylor's book *Respect for Nature: A Theory of Environmental Ethics*, Princeton University Press, 1986 is one of the most thorough and philosophically rigorous theories of environmental ethics to have been written. It is mostly quite readable, and only occasionally technical, but is rather long. There is a briefer presentation of the main argument in his essay, 'The ethics of respect for nature', *Environmental Ethics*, vol. 3, no 3 (Fall 1981), reprinted in *Environmental Philosophy,* edited by Michael E. Zimmerman, Prentice Hall, 1993. Sumner's *Welfare, Happiness and Ethics*, Oxford University Press, 1996 is a contribution to an interesting current debate about the nature of well-being. Although not an introduction, it is not written in a forbidding style, and would be a good way of getting further into the issues raised in this chapter and in Chapter 2. On the issue raised at the very end of the chapter, which divides animal liberationists and conservationists, much more needs to be said than I have been able to do. The issue is stated very clearly by Mark Sagoff, 'Animal liberation, environmental ethics: bad marriage, quick divorce', originally published in *Law Journal*, vol. 22, no 2 and reprinted in Zimmerman (1993). The essay by Bernard Williams briefly discussed in this chapter, and referred to again in Chapters 6 and 7, is a concise and incisive review of how – and how not – to answer the question of its title: 'Must a concern for the environment be centred on human beings?' (Williams (1995)).

Notes

[1] Speciesism is a position which does not take the interests or suffering of animals into moral account, rather in the way that racism is the failure to take the interests of members of other races into account (see Book 2, p.27).

[2] A prima facie duty is one that ought to be carried out unless there is, in the particular circumstances, another moral duty of over-riding importance.

[3] If you have read the appendix to Book 1 on reasoning, and/or consulted the entries in *Thinking from A to Z* you may have gained the impression that arguments are either deductive or inductive, and that inductive arguments are inferences from empirical observations to an empirical generalization. The argument of Taylor under discussion is plainly neither deductive nor inductive. In reality induction is only one variety of non-deductive (informal) argument. Any argument in which the premises support the conclusion without logically entailing it is a non-deductive argument. Practical arguments, supporting such conclusions as 'The best thing to do is...', and moral arguments, supporting such conclusions as 'One ought to...' are typically non-deductive. One important type of informal argument is argument by analogy, which is fully discussed in Book 2, pp. 146–8.

[4] 'Teleological' means 'goal-directed'. 'Telos' is the Greek word for an end, aim, or goal. 'Anthropomorphizing' means, literally, representing the non-human, e.g. gods or animals, in human form; here it means fitting the non-human out with human thoughts, feelings, etc.

[5] Hare does not make the distinction that Taylor makes between having an interest and something's being in one's interest, in those terms, but his argument is not affected by that since he does distinguish between interests that a being is aware of having and interests that a being is unaware of having. Hare's target is not Taylor's theory but a similar one advanced earlier than Taylor's by Robin Attfield (Attfield (1981)).

CHAPTER 6

Relating to Nature 1: Following Nature

OBJECTIVES

When you have worked through this chapter you should:

■ Realize the multiple ambiguity of the word 'nature' and the dangers in not being aware of its different senses.

■ Be able to assess Mill's criticism of the attempt to make nature the standard of human conduct, and understand alternative ways in which we may learn from nature.

■ Understand the problem of arguing from fact, especially from biological fact, to value.

■ Have grasped the distinction between absolute and relative senses of 'natural'.

Introduction

> The idea of ascribing interests to species, natural phenomena, and so on, as a way of making sense of our concern for these things, is part of a project of trying to extend into nature our concerns for each other, by moralizing our relations to nature. I suspect, however, that that is to look in precisely the wrong direction. If we are to understand these things, we need to look to our ideas of nature itself, and to ways in which it precisely lies outside the domestication of our relations to each other.
>
> (Williams (1995), p.237)

Animal liberation theories expand the moral circle. Starting from some primitive moral group – the family or the tribe – the boundary is pushed further and further out, each stage of the expansion being motivated by recognition of common interests or shared characteristics with beings formerly regarded as essentially different from 'us'. This process can involve a shift in the perception of what is important about 'us'. Thus Bentham's remark that the important question about animals is not 'Can they reason?' but 'Can they suffer?' marks such a shift. But the process is inevitably one by which outsiders are assimilated into our community. The human moral community provides the model for our understanding of our relations with other animals. This is not without strains even in this context: what, for instance, should we do about the behaviour of predators – control it, provide vegetarian diets for wild carnivores? The absurdity of such proposals stems from the misguided attempt to construe our relations with animals in general by analogy with our relations with one another. The strain becomes greater, the sense of community more stretched, when all living things are brought into the circle, and becomes intolerable when ecosystems and species are brought in.

We should, say some exponents of deeper green theories, refrain from trying to understand our relations with nature by analogy with our relations to one another. This is still too human centred. Instead, we should adopt a different perspective, viewing human beings as one species among others, part of nature at large, not apart from it. In these final two chapters we shall look at some aspects of this idea. In this chapter we consider the question whether a study of nature can provide us with a guide to our own behaviour, towards one another and towards the non-human.

John Stuart Mill on nature

In his essay 'Nature' Mill does two things. He distinguishes between two senses of the word 'nature', and he then argues that in neither sense can the injunction 'Follow nature' be accepted as a principle by which to regulate human behaviour.

Try to analyse Mill's argument by answering the following questions after you have completed the reading.

EXERCISE 21

Mill's essay 'Nature'

1 First make a note of the two senses of 'nature' that Mill distinguishes, picking out of the text phrases that capture each sense. With what is nature in each sense contrasted?

2 How many ways of following nature does Mill identify? Note briefly what they are, and what Mill thinks of them.

3 In what way does Mill believe that religion has led to inhibitions regarding the human attempt to improve nature?

4 Does Mill in your opinion believe that nature is immoral? (Yes/no/unclear.)

5   What is the third possible sense of 'nature' that Mill considers, and why does he dismiss it?

Now read the extracts from Mill's essay, Reading 11, pp.251–66.

Check your answers against those at the back of the book before reading on.

DISCUSSION   Mill's firm view is that there is no sense of 'nature' in which 'follow nature' is sound advice to human beings. He is surely right in dwelling on the ambiguity of 'nature', drawing attention to the different meanings that attach to 'following nature' depending on the sense in which it is understood. He recognizes that the word is multiply ambiguous.[1] But the two senses Mill identifies as particularly relevant seem to deserve the prominence he gives them. We seem often to mean by nature the world, including human beings, but also, as often, what is left of the world when we subtract human beings. Three points should be noted about this distinction:

1   In the comprehensive sense, which Mill calls the 'true scientific' sense, human activity, the powers by which men make things, and the things they make, are natural. In this sense the only contrast with the natural – though Mill does not point this out – is the supernatural: whatever exists and happens in the world is nature.

2   Mill contrasts nature, in the second, narrower sense, with art. The term 'art' he uses in a very broad sense, comprehending both the products of human activity: a garden, a bed, a poem; and the productive activities: tilling the ground, making a bed, writing a poem.

3   The comprehensive sense includes 'all the powers existing in the outer or the inner world'. By the 'inner world' Mill means the human mind, including its capacity for voluntary action. The narrower sense includes only those motivating forces in human lives which do not depend on deliberation.

For convenience in discussing the argument I shall call nature in Mill's first sense 'universal nature', and nature in his second sense 'wild nature'.

Mill considers first the injunction to follow nature as meaning to follow universal nature and so understood he declares it to be absurd and unmeaning. The argument for this is given in paragraph 11, and may be summed up in one sentence from that paragraph:

> To bid people conform to the laws of nature when they have no power but what the laws of nature give them – when it is a physical impossibility for them to do the smallest thing otherwise than through some law of nature, is an absurdity.

This actually understates the force of the argument, for if everything happens according to some natural law, then it is not just a physical but a *logical* impossibility for anyone not to conform. Why does this show that the injunction to follow universal nature is absurd? It may strike you that the answer is obvious, because you can easily supply what is needed to make the argument complete. Let us state the obvious, for only by displaying all of Mill's premises can we be sure of identifying something questionable.

Premise 1   An injunction to act in a certain way has a point only if it can guide the person to whom it is addressed to act in that way rather than some other.

Premise 2   The injunction can do this only if the person addressed has the choice between acting or not as directed.

Premise 3   No one has the choice to follow universal nature or not.

Conclusion   The injunction to follow universal nature is 'superfluous and unmeaning'.

The conclusion does follow from the three premises, so the argument is valid.

Mill next turns to the injunction understood as telling us to follow wild nature. This takes him longer to dispose of; it cannot be dismissed as unmeaning. Note that in his summing up at the end of the essay Mill makes two criticisms of the injunction to follow wild nature: that it is *irrational* and that it is *immoral.* I think he has in mind two rather different ways in which wild nature – nature unmodified by deliberate human activity – might be taken as a rule for human activity. The first way would be to take the unmodified processes of nature as good, incapable of improvement, and therefore to be left alone, not modified or interfered with by man in any way whatever. This rule he thinks is 'absurd and self-contradictory' because it is at variance with 'the very aim and object of action', which is 'to alter and improve Nature' (i.e. wild nature). The second way of taking wild nature as a rule for human activity is to imitate it, to behave as wild nature behaves, and this he condemns as immoral. Mill moves from criticism of the first, as irrational, to criticism of the second, as immoral, without marking the transition, and some of his observations about wild nature are intended to support both.

First, then, the criticism of the injunction to leave wild nature alone. Why does Mill say that this is absurd and self-contradictory? I suspect that he is here conflating two quite different points. This is evident in his summary (paragraphs 30–2):

> the doctrine that man ought to follow nature, or in other words, ought to make the spontaneous course of things the model of his voluntary actions, is ...

irrational, because all human action whatever, consists in altering, and all useful action in improving, the spontaneous course of nature.

Two different notions of rationality are involved here. If voluntary action necessarily alters the course of nature, then to tell someone to act but not alter the course of nature, is to command the logically impossible. On the other hand, if *useful action* consists in improving the course of nature, then to tell someone to avoid trying to improve the course of nature is to command action which is possible but foolish. I think we can ignore the point about self-contradiction. Mill's discussion shows that he is attacking a doctrine that it is possible to put into practice but irrational, in that to do so would frustrate ends that any sane person must have.

Mill insists that wild nature is capable of improvement, and reminds his readers of improvements that everyone is in favour of, pointing out that

> to commend these and similar feats, is to acknowledge that the ways of nature are to be conquered, not obeyed: that her powers are often towards man in the position of enemies, from whom he must wrest, by force and ingenuity, what little he can for his own use, and deserves to be applauded when that little is rather more than might be expected from his physical weakness in comparison to those gigantic powers.

(Reading 11, paragraph 15)

The manifest improvements brought about by art (a modern writer would be more likely to say technology) mean that no one seriously upholds the anti-improvement rule in this extreme form, but there is widespread reluctance to reject it outright and embrace the contrary doctrine of improvement. Religion is the culprit. If nature is believed to be the direct handiwork of a just and benevolent creator, then there must be a prima facie objection to any new attempt to modify it. In order to counteract this presumption against attempts to improve on nature, Mill argues that the operations of nature suggest it is not the creation of a just and benevolent being or beings. Hence the splendid purple passage (paragraphs 19 and 20): 'In sober truth, nearly all the things which men are imprisoned for doing to one another, are nature's every day performances'. The spontaneous forces of nature are in many ways injurious to us, and it would be irrational not to take what measures we can to protect ourselves.

refutation I take this indictment of nature to function in two ways in Mill's **refutation** of the injunction to follow wild nature. It is part of an argument for the irrationality of a rule that enjoins leaving wild nature alone, not attempting to find ways of defending people from disease, famine, cold, etc. But it also functions as part of an argument that attempts to refute the injunction interpreted in the second way I indicated, that is, as the injunction to human beings to *imitate* nature, to behave as nature behaves. In fact we are really dealing with two rules expressed in the same words: (a) the imitation rule, and (b) the non-improvement rule. Separating them, and the arguments offered in refutation of them, enables us to see why Mill castigates the injunction to follow nature as both immoral *and* irrational. These charges are not the same, but the purple passage provides evidence that supports both. So how good are the arguments?

The imitation rule

The argument for the immorality of the imitation rule is simple and compelling.

Premise 1	A rule that enjoins plainly immoral actions is itself immoral.
Premise 2	The rule enjoining human beings to imitate nature enjoins plainly immoral actions.
Conclusion	Therefore that rule is immoral.

Does Mill imply that nature is immoral? His language seems to suggest that it is. But his argument does not depend on that claim. It requires only the claim that many of the things that happen by natural agency are wrong if they are done by human beings.

The non-improvement rule

The argument for the irrationality of the non-improvement rule is more obviously relevant to environmental ethics than the imitation rule. It is also more difficult to assess. This is the argument.

Premise 1	A rule that prevents us from acting in order to improve the conditions of life is irrational.
Premise 2	A rule that forbids us to deliberately modify nature prevents us from acting to improve the conditions of life.
Conclusion	Therefore that rule is irrational.

Mill is not here suggesting that if we reject the non-improvement rule we are therefore committed to an alternative rule that tells us to modify nature without restraint. The rule tells us that we should never seek to improve on nature because nature is *always* right. Mill's objection is that nature is *sometimes* wrong, so it cannot be sensible never to try to improve it. No doubt a sensible rule would tell us to be cautious. But whatever reasons there may be for caution in modifying nature, telling us to look to nature for guidance is useless. If we are to follow nature only sometimes, we need some guide other than nature to tell us when to follow it and when not to. To repeat the point, Mill does not need to argue that nothing natural is good, only that not everything is, and that consequently we need some independent standard to discriminate what is good from what is not good.

Mill lays himself open to objection on three scores. First, his highly charged rhetoric implies a view of nature as hostile, an enemy to be conquered, a setting for human beings that is dangerous and entirely lacking in the amenities needed to make life tolerable. This is a view of nature and the human relationship to it that many contemporary environmentalists take to be responsible for our destructive and wasteful treatment of the natural environment. Secondly, he is an enthusiastic advocate of the use of art (or technology) to shape nature more to our liking. He admits to the limited nature of our powers, but endorses the attempt to use them to their limit. This preference for nature that has been transformed by human activity, and apparent approval of the pursuit of a humanized nature as a central aim of human life, are in strong contrast with the preference of contemporary environmentalists for minimal interference in natural systems, a policy of 'treading lightly on the earth'. Thirdly, his insistence that what is of value in human character is created by deliberate alteration of our animal nature, so emphasizing that we exist apart from nature, contrasts with another common theme of contemporary environmental writing, that of *belonging to nature*, which we shall be looking at in the final chapter.

What is and what ought to be

Mill has identified two senses of 'nature', and has produced very strong arguments for his conclusion that in neither sense is the injunction to follow nature acceptable. But has he overlooked some other sense in which the injunction to follow nature is sound advice? What is his justification for supposing that the two senses are the only relevant ones to be considered? It might seem a difficult thing to do to review all possible senses. How could one know that one had completed the review? We shall see later in this chapter that there is more to be said about the possible interpretations of following nature.

Mill discusses a possible third sense of 'nature' and considers whether it could yield a defensible version of the 'follow nature' rule. In doing so, he introduces us to a topic of the utmost importance, not only to environmental ethics, but to ethics in general. His remarks occupy one paragraph of the essay, but they deserve close attention.

Read again carefully paragraph 9 in Reading 11, pp.254–5.   **READING**

In paragraph 8 Mill briefly discusses the longevity of the idea that to use the term 'nature' is to convey commendation, approval, even moral obligation, and that to say that something is unnatural or contrary to nature is to condemn it. Does this approval-conveying use indicate a third sense of 'nature', one that might yield a sensible interpretation of the injunction to follow nature?

The critical distinction is between *what is* and *what ought to be*, and terms that refer to each, which we might call 'factual' and 'ethical' terms respectively. If 'natural' is used as an ethical term, so that calling some kind of behaviour natural is to say that one ought to behave in that way, then we cannot also say that *the reason why* one ought to so behave is that to do so is natural *in that sense*, for that would be to utter a tautology: that one ought to because one ought to. Mill is surely right in saying that 'those who set up Nature as a standard of action' cannot have been using the term in an ethical sense, but were saying 'that what is constitutes the rule and standard of what ought to be' (paragraph 9).

We may take Mill's point further, as implicitly he does himself. The doctrine he is considering is that 'nature' in a factual sense is the standard for what we ought to do. This means that arguments which have as conclusions something of the kind 'one ought to do so and so' will have premises that cite as reasons for the conclusion statements about what is natural in a factual sense. For example, suppose that a woman is told that she ought to breast-feed her baby because she is a mammal and it is natural for all mammals to suckle their young. The usual response is 'so what?'. Something needs to be added to connect this 'is' with that 'ought', to explain why the fact gives a reason for the moral judgement. What needs to be added is 'one ought always to do what is natural' or something equivalent. This is a general ethical premise. The factual premise is presumably true if nature is taken in Mill's second sense ('wild nature'). The most obvious strategy to defeat the conclusion, then, is to question the general ethical premise. This is precisely Mill's strategy in attacking all attempts to justify moral prescriptions by appeal to what is natural. That we ought to follow nature always is completely unacceptable as a rule of conduct. But even if it were acceptable it would be necessary to give reasons for accepting it. 'Because it's nature' won't do as a reason.

A possible objection to Mill's rejection of nature as a guide to human behaviour is that he was writing at a period before important discoveries, especially in the life sciences, that revolutionized our knowledge of nature precisely in those areas where it is most relevant to an understanding of human beings and their relationship to other species. The essay 'Nature' was written between 1850 and 1858 (although not published until 1874), before the publication of Darwin's *Origin of Species* (1859).

It will help us to assess this objection to consider Paul Taylor's view of the matter. Taylor, a convinced biocentrist, writing very much in the ethos of post-Darwinian science, devotes a section of his book *Respect for Nature* to assessing the relevance of contemporary biology to the choices we make as moral agents.

Taylor is in agreement with Mill on the logical relation between what is and what ought to be. We are animals, but we are also moral agents. There are many features of our lives which we owe to our biological nature, but it is as moral agents that we choose by what principles we ought to live, and '[o]ur proper role as moral agents is not deducible from facts about our biological nature' (Taylor (1986), pp.49f.).

> From an evolutionary point of view, we perceive ourselves as sharing with other species a similar origin as well as an existential condition that includes the ever-present possibility of total extinction. If we now move to an ecological point of view, our animal nature makes itself evident in another way. We see ourselves subject to the inexorable constraints of biological necessity. We find that our physical survival as living organisms is explainable by the same laws and theories that account for the physical survival of other species. Our ecological relations with non-human animals and plants and our need for an environment free of pollution are not at bottom any different from what has been found to be true of other forms of life on Earth. Like them we are an integral part of the natural universe.
>
> (Ibid., p.49)

These are biological facts about us; they describe our animal nature. But, unlike other animals, we have the ability to choose how to conduct our lives, and by what norms to regulate ourselves.

> Understanding ourselves as biological entities, however, does not provide us with any particular directives as to how we should direct our lives. Our proper role as moral beings is not deducible from the facts about our biological nature... Even the goal of self-preservation cannot be shown to be an end that humans *ought* to seek as moral beings.
>
> (Ibid., pp.49f.)

Taylor applies this in particular to the attempt to derive moral directives from ecological premises:

> The claim is frequently made that ecology shows us how to live in relation to the natural environment. Thus it is held that ecological stability and integrity themselves constitute norms for environmental ethics. The very structure and functioning of the Earth's ecosystems, it is said, make known to us the proper

relationships between ourselves and the natural world. The ecological balance holding among organisms and between organisms and environment in a healthy ecosystem should be our guide in shaping a human culture that fits harmoniously into the order of nature. The conclusion drawn from these considerations is that the science of ecology provides us with a model to follow in the domain of environmental ethics.

(Ibid., pp.50f.)

This line of reasoning, Taylor says, confuses fact and value, 'is' and 'ought'. To ask how human culture *should* fit into the order of nature is to ask an ethical question, not a question of biological fact. Taylor does not of course deny that human beings are subject to ecological constraints. There are, for instance, limits to the damage we can do the biosphere without threatening our own extinction. This is an example of the way in which factual information about the consequences of our adopting some course of action can be relevant to our decision to adopt it or not. But it is not the information alone that dictates the decision.

Nothing in ecology, for example, can tell us that it is wrong to have a wholly *exploitative* attitude towards nature. As far as ecology is concerned it is perfectly possible for humans to choose not to adopt the attitude of respect for nature, but rather to consider wild living things as so many objects that are there to be used for the exclusive benefit of humans.

(Ibid., pp.51f.)

Other ways of learning from nature

Suppose we accept the impossibility of deducing moral guidance from facts about nature. Is that the end of the matter? Mill himself points out that there is such a thing as *studying* nature:

If, therefore, the useless precept to follow nature were changed into a precept to study nature; to know and take heed of the properties of things we have to deal with, so far as these are capable of forwarding or obstructing any given purpose; we should have arrived at the first principle of all intelligent action, or rather at the definition of intelligent action itself.

(Reading 11, paragraph 12)

This is to cast knowledge of nature in an instrumental role. Understanding the properties of metals enables us to build bridges and cars; understanding the genetics of certain diseases makes it possible to engineer human beings with no predisposition to those diseases. Such knowledge does not dictate our purposes, but it is necessary to our carrying them out. It can also show us whether it makes sense for us to have the purposes in the first place: there is no point in having a purpose that it is impossible to carry out. But all this has to do with knowledge in the service of our manipulation of nature.

Paul Taylor sees other possibilities. While holding as firmly as Mill to the impossibility of deriving moral precepts from facts about nature, he does not believe that knowledge of such facts has only instrumental value. He recognizes that factual knowledge can affect the way we think about ourselves, what we take ourselves to be, what we have in common with other species, and how our fate is bound up with theirs.

> The first thing we do when we accept the biocentric outlook is to take the fact of our being members of a biological species to be a fundamental feature of our existence. We do not deny the differences between ourselves and other species, any more than we deny the differences among other species themselves. Rather we put aside these differences and focus our attention upon our nature as biological creatures. As far as our relation to the Earth's ecosystems is concerned, we see ourselves as but one species-population among many. Thus we keep in the forefront of our consciousness the characteristics we share with all forms of life on Earth. Not only is our common origin in one evolutionary process fully acknowledged, but also the common environmental circumstances that surround us all. We view ourselves as one with them, not set apart from them. We are then ready to affirm our fellowship with them as equal members of the whole Community of Life on Earth.
>
> (Taylor, op. cit., p.101)

Taylor is now mentioning certain facts about our situation, not in order to draw attention to the logical gap between them and our moral commitments, but to draw attention instead to the way in which reflecting on those facts can lead to our adoption of a moral attitude, not as logically inescapable, but as suitable, fitting or appropriate. The expressions he uses at the end of this paragraph, 'fellowship' and 'community of life' already have strong moral overtones. If we accept the appropriateness of using them to describe our relationship with other species we are well on the way to adopting respect for nature in Taylor's strong sense as a moral attitude.

We have to ask whether 'fellowship' and 'community of life' *are* appropriate. In the previous chapter we considered another element of Taylor's characterization of the biocentric outlook, 'the belief that all organisms are teleological centres of life in the sense that each is a unique individual pursuing its own good in its own way'. We also encountered objections to Taylor's view that this feature of living organisms is a sufficient factual basis for conferring independent moral status on them. The serious doubt about that applies also to the view that we can use the terms 'fellowship' and 'community' of our relations with all other species in a sense that preserves the moral significance that the terms have when applied to our relations with other human beings.

Taylor is vulnerable to the criticism that he 'domesticates' our relationship with nature. His way of conceiving our relationship to nature turns out to bring us back to the human moral community as a model.

There is one undoubtably valuable thing about this approach, and that is his account of the way in which our understanding of nature can change, and lead to a revision and revaluation of our attitude to nature. He helps us to see how our value judgements, while not being deducible from the facts of our situation, can be suitable, fitting or appropriate to it. Doubts remain about the conclusion he reaches by this method of argument, but the *method* of argument is surely sound.

I bring this discussion to an end by suggesting that you read part of a paper by another venerable American environmental philosopher, Holmes Rolston III. The prose of this is very different from the correctly academic clarity and austerity of Taylor. It comes from a richer literary tradition; some will find it a refreshing change, others just maddeningly allusive and elusive. Rolston's conception of the nature to which we have to relate is also very different; there is little suggestion of the chumminess that we get in Taylor's account.

Now read Rolston's 'Following nature in a tutorial sense' (Reading 12), and then turn to the exercise below.   **READING**

Rolston writes with Mill's view of nature very much in mind. Before reading my brief discussion, note your answers to these questions:

EXERCISE 22
'Can and ought we to follow nature?'

1   What does he mean by 'natural resistance' and 'natural conductance'?

2   What do you consider to be the main point or points of disagreement with Mill?

3   Are there points on which he agrees with Mill?

4   Here is the passage from Mill's *Principles of Political Economy*, from which Rolston quotes. Is it inconsistent with the views set out in 'Nature'?

There is room in the world, no doubt, and even in old countries, for a great increase of population, supposing the arts of life to go on improving, and capital to increase. But even if innocuous, I confess I see very little reason for desiring it. The density of population necessary to enable mankind to obtain, in the greatest degree, all the advantages both of cooperation and of social intercourse, has, in all the most populous countries, been attained. A population may be too crowded, though all be amply supplied with food and raiment. It is not good for man to be kept perforce at all times in the presence of his species. A world from which solitude is extirpated , is a very poor ideal. Solitude, in the sense of being often alone, is essential to any depth of meditation or of character; and solitude in the presence of natural beauty and grandeur, is the cradle of thoughts and aspirations which are not only good for the individual, but which society could ill do without. Nor is there much satisfaction in contemplating the world with nothing left to the spontaneous activity of nature; with every rood of land brought into cultivation, which is capable of growing food for human beings; every flowery waste or natural pasture ploughed up, all quadrupeds or birds which are not domesticated for man's use exterminated as his rivals for food, every hedgerow or superfluous tree rooted out, and scarcely a place left where a wild shrub or flower could grow without being eradicated as a weed in the name of improved agriculture. If the earth must lose that great portion of its pleasantness which it owes to things that the unlimited increase of wealth and population would extirpate from it, for the mere purpose of enabling it to support a larger, but not a better or a happier population, I sincerely hope, for the sake of posterity, that they will be content to be stationary, long before necessity compels them to it.

(Mill (1963–77 edn), vol. 3, p.170)

DISCUSSION

1   Rolston's main thought is that we learn how to live by the experience of acting on and being acted on by nature: 'living well is the catching of certain natural rhythms'. By that he seems to mean both rhythms in the nature outside us and in the natural processes within ourselves. The most important distinction he makes is between what he calls 'natural conductance' and 'natural resistance'. (The odd word 'conductance' is explained when Rolston contrasts resistance with assistance.) Natural resistance includes those aspects of nature that Mill describes as hostile to life and frustrating of our purposes; but it is also nature that is responsible for our existence, for our having evolved the dispositions, abilities and cultural institutions that enable us to cope with a difficult environment; it is in these ways that nature assists (conducts) us.

2   As he makes explicit, Rolston does not claim that our living encounter with nature teaches us how to treat one another; its lessons are directed to showing how we should regard nature. So he agrees with Mill that we cannot follow nature in what Rolston calls 'an imitative ethical sense'. And he agrees that what is natural in Mill's second ('wild') sense is not always good, and is capable of improvement by human effort.

3   His main disagreement with Mill is over Mill's seeming to think that 'wild nature' is wholly inimical and recalcitrant, that it submits to some degree to our transforming efforts, but in no way cooperates in or facilitates them. If our life is good, then, it is despite nature, and due only to the degree of success we have achieved in mastering it. Mill gives the impression that nature and civilization are quite distinct spheres, and that we do well to have as little to do

with nature as possible. Rolston, by contrast, emphasizes that although 'part of nature opposes life' and must be resisted, it is also nature that makes possible the only kind of life we have: 'She is also the bosom out of which we have come, and she remains our life partner, a realm of otherness for which we have the deepest need.' Interestingly, Rolston is able to call Mill as a witness on his own side of the dispute in a passage quoted from Mill's *Principles of Political Economy*. That passage, in full, is quoted above (pp.129–30).

4   The sentiments expressed in that passage are not entirely at odds with his view in 'Nature', for in the latter he writes of the capacity of nature to inspire awe, and induce a sense of our littleness and impotence, but his main concern is not to underline the importance of these feelings, but to distinguish them from admiration as a moral sentiment. Nature is *grand* but not *good* in a sense which should inspire emulation. Thus he does not deny that nature can have value for us, but in his pursuit of the aim of showing that it is not a model for imitation he fails to give any weight to the kind of value that it does have.

Absolute and relative wildness

The distinction between nature and art, in which 'nature' is defined as that which has not been modified by human activity, makes nature an absolute notion, and one that is exemplified to a minute extent in most parts of the world, in large part because of the failure of the hope that Mill expresses at the end of the passage just quoted. There may be good reason to claim that naturalness, in this absolute sense, has a distinct kind of value, but it cannot represent the whole of what most people have in mind when they think about nature, and why they are keen on it. Many defenders of deep green views have taken the distinction in this absolute sense, and have been particularly concerned to articulate their sense of the value of 'raw' nature. There may be good reason to be concerned about the survival of areas of raw nature on a planet so extensively occupied by the human species, since it is necessarily irreplaceable by human effort. Its value lies in the fact that it is independent of human beings; it goes on in its own way without any reference to human concerns, and so makes us aware that there are limits to our importance in the scheme of things (supposing there were a scheme). The seas and the atmosphere may be thought of as wildernesses, their uncontrollability constantly reminding us of the limits of our powers. But there can be no doubt that to equate environmental ethics with this particular concern is to narrow its field very drastically. For most people, at least most of those who inhabit densely populated parts of the earth, the environment they care about and need to defend is not wilderness.

Things can be more or less natural, and natural in one respect, not in others. Planting a row of trees and erecting a line of pylons both modify a valley. A plough-horse and a tractor are both artefacts, objects whose character has been designed and realized by human activity. A sandcastle and a computer are both artefacts, so is a computer program or a mathematical proof. That such differences among things that are only in part natural can have significant value consequences is obvious when one thinks of hedges replaced by stock-proof metal fencing, or imagines a moorland landscape with the dry stone walls replaced by neat brick walls. Working with seasoned wood and with green wood both involve imposing form on a natural material, but there are two differences. Both materials have been modified by cutting the tree down and converting it into convenient lengths and sections. Seasoning modifies the material further, so it is twice removed from its natural state. A second difference is that the worker with green wood has a less inert material to work than the worker with seasoned wood. Both need to have regard to what the material will let them do, but the latter has more latitude than the former. A chair made from green wood reveals more about the natural origin of the wood than does a chair made from seasoned wood.

One of the motives behind present environmental concern is fear that we shall have nothing left that is not transformed by human activity. Wilderness preservation is only one expression of this anxiety, one that is more relevant in some countries than others. The term 'wilderness' applies to relatively extensive tracts of land in which none of the characteristics, land formation, vegetation, species diversity has been influenced by human beings. In countries such as Britain little or nothing comes into this category. There is country that is relatively wild, but much more that is thought of as being natural because its character is the result of many generations of unchanging pastoral and agricultural practices. In the recent past, of course, these practices have been changing, and the character of the rural landscape has changed in consequence. There is distress at the loss of countryside to residential and industrial development, but also distress at the loss of familiar character in the rural landscape brought about by intensive and mechanized agriculture and forestry. This is not a matter of valuing the natural in the sense of wild nature, but a combination of several value preferences: valuing the rural over the urban, valuing growing things over constructed things, valuing the familiar over the new and unfamiliar.

The landscape that results from new forms of cultivation is less natural in Mill's second sense: it is further removed from the wild. But a different sense of natural is also at work. We speak of natural ways of doing things when they have become habitual, familiar, not needing deliberation. If you have always made pastry in a certain way, that is the natural way to do it. There are different ways of using knitting needles; I was taught to do it by someone who had learned to knit in France; her way seemed quite unnatural to knitters who had been brought up to do it in the English way. There is an analogy, but also an essential difference, between this sense of 'natural' and the sense in which nature is contrasted with art (which, borrowing the term from Rolston, we might call the 'non-artifactual' sense). The analogy is that both involve a contrast with what happens spontaneously. What is natural in a non-artifactual sense is what happens if no human being intervenes, imposing a new form. What is natural in a cultural context is what you do spontaneously if no one stops to consider how else it might be done. There is a temporal aspect to this notion of the natural as the familiar. What is natural in our cultivation of the land is a kind of manipulation that has not changed recently.

The sense that the transformation of the rural scene involves a loss of value is not, however, to be explained just by a preference for the familiar: dislike of change as such might just as well be thought an unfortunate human limitation. But to the extent that one is aware of the part that human shaping has played in the evolution of the character of a particular rural landscape, another reason for valuing it is the testimony it bears to the virtues and skills of the generations of our forebears. It would by quite perverse if, in the effort to avoid a human-centred environmental ethics, this aspect of the value of the semi-natural were to be put aside as of no account. All human beings live in environments which they and their predecessors have shaped in various ways: they value not only the raw material they have shaped, but the shapes they have imposed on it, and of course the combination of the two. (Cf. Jane Howarth on the importance of past interactions with cherished objects, in Reading 9, pp.232ff.)

Conclusion

'Natural' has a number of senses but in none of them can we move from 'this is natural' to 'this is good' or 'this ought to be done'.

Things that have not been transformed by human activity have a special kind of value, but all human environments bear the marks of human activity; these may be no less valuable than wholly wild places and features, and part of their value may derive precisely from their being shaped by human hands.

Chapter summary

The attempt to assimilate our relations to nature to our relations to one another leads to difficulties. How then should we relate to nature? One influential idea has been that, as natural beings, we should look to nature as a guide to our behaviour. Mill subjects this idea to critical scrutiny. He distinguishes two senses in which 'nature' may be understood, a comprehensive sense in which everything that happens is natural, and a narrower sense in which everything is natural except human activity and its products. He concludes that in whichever sense it is understood, the injunction to follow nature must be rejected. Understanding the workings of nature is necessary if we are to achieve our ends, but we cannot infer what ends we ought to have from facts about nature: that involves fallacious reasoning from fact to value, or from what is to what ought to be. Although he is as strict as Mill in ruling out the possibility of deducing moral judgements from biological facts, Taylor draws attention to the way in which a thorough acquaintance with those facts can make the adoption of a certain moral attitude reasonable. Holmes Rolston too accepts the impossibility of the deduction from fact to value, but draws attention to ways of learning from nature that Mill's essay neglects. Both Taylor and Rolston accept the soundness of Mill's argument, but question the sharp contrast he draws between wild nature and human civilization, and his locating value exclusively in the latter, as too extreme. Some of what we value, in ourselves and in external nature is not due to our own creative efforts. But if Mill is mistaken in assigning all value to civilization, it is equally a mistake to assign all value to what human activity has not touched. Most conservation efforts are directed to the preservation of nature that has been significantly modified, and whose value depends on the mix.

Further reading

Much of the chapter entitled 'Preservation' in Passmore's book (see 'Further reading' Chapter 1) is relevant to the question of the value of wilderness. A book that is fully aware of the value of humanized nature, made landscape, is *Future Nature* by W.M. Adams, Earthscan, 1996. The writer is a geographer, not a philosopher, so his book contains information as well as ideas.

Notes

[1] Indeed, A.O Lovejoy has identified eighteen distinguishable senses in eighteenth-century writings (Lovejoy (1948)).

Relating to Nature 2: On Being a Part of Nature

When you have worked through this chapter you should:

- Understand a naturalistic view of the relationship of human beings to the rest of nature.
- Be able to understand a number of deep green views about how human beings can be part of nature.
- Be able to assess the claims of deep ecologists such as Naess and Fox that human beings can identify with nature.

Introduction

A common theme, especially in writers who espouse a variety of deep green theory called 'deep ecology' (see p.141), is that Western attitudes in particular are formed by the belief that human beings are not a part of nature, and that an examination of the human self in relation to nature is prior to the task of developing environmental ethics. Val Plumwood, whom you encountered in Chapter 1 as Val Routley, writes:

> One key aspect of the Western view of nature, which the ethical stance neglects completely, is the view of nature as sharply discontinuous or ontologically divided[1] from the human sphere of reason. This leads to a view of humans as apart from or 'outside of' nature, usually as masters or external controllers of it.
>
> (Plumwood (1991); in Elliot (1995), p.155)

The phrases 'part of' and 'apart from' are not at all technical, but they are extremely vague. In this chapter we shall try to see what they might mean. We shall see that, although it is indisputable that we are part of nature in a plain biological sense, various attempts by deep ecologists to show that we are, or could be, part of nature are unsatisfactory.

A naturalistic view of the human situation

By a 'naturalistic view' I mean a view that is agnostic about the existence of supernatural beings of any kind and is broadly consistent with current scientific theory. I am simply going to state it, not to justify it. That is not to say that it is not in need of justification. Some controversial elements in it will be discussed in detail in Books 4–6.

In its widest possible sense 'nature' encompasses the whole material universe, in which all objects that exist in space and time are included (universal nature). The only possible beings outside of nature in this sense are supernatural beings, such as gods, which are defined negatively as non-spatial and non-temporal. Whether or not there are any such beings, we are certainly not among them, not at any rate entirely. But many people have entertained the idea, and a few still do, that a bit of each of us, the soul, is supernatural, even that it is the most important bit, even that this bit is what each of us essentially is. That we are also animals, if only temporarily, is something that those who have held this belief have been obliged to recognize, some with reluctance and distaste, others with equanimity and even relish. If our being here, members of the natural world, is fortuitous, a question may seem to arise of what we are here for. Have we been co-opted to take charge, with despotic powers?[2] This, as David Hume said of the belief that we live forever, is a most unreasonable fancy. It may none the less have exerted a considerable influence on human attitudes and behaviour towards the natural world. Some writers have attributed our present environmental crisis to religious traditions, such as Christianity, which incorporate this fancy. Others have drawn attention to a strand of Christianity that gives us the role of stewards of nature, rather than despots, a hardly less fanciful idea, even if more benign in its effects on human behaviour. Questions about the influence of these and other beliefs on attitudes to nature are not our topic here. As for the question 'what are we here for?', the question of what our mission is only arises if we have one, and that is an issue for philosophers who enquire into the truth of religion – one of the topics in Book 6.

The sense of apartness from nature briefly discussed in the previous section is a radical one: it is what is essential to us that makes us distinct from everything in the natural world. An element of that view has generally been that the part of us which puts us apart from nature is our reason. If we reject, or leave in the air, the notion that we are not natural beings, we can still be left with the notion that although we are animals we are animals possessing unique capacities, having nothing of importance in common with other animals.[3] Here are some considerations bearing on that notion.

1   Our capacity for thought, though not unique, is immensely greater than that of any other terrestrial creature. Among other things, our mental capacities enable us to see much further into the consequences of events, including our own doings, than other creatures, and to deliberate about what to do about them. We can envisage alternative futures and review possible ways of reaching them or averting them. We can engage with others in gathering information and making plans. We can raise questions about who we are and how we should relate to the non-human world. We are language users, and whether all mental activity depends on the use of language or not, the range and complexity of our mental activity would not be possible without language. Does our possession of these powers mean that we are discontinuous with the rest of nature? If we accept a Darwinian account of evolution we are bound to suppose that the powers that we now have are the result of a long series of transformations through which the brains of pre-humans and proto-humans successively acquired new and more powerful functions. We did not spring from the earth fully armed with our present equipment. Many of the functions of our brains are similar to those of related animals. So we are continuous with other animals both by similarity and by the continuity of evolution. Difference does not mean discontinuity.

2   Our bodily appetites and our emotions are as much part of what we are as our intellectual capacities, and in the former our similarity to other animals, especially to other mammals, is more evident than in the latter. If there is a discontinuity here, it is a psychological and ethical one. Human beings have the ability to modify their innate inclinations, redirecting them, moderating their strength, or suppressing them according to the perceived tendency they have to good or evil. As we saw in Mill's essay (Reading 11), he is determined to show that nature does not provide a standard of what we ought to do; he insists that what is good in humanity 'is the result, not of instinct, but of a victory over instinct', a victory that is secured in some part by personal reflection, but in larger part by the wisdom transmitted by education. In a revealing passage Mill contrasts the artificially created virtues of human society with the 'odious scene of violence and tyranny which is exhibited by the rest of the animal kingdom, except insofar as tamed and disciplined by man'. This horror of the prevalence of predator-prey relations, of 'nature red in tooth and claw' was a common reaction among Mill's contemporaries to the revelations of natural history. Man is the self-tamed animal. If only he could tame the others what an improvement that would be!
    The sharpness of the contrast that Mill draws between the innate tendencies common to humans and other animals and the artificial virtues of humans is exaggerated in both directions. Animals are not engaged all the time in

devouring one another. Many of their behaviours are concerned with quite other things such as caring for their young. Whether any of their behaviours should be described in moral terms is debatable, but if they are not to be commended for caring for their offspring they should not be blamed for eating their neighbours. Care should be taken in using such terms as 'cruelty' and 'tyranny'. The exaggeration in the other direction is to place all the weight on art (technology) and none on what the art is exercised on in the development of virtue in humans. Mill acknowledges at several points that there must be something there in human nature to begin with if virtues are to be acquired. There must be, say, some primitive form of sympathy; but also there must be an innate capacity to respond to influences directed to developing that primitive instinct into a fully formed altruism. The language of conquest or victory is quite inappropriate.

3   A further characteristic of humans that is often held to divide them from other animals is their ability to manipulate their environment. There is certainly a great difference in the scale of the changes that human beings can bring about compared to any other species. The application of scientific knowledge to technology is the cause of this extended ability, and this is a consequence of the development of the human mental powers already mentioned. But do these differences put us apart from nature? Several considerations should make us hesitate to agree. First, other species provide some examples of tool-using and building, however modest by comparison with ours. Secondly, a more fundamental point is that the mental powers that enable us to transform our environment are those of an animal with a highly developed brain, but still those of an animal. Thirdly, none of our activities sets us apart from nature in Mill's first sense (universal nature). He makes this point himself: 'Art is but the employment of the powers of Nature for an end' (Reading 11, paragraph 5); and in a later paragraph he suggests, as noted previously, that although the injunction to follow universal nature is absurd, to study nature so as to be able to adopt means that, by the operation of natural laws, will bring about the results we desire, is 'the first principle of intelligent action'. Finally, another platitude, our ability to control natural forces is, however great, extremely limited. Winds, tides and earthquakes wipe away in a few minutes the most ambitious constructions of human beings, along with their makers, giving the strongest possible proof that we are part of nature.

4   One of the chief sources of inspiration behind the development of environmental awareness and the revision of traditional ethical thought is the science of ecology, or at least, of ideas derived (sometimes loosely) from that science. A key concept is that of the *ecosystem*, an association of plant and

animal populations, and inorganic elements, bound together by complex relations of interdependence, each population depending for its existence on others and performing its own function in maintaining the system. A human population, and its members, belongs to an ecosystem, and could not live in isolation from it. We do not only live alongside other species, plant and animal, and have features in common with them, we are part of the same system of life.

Let us try to sum up the results of this collection of observations. First, it is useful to keep in mind Mill's two senses of 'nature'. In the first sense, we could be apart from nature only if we were supernatural beings equipped with mental and creative powers that were wholly independent of natural laws. To believe oneself to be apart from nature in this sense is to be the victim of a delusion. If viewing ourselves as masters or external controllers of nature implies being apart from nature in this sense, then it is a serious form of insanity. It does not seem that it is this sense that Plumwood primarily has in mind, because she goes on to characterize the human–nature discontinuity in a way that involves the second sense of nature (wild nature):

> What is taken to be authentically and characteristically human, defining of the human, as well as the ideal for which humans should strive, is *not* to be found in what is shared with the natural and animal (e.g. the body, sexuality, reproduction, emotionality, the senses, agency) but in what is thought to separate and distinguish them – especially reason and its offshoots.
>
> (Plumwood, op. cit., p.156)

So we may say that, according to Plumwood, to define the human as constituted solely by attributes that are not shared with other natural beings, and especially not by those that we have in common with other animals is to believe oneself 'apart from nature'.

Now, if this is what it is to believe that human beings are 'apart from nature', it is surely unjustified. But does one have to resort to a deep green position to reject it? To define the human in such a way is surely quite arbitrary. There would have to be some reason to think that what a thing *is* is identical to the ensemble of features that it alone possesses. In the absence of such a reason it is reasonable to say that we are animals with some features that distinguish us from other animals. That is scarcely more than a platitude. To dwell on the similarities and continuities, however, rather than solely on the differences, serves to induce a realistic conception of the place of human beings in nature. Such realism – an undistorted view of the facts about what we are and how we relate to other beings, living and non-living – is a **necessary condition** (though not a **sufficient** one) of working out what our attitudes and behaviour towards other beings should be. (In moving from reflections on our place in nature to attitudes and commitments we need to recall the hazards involved in

necessary and sufficient conditions

139

moving from statements about what *is* to judgements about what *ought to be*.) To realize that human beings are one species among many, subject to the same contingencies of existence as others, and dependent upon many of them should, if the realization is more than a notional assent, induce humility, banishing exaggerated ideas about our importance in the general scheme of things. To the extent that an undue pride is based on misconceptions about our biological nature, a dose of biological reality is salutary. But biological realism is not only the province of deep green philosophy.

Extended communities and extended selves

We may agree that we are not 'apart from nature', and therefore, in a platitudinous sense, we are part of it, but is there some other, non-platitudinous, sense in which we are part of nature?

Several philosophers who adhere to one of the deeper green views emphasize the importance of our having a deeply felt sense of being part of nature. One of Taylor's main aims in his elaboration of the biocentric outlook is to make his readers recognize and give intellectual and emotional assent to a view of ourselves as part of nature, existing on equal terms with all other living things. In his writing, the idea of a community, as I suggested in the previous chapter, plays a crucial role in making the transition from an intellectual recognition of common origin and mutual dependence to the emotional and moral commitment implied by respect. The term 'community' can do this because it combines the ideas of mutual dependence on the one hand with mutual obligation and care on the other. Whether it can do it legitimately is another question. What do the members of a group have to have in common for the group to be a community? Mutual awareness seems to be one necessary condition. Having some common interests that the members cooperate in promoting is another. The members having individual interests that are reciprocally acknowledged is another. On that basis mutual obligations can arise. It is doubtful whether all human beings constitute a community, but at least they have the capacity to recognize one another as potentially fellow members of a community of interest. Most living things are not even potential fellow members of a community satisfying those conditions. It may be quite harmless to speak of our belonging to a single community of life, but we need to avoid sliding from the 'thin' sense of 'community' in which it means nothing more than interdependence to the 'thick' sense in which it implies the conditions just mentioned.

So, according to Taylor, our being 'part of nature' is our being members of a community of living things. In the 'thin' sense of 'community' this is true and something nearly all of us would recognize, but in the 'thick' sense of 'community' it is something nearly all of us would recognize as false.

A different deep green account of our oneness with nature is a central feature of deep ecology. The father of this theory is Arne Naess (whom you encountered in Chapter 1 (p.21)). The views of Taylor and Naess have important common features. These include the interdependence of living forms throughout nature; the possession by all living things of a value that is independent of human interests, and the possibility of understanding the needs of other living things from their point of view. But there are two further features of Naess's view that make it quite definitely different from Taylor's.

1   The first plank of the platform of the deep ecology movement[4] is that the 'flourishing of human and non-human life on Earth has intrinsic value. The value of non-human life is independent of the usefulness these may have for narrow human purposes'. In a note on this, Naess says, 'The term "life" is used here in a comprehensive non-technical way to refer also to things biologists may classify as non-living: rivers (watersheds), landscapes, cultures, ecosystems, "the living earth"' (Naess (1989), p.29). In contrast, Taylor restricts the scope of moral status strictly to living individuals.

2   An even more notable difference, however, is in the central place Naess gives in his theory to the idea of self-realization, and more particularly in the way he develops that idea. In its usual sense, the term 'self-realization' refers to the process or activity by which a living being develops its natural capacities, so self-realization is synonymous with the realization of a being's good. So far there is no difference between Taylor and Naess. The difference emerges when Naess distinguishes between self-realization and Self-realization. For Naess, to be one with nature is to become part of 'the great Self'. Here is a passage in which Naess brings out the connection between this concept and an ecological understanding of nature.

> Modern ecology has emphasized a high degree of *symbiosis* as a common feature in mature ecosystems, an interdependence for the benefit of all. It has thereby provided *a cognitive basis for a sense of belonging* which was not possible earlier. Family belonging, the tie of kinship, has a material basis in perceived togetherness and cooperation. Through the extension of our understanding of the ecological context, it will ultimately be possible to develop a sense of belonging with a more expansive perspective: *ecospheric belonging*.

> 'The task is to find a form of togetherness with nature which is to our own greatest benefit. Any other definition is hypocritical.' If such a statement is accepted, 'our own benefit' must then mean 'that which serves the great Self, not merely the individual ego or human societies. If a lesser self is implied, the

sentences are misleading. One can desire well-being for an animal or a plant just as naturally as one can for a person. For some dog owners, their dog's well-being is more important to them than that of their neighbour. The identification is stronger, and empathy is greater. One can, without hypocrisy, *desire something which is for the benefit of other living beings* – and one normally obtains great, rich satisfaction from it.

(Naess (1989), p.168)

The key to the distinction between lesser and greater selves – between self and Self – is the notion of identification. People often speak of themselves as identifying with others, meaning, for example, that they understand what it is like to be some other person, either in general, or in a particular situation. That is one aspect of the concept as Naess uses it, but the work he puts it to extends well beyond such familiar uses. In fact, the concept is far from clear, so we shall have to examine it critically. But first, read a longer extract from Naess. It comes a little later in the same chapter of *Ecology, Community and Lifestyle* as the one just quoted.

EXERCISE 23

Identification, wholeness and self-realization

Read Naess in Reading 13, and then answer the questions below.

1   Naess supposes that we can identify with a variety of different things, including human beings, animals, plants, mountains and landscapes. Can the same process of identification be involved in these different cases? If not what different processes might be involved?

2   How does identification with other beings result in an expansion of self into Self?

3   How does the notion of an expanded self help to explain concern for other living things?

DISCUSSION

1   The most familiar and intelligible case is that of identification with another human being. This can have various grades or stages. Knowing what it is like to be embarrassed when I forget someone's name means that I can identify with another person's embarrassment in the same situation, in the sense of knowing what it feels like. This is a minimal kind of empathy, minimal because it does not imply that I have any feeling for the person concerned – I may be quite indifferent to them. Even this minimal sense, however, does not carry over to all the various beings that Naess believes we can identify with. It may carry over to sentient beings to the extent that we have reasonably well-grounded beliefs about how various species of animal feel about the things that befall them. It cannot carry over to plants and mountains. Identification in the sense of empathy cannot be what is needed. There is another sense of 'identification' that can apply to human relationships that may be of more help.

With close family and friends, it can happen that a person wishes the other's good with the same directness that she wishes her own – the other's good is her own good. In principle, it might seem that this sort of identification could carry over to any being that has a good of its own. But there are two problems: first, it is not clear that all the kinds of entity that Naess wants us to identify with can be said in any real sense to have a good of their own (do mountains and rivers, for example?); and secondly, there may be limits to the number of beings with which a single person can identify at any one time – the problem of limited sympathies.

2   The Self with a capital 'S' comprises all the beings whose good I wish as though it were my good. The greater the number of beings with whom I identify in this way, the larger the Self.

3   'We seek what is best for ourselves, but through the expansion of the self, our "own" best is also that of others'.

The concept of the extended or expanded self does not meet with the approval of all philosophers who adopt a deep green position. Val Plumwood is among them. Reading 14 is the article from which two brief passages have already been quoted in this chapter.

First, to understand where Plumwood locates herself in the deep green position, read pp.285–90 of Reading 14, bearing in mind the questions and answers to Exercise 23 above. Then read the next section of the Plumwood article, Reading 14, pp.290–1 and answer the following questions.

EXERCISE 24
The expanded self

1   What do you understand the objection(s) to be to the use Naess makes of the concept of the expanded self?

2   On a charitable reading of the passage from Naess, try to sketch a reply that might be made on his behalf

---

DISCUSSION

1   An explicit objection is that 'the widening of interest is obtained at the expense of failing to recognize unambiguously the distinctness and independence of the other'. Less explicit, but implied by the remark that deep ecology does not question 'the structures of rational egoism', is the objection that Naess fails to allow for the possibility of genuine altruism.

2   To the first objection, Naess could reply by pointing to such remarks in his text as 'each living being is understood as a goal in itself'. The self expands by understanding the goals of other living beings and making them its own. To the second, he could reply that to make another's goal one's own in this way

entails protecting or fostering it for its sake, not one's own, and that this is just what altruism is.

It seems to me that these possible replies are not implausible. But the more satisfactory they are the more they reduce the Self to nothing more than a picturesque way of saying, as Naess does in the passage quoted in the text, that 'one can, without hypocrisy, desire something which is for the benefit of other living beings'. It is less confusing to say this plainly without expressing it in a way that seems to concede that self-interest is the only motive we can act from. There is another important point that talk of the Self is likely to gloss over. The goals of individuals often conflict. Another individual may have goals whose achievement would entail my not achieving mine, and in the extreme may threaten my destruction. If your goal is to eat me, am I to identify with your goal? Does the Self have a harmonious set of goals? If so, how is the reconciliation of the conflicting goals of innumerable selves achieved?

But the fundamental objection is to the possibility of the kind of extensive identification with other life forms that the concept of the expanded self – the Self – presupposes. Like Taylor's biotic community, Naess's Self is a fiction, at best a somewhat extravagant metaphor for more homely kinds of concern for the natural world and a sense of connection with it. If there really were a larger Self that encompassed the entire ecosphere then no doubt Self-interest would be the appropriate and quite sufficient motive for environmental concern. But that motive is no more real than the Self.

This criticism does not imply total rejection of the possibility of identification with natural objects and other living things. One can certainly identify with a locality, a landscape, a particular animal, or a particular tree, to such an extent that their presence, or at least existence, is part of one's sense of who one is. This possibility is one of the roots of Naess's view, which must derive in large part from his own intense relationship with the Norwegian countryside. But it is of the essence of such relationships that they are to particular places and beings. (For a telling expression of the intense particularity of this kind of identification, read Hopkins's poem 'Binsey Poplars' (Reading 16). See too, Jane Howarth on the irreplaceability of cherished objects in Reading 9, pp.229–33.) Concern for natural beings in general must have other sources.

There is, however, a rejoinder to the final objection that must be considered. It is that the objection overlooks the possibility of other senses of 'identification' than those I have considered, and here assumed that Naess had in mind in the passages discussed. One alternative sense of 'identification' in particular is put forward as the basis for an expanded Self by Warwick Fox, a philosopher who has developed a version of deep ecology which he calls 'transpersonal ecology'.

Read Fox's account of the varieties of identification in Reading 15, 'Transpersonal ecology and the varieties of identification', and then answer the following questions.

1   In what way is the personal basis of identification limited?

2   In what way is the ontological basis of identification limited?

3   Summarize, in a few words, cosmologically based identification (or you might instead pick out a couple of key sentences in the Reading).

4   What, in Fox's view, is the main advantage of the cosmological over the personal basis of identification?

DISCUSSION

1   The personal basis limits identification to other entities with which one has had personal involvement. The self is not enlarged sufficiently to encompass the whole of nature, or even any extensive portion of it.

2   The ontological basis is limited in a quite different way. It can encompass everything, but the process of identification requires an arduous discipline which not many people are prepared to undertake.

3   There are two phases, or aspects, of cosmologically based identification. The first is 'a deep-seated realization that we and all other entities are aspects of a single unfolding reality'. This gives rise to the second phase: 'experiences of commonality' with all the other entities that are, equally with ourselves, parts of this unfolding reality. I am not sure whether there is a third phase, or whether the experience of commonality – not a very perspicuous phrase – is meant to include 'an orientation of steadfast (as opposed to fair-weather) friendliness'.

4   The advantage claimed for cosmologically based identification is that it yields an impartial concern for all entities, and avoids the partiality towards one's particular friends – whether human or non-human – that person-based identification is necessarily prone to.

Now return to Plumwood and read the next section of Reading 14, pp.291–2, and answer the following question.

What is Plumwood's response to Fox's version of the expanded self ?

DISCUSSION She objects to the emphasis on impartial concern for all things, at the expense of 'our own particular concerns, personal emotions, and attachments'. The objection is twofold: the cosmological concern she derides as 'vague, bloodless and abstract', while the rejection of particular attachments discounts the attachment to particular places 'that has motivated both the passion of many modern conservationists and the love of many indigenous peoples for their land'.

What surfaces here as a disagreement about the source of environmental concern is in fact a particular manifestation of a very general division among moral philosophers. Some see moral concern as based on feelings of sympathy, as involving careful consideration of particular cases, rather than following general rules, and as allowing some partiality for those with whom the agent has a special relationship. In opposition to this there are philosophers who view feelings as an untrustworthy basis for morality, preferring universal principles, which are to be applied impartially and without regard to whether one is dealing with friend or stranger. To describe the opposition in this schematic way is of course to invite the response that there need not be an 'either/or' about this. It may well be that an adequate moral philosophy must effect some kind of compromise between these extremes. A good example of a position that attempts to reconcile these extremes is Mary Midgley's. You might recall Midgley's view, discussed in Book 2, that sometimes we should be impartial, sometimes partial (Book 2, pp.151–9).

Returning to the specific controversy, one might accept Fox's advocacy of concern for nature based upon cosmological identification, without also accepting his dismissal of particular attachments. He may be right that attachment to family, mates, fellow nationals, fellow fans and so on, is a source of destructive competition. That does not prevent it from being also the source of many good things. Why cannot we have both universal and particular bases for environmental concern? Perhaps we can, but there is room for some scepticism about Fox's claims for his particular route to universal concern. His description of the friendliness towards all entities is pretty strong: 'a clear and steady expression of positive interest, liking, warmth, goodwill, and trust' – that's stretching the notion of friendliness surely? Can a sense (however deep-seated) that I, together with every other entity, am part of a single unfolding reality, really be an adequate object for that array of feelings and attitudes? A cool respect, a willingness to let be as much as possible, perhaps. But warmth? How warm can feelings be if so widely spread? Friendliness on this scale sounds like the exceptional virtue of the rare ecological saint. We should perhaps be thankful for the more frequent if less exalted virtue of those who are attached to a place and are aware of and respect the similar attachments of others.

Attitudes to nature – a cautionary note

General statements about being part of nature can capture something important, but can also dissolve into something ludicrous if taken uncritically. They have a function as slogans or proverbs. Bernard Williams, in the essay quoted in Chapters 5 and 6 (Williams (1995), pp.236ff.), writes of a kind of respect for nature that is based, not on a sense of community, but rather on the sense of a different but equally intimate involvement: 'a sense of opposition between ourselves and nature, as an old, unbounded, and potentially dangerous enemy'. On this basis 'our sense of restraint in the face of nature, a sense very basic to conservation concerns, will be grounded in a form of fear: a fear not just of the power of nature itself, but what might be called *Promethean fear*,[5] a fear of taking too lightly or inconsiderately our relations to nature'. No doubt there is something healthy about this attitude, but it can easily tip over into superstitious dread of the kind castigated by Mill (see Reading 11, paragraph 16). It works best as a warning not to blast on without thinking, but it gives no real guidance when it comes to deciding whether some piece of biomedical research, or the damming of a great river, transgresses the proper bounds of our invasion of nature or not.

Some ways of thinking about nature do seem to imply falsehoods or indefensible attitudes. Thinking of nature as an enemy to be conquered, subdued or outwitted may be a harmless way of talking about quite justifiable ways of surviving in adverse circumstances, but as a metaphor it is puerile boastfulness, and if taken seriously can be used to justify monstrously destructive behaviour. Other more or less mistaken or misleading ways of thinking about nature include: taking it as a model for human behaviour; absorbing the multiplicity of natural objects into the self, even with a capital 'S'; thinking of nature and of human culture as though they were independent worlds, and ascribing value exclusively to one or the other – both Mill and some of his wilderness-loving opponents go wrong in wanting to hog value for human artifice on the one hand, or for the absolutely natural on the other.

We should not expect any single answer to the question about how we should relate to nature. We have noted some mistaken ways of thinking about that relationship. But there are many ways in which we can legitimately relate to it, and each has its own way of valuing built in. Using things is one way. Being in a place, walking through a wood, studying natural phenomena scientifically, painting or writing about natural things, viewing things aesthetically are others. In all these activities there are forms of value to be discerned and responded to. Cosmologically based contemplation is another, rather rarefied form of activity, which has its place for those with a taste for that sort of thing, but it has no particular pre-eminence as a way of getting to the heart of the matter.

Conclusion

That we are part of nature in a plain biological sense is not worth disputing. We are animals with certain highly developed capacities. Whether the differences between human beings and other species constitute a 'sharp discontinuity' is not a very clearly formulated question: how great would the differences need to be? At any rate, a sober realism about our place in nature provides no basis for fantasies about dominion. Actual experience of nature can bring a livelier sense of relationship to parts of it, but attempts to form 'thick' community relationships with all other living things, or to become united with the whole of it in one Self seem unlikely to succeed.

Chapter summary

The belief that there is a sharp discontinuity between human beings and the rest of nature, that we are 'apart from' nature, has been blamed for attitudes of superiority and exploitativeness towards nature. A naturalistic view of our relationship to nature sees us as animals who share many characteristics with other species, though we have evolved to have certain capacities that other species lack, or have to a lesser degree. We are linked to other species in three ways: by origin, by similarity and by mutual dependence. Nothing in a realistic view of human nature provides grounds for our supposing that we have the right to exploit nature as we think fit. It is more likely that such a view would tend to discourage an exaggerated sense of species importance. Attempts to argue for closer links than the three just mentioned, and to draw stronger conclusions about what our attitude to nature should be, take several forms. One is Taylor's use of the notion of living things as forming a community, which fails by sliding from a 'thin' sense of 'community' to a 'thick' sense. Another is Naess's notion of belonging to an extended Self through identification with a wide range of natural beings. Naess's own examples of identification do not extend far enough for the purpose, but that is overcome by Fox's notion of cosmological identification. That, however, imposes impossibly high demands on our capacity for friendship. Finally, there are many attitudes to nature and ways of relating to it. Some can be disqualified because they are based upon false beliefs, but many are left, including some quite unpretentious ones.

Postscript

Some readers will have found the treatment of deep green theories, especially of deep ecology, much too short and unsympathetic. There is much more to deep ecology than I have indicated, in at least two respects. First, it is not just a position on the issue of how we should value natural beings. In addition, it incorporates principles of political and economic organization, national and international, whose implementation is needed, in the view of its exponents, to prevent environmental catastrophe. It offers a comprehensive world view and an answer to the question 'How should we live?', in some ways comparable to a religious system (in its comprehensiveness, rather than in its having theological foundations). Secondly, for some of its adherents, deep ecology is a world view that rests on a metaphysical theory, a theory about the ultimate nature of reality, of which you will have encountered some indication in the readings for this chapter. Two questions about this theory arise: whether it is tenable, and whether its acceptance is a prerequisite of an acceptable environmental ethics. The first of these questions would take us into a new area of philosophy, metaphysics, which is large and complex. The answer to the second question is 'It had better not be', because the theory in question is very abstruse and highly controversial; our problems are too urgent to wait until everyone has understood and accepted it. A main aim of this book has been to suggest that a more adequate understanding of the value of non-human nature rests on foundations that are more familiar and more easily acceptable.

It remains true that deep ecology is to some people a revelation of a new way of looking at things. Naess is an inspirational writer and teacher who combines philosophizing of a headily speculative kind and an earthily practical approach to the possibilities of living in communities of many different species. Taylor is not a deep ecologist; his biocentrism rests on naturalistic foundations, and his discourse remains within the bounds of academic philosophy. But he is a coolly passionate advocate of a profound change in the way we look at ourselves and our relations with other life-forms. The medium may not inspire, but the message may well do so. I have argued that there is a doubt whether Taylor has established as much as he wants to establish, but not that his argument establishes nothing at all. Just as it is unlikely that an open-minded reader could emerge from a reading of Singer's *Animal Liberation* with unchanged views about animals, so it is unlikely that the same reader would survive a reading of Taylor's *Respect for Nature* with unreconstructed views about living things.

The final comment must be that much as philosophers may seek to advocate changes in belief and behaviour, they are committed by the rules of the trade to support their proposals with good arguments, and as students of philosophy we inherit the Curse of Socrates, the obligation to accept nothing that is unclear or unsupported.

Further reading

There is much more to deep ecology than is dealt with in this chapter. Further reading in the books by Naess (1989) and Fox (1990) would fill out your knowledge (but parts of Naess's book are hard to follow). Deep ecology is only one variety of deep green theory. Another, calling itself 'deep green theory', is expounded, and its differences from deep ecology explained, in Richard Sylvan and David Bennett, *The Greening of Ethics*, The White Horse Press, 1994. The influence of various strands of Christian teaching about the relationship of human beings to nature is explored by John Passmore in the first part of his book, *Man's Responsibility for Nature*, Duckworth, 1980 (2nd edn).

Notes

[1] [The phrase 'ontologically divided from' uses a technical term in philosophy. But the phrase, as used in this quotation, adds little if anything to the preceding phrase 'sharply discontinuous'. Ontology is the study of being, and is concerned with the way the world divides into fundamentally different sorts of existent, for instance (but controversially), minds and bodies.]

[2] Recall the discussion of the passages from Genesis and St Augustine in Book 2 (pp.76–7) which spoke of human beings having dominion over the rest of the natural world.

[3] The differences between humans and other animals was discussed at length in Book 2, Chapter 3.

[4] The deep ecology platform is a sort of manifesto drawn up by environmental philosophers in the US with Naess's collaboration. It can be found in Chapter 1 of Naess (1989).

[5] Prometheus was the character in Greek myth who stole fire from the gods so that human beings could keep warm and cook, for which transgressive act he was impaled by the gods on a mountain for eagles to peck at his entrails for all time. A greater miscarriage of justice would be hard to imagine.

Afterword

Values and valuing

Early on in the book (Chapter 1, p.32; Chapter 2, pp.42–3) I alluded to an ambiguity in the term 'intrinsic value' and promised to return to it.

The ambiguous senses are these:

1   Intrinsic value = non-instrumental value: the value we ascribe to something that we value not for its usefulness but for its own sake.

2   Intrinsic value = value that something has independently of the existence of any being who evaluates.

The first sense has been extensively discussed in the book, but the second sense has not, although some of the writers discussed use it in the second sense, or use terms that have the same sense. Taylor's term 'inherent worth', for example, is intended to mean value that is not only independent of human needs and purposes (non-instrumental value), but independent of human *valuing*.

This second sense immediately raises a fundamental philosophical issue that has divided philosophers throughout the ages, and now divides philosophers who think about environmental ethics: 'Are there any such values?'.

The issue has been put in various ways. An ancient way is the question, 'Do we value good things because they are good, or are they good because we value them?' If we say the first, then we imply that goodness is a property of good things that they just have, which we recognize when we value them, but which they have even if we fail to recognize it. If we say the second, we imply that goodness is somehow conferred on things by our valuing them. According to the first answer we could say that goodness is *real*, meaning by that, that it is part of the world as it is in itself, independently of the way in which we experience it. According to the second answer, the existence of goodness is a result of the way we experience the world.

It has seemed to some philosophers important to maintain that when we find value in nature we do not put it there, that it is not a projection of our valuing minds. They believe that if value is not in nature, part of a mind-independent reality, then its value depends on whether human beings care about it. If there really are values in nature, then they are still there even if we do not recognize them, and our failure to recognize them would be an *error*.

The philosophical question about the reality of value is such a difficult one, and so much weighty philosophizing has been spent on it, that to attempt a quick answer here would invite ridicule. But you may well wonder how I have managed to side-step such a fundamental issue that has seemed so crucial to some environmental philosophers. That I can try to explain.

It seems to me that the view that nature must be valuable in the second sense of intrinsic value is encouraged by the failure to make a clear distinction

false dichotomy

between it and the first sense. The confusion sets up a **false dichotomy** between instrumental value and value as a real, mind-independent property of things. What seems to happen is this. One begins by objecting to some of the ways in which human beings *use* nature, and is then moved to protest that it has value that is independent of the purposes for which human beings use, consume and manipulate it: value beyond instrumental value. One then concludes that nature has value which is independent of its being valued. But this is to confuse independence of our *purposes* and independence of our *valuing*. What the false dichotomy leaves out is the whole range of values that are revealed to the contemplative gaze, the values that are discovered in the activities that exercise the capacity for disinterested attention: the scientific study of nature, aesthetic appreciation, the physical activities of walking, climbing, sailing, and so on. Whether or not these values are independent of our valuing them, they are values for us. And if values are real, valuer-independent properties of things, it is only in experience of them that values reveal themselves, either to our thinking or to our feeling. It is difficult to see what philosophers who insist on the independence of value from valuing hope to gain over and above what is gained by the recognition of these non-instrumental values. What environmental ethics needs is to uncover reasons that can weigh in the deliberations and decisions of human beings in their dealings with nature, reasons that go beyond the (also important) reasons for conserving resources, and preserving the natural world as our life support system. It does not help us to decide what these reasons are to know that they are independent of our valuing.

That is why I have evaded the issue of the reality of values, and have instead emphasized the contemplative values in contrast to instrumental values. In doing so I have no doubt under-emphasized the importance of instrumental values. But then, no one is likely to undervalue them.

Revision Test

This test is intended to help you revise some of the main points covered in this book. Try working through the questions without using your notes or referring back to the text. Then compare your answers with those at the back of the book.

Chapter 1

1   Deep green environmentalists believe that sentience is

  (i)   necessary and sufficient

  (ii) necessary but not sufficient

  (iii) sufficient but not necessary

for a being to have independent moral status.

Tick at least one.

2   The Routleys believe that

  (i)   traditional Western ethical principles impose no restrictions on the treatment of non-human beings;

  (ii) there is no difference in practice between adherents of traditional principles and adherents of new principles;

  (iii) only new principles can adequately protect the environment.

Which if any is/are true?

3   According to the Routleys, the last man

  (i)   does nothing wrong;

  (ii) does wrong if he destroys sentient animals, but not otherwise;

  (iii) does wrong because he can't be sure that he is the last conscious being;

  (iv) does wrong because he destroys things that have value.

Which if any is/are true?

4   *Premise 1*
No human action is wrong unless it harms some human being.

Premise 2
The last man's action harms no human being.

Conclusion
So the last man does nothing wrong.

Which of the following criticisms of the argument do the Routleys make?

    (i)   the argument is invalid;

    (ii) the argument is unsound;

    (iii) the first premise is false;

    (iv) the second premise is false.

Chapter 2

1   According to the view presented in Chapter 2, things in nature have, on a human-centred account:

    (i)   instrumental value only;

    (ii) non-instrumental value only;

    (iii) both instrumental and non-instrumental value.

2   *Premise 1*
If two experiences are indistinguishable by the person who has them they have the same value.

Premise 2
The experience machine gives an experience indistinguishable from the experience of walking through a wood.

Conclusion
The experience of walking through a wood and the experience given by the machine have the same value.

According to Nozick:

    (i)   the argument is valid;

    (ii) the argument is unsound;

(iii) the first premise is false;

(iv) the second premise is false.

3   (a) Which of (i)–(iv) is/are asserted by the authors of *Blueprint for a green economy?* (b) Which of (i)–(iv) is/are denied by the main criticism of cost benefit analysis discussed in Chapter 2?

(i)   environmental goods have economic value;

(ii)   costs and benefits can be measured by the yardstick of money;

(iii) there is no way of assigning monetary values to such goods as beauty and tranquillity;

(iv) willingness to pay is a measure of the contribution to a person's well-being of such goods as beauty and tranquillity.

4   What is it about Rangitoto or Windermere that makes it, according to the criticism discussed in Chapter 2, not measurable in monetary terms?

Chapter 3

1   According to Warnock and Mackie, things are apt to go badly for us because:

(i)   no one cares about anyone else;

(ii)   no one cares much about anyone else;

(iii) we care a lot about some others but little or nothing about others;

(iv) we are not sufficiently reasonable.

2   According to Warnock and Mackie:

(i)   human beings are incapable of cooperating without coercion;

(ii)   morality is loving everyone as we love ourselves;

(iii) morality goes some way to making up for the fact that we do not love everyone as we love ourselves;

(iv) a function of morality is to make cooperation possible.

3   In situations like that of Tom and Dan (the prisoners' dilemma):

(i)   if each individual reasoned better regarding his own interest they would reach their best joint outcome;

(ii) a prior agreement to cooperate would enable them to reach their best joint outcome;

(iii) only external coercion would make the best joint outcome reachable;

(iv) their both having moral dispositions would make the best joint outcome reachable;

(v) their knowing that they may be in the same situation in future makes no difference.

According to Mackie's account which of (i)–(v) are true, which false?

4   According to the account in Chapter 3 of the need for cooperation in producing environmental goods that benefit every individual:

(i) self-interest dictates that one should cooperate;

(ii) it is in one's interest to have a disposition to cooperate with others who are willing to cooperate;

(iii) agreements between cooperators must be in the form of formally binding contracts;

(iv) coercion is the only effective method of reinforcing agreements;

(v) coercion is sometimes a necessary method of reinforcing agreements;

(vi) considerations of self-interest are always enough to rule out free-riding as a rational policy;

(vii) some free-riders are imprudent.

Which of (i)–(vii) are true, which false?

Chapter 4

1   According to Hepburn:

(i) wonder is a response to surprising phenomena that always wears off as we come to understand the phenomena – true or false?

(ii) wonder can be an appropriate response or a misplaced one – true or false?

(iii) Wonder is an attitude in which we attend to what kind of value in its objects – their instrumental value or their non-instrumental value?

(iv) wonder is associated with which moral virtues? Give examples.

2   According to O'Neill:

   (i)   what is the use of the senses that is distinctively human?

   (ii)   why can science be a component of human well-being?

Chapter 5

1   According to Taylor:

(a) That a thing can be benefited or harmed is:

   (i)   a necessary condition

   (ii)   a sufficient condition

of its having a good of its own – (i) only, (ii) only, both (i) and (ii)?

(b) Which of these has a good of its own?

   (i)   my canary;

   (ii)   my washing machine;

   (iii) my aspidistra;

   (iv)   my lungs;

   (v)   my stick insect.

(c) The statement that a being has a good of its own:

   (i)   conveys a piece of biological information;

   (ii)   expresses a moral commitment;

   (iii) gives a logically compelling reason to respect the being;

   (iv)   states a necessary condition of its deserving respect.

2   Sumner believes:

   (i)   only beings which are capable of suffering and enjoyment can have a good;

   (ii)   Taylor gives no reason to promote the good of non-sentient beings;

   (iii) only beings which are capable of suffering and enjoyment have a welfare;

   (iv)   we ought to promote the perfection of living beings.

Which of (i)–(iv) is/are true, which false?

Chapter 6

1   According to Mill:

   (i)   there is a sense of 'nature' in which we cannot help but follow it – what is it?

   (ii) there is a sense in which we can follow nature – what is it?

   (iii) there are two ways in which we can follow nature in this sense – what are they?

2   What is wrong with the following argument:

   A

   It is natural for human beings to eat meat.

   Therefore it is morally permissible for them to eat meat.

Is this one any better?

   B

   It is unnatural for human beings to eat meat.

   Therefore it is wrong for human beings to eat meat.

What is required to put them right?

3   Taylor believes that:

   (i)   moral conclusions can be deduced from biological facts – true or false?

   (ii) biological facts can support moral conclusions by showing them to be reasonable – true or false?

4   According to a naturalistic view there are both similarities and differences between ourselves and other species. What is essential to being human is to be defined by what makes us different – true or false?

Chapter 7

1   Taylor and Naess have which of the following features in common:

   (i)   an emphasis on the interdependence of living forms throughout nature.

   (ii) the possession by all living things of a value independent of human interests.

(iii) among living things are included rivers, landscapes and ecosystems.

(iv) a belief in the possibility of understanding the needs of other living things from their point of view.

(v) the belief that to understand nature ecologically is to identify with other living things in such a way that one's interests and their interests come to be felt as the interests of a unified Self.

2   According Naess and Fox we should incorporate as wide a variety of other species into the self (Self) as possible. Four of the sentences below express points in favour of their view. Each of these pros can be matched with a con among the remaining four sentences. Match the pairs.

(i)   One will defend the interests of members of other species because they are one's own interests.

(ii)   Nature is understood as a unified whole, not a collection of units with opposing interests.

(iii) Feelings of friendship are necessarily restricted to a circle of beings with which we have particular relationships.

(iv)   Concern for nature is rooted in intense emotional attachments to particular place.

(v)   Concern for nature should be genuinely altruistic, not a form of self-interest.

(vi)   Concern for other natural beings should be universal and impartial.

(vii) Genuine moral concern requires distance and recognition of the distinctness of others from self.

(viii) Universal and impartial concern for natural beings is compatible with warmth of feeling.

Readings

'Environmental Ethics in Practice'

Richard and Val Routley

The authors consider the suggestion that the new environmental ethics that they have contended for does not have any *practical* consequences different from those of conventional ethics. They have already, in the paper* from which this Reading comes, argued that in a number of hypothetical situations, such as that of the last man, the two ethical systems would justify very different actions. They now argue that the same can be seen to be true in a series of real life situations.

Since it is sometimes charged – despite all that has been said – that an environmental ethic does not differ in practice from that of more conventional 'chauvinistic' ethics, there is point in spelling out in yet other ways how it can differ in practice. Firstly, many conventional positions, in particular social contract and sympathy theories, cannot take proper account of moral obligation to future humans (who are not in the immediate future). Since the usual attempt to argue, in terms of value and benefit to humans, that natural areas and ecosystems generally should not be destroyed or degraded depends critically on introducing possible future humans who will suffer or be worse off as a result of its destruction or degradation, it is plain that an environmental ethic will differ radically from such conventional positions. That is, the usual argument depends on the reduction of value of a natural item to the interests of present and *future* humans, in which reduction future humans must play a critical role if conclusions not blatantly opposed to conservation are to be reached. Hence there will usually be a very great gulf between the practical value judgements of conservation ethics and those of conventional positions which discount the (non-immediate) future.

Secondly ... there are practical differences between an environmental ethic and conventional instrumental views which *do* take account of the interests of past, present and future humans, differences which emerge sharply at the hypothetical (possible world) level. It is, however, unnecessary to turn to possible world examples to see that normally there would be very great differences in the practical valuations and behaviour of those who believe that natural items can have value and create obligations not reducible (in any way) to human interests and those who do not, as the following... examples show.

Example 1   We need only consider the operation of... *concepts within the actual world*, for example, the concept of *damage* to a natural item, and the associated notion of *compensation* for that damage. Thus C. Stone, for instance, in *Should Trees Have Standing? Towards Legal Rights for Natural Objects*[1] notes the practical legal differences between taking the damage to a polluted river as affecting its intrinsic value, and taking it as just affecting human river users. In the one case one will see adequate compensation as restoring the original state of the river (rectifying the wrong to the river) and in the other as compensating those present (or future) humans who will suffer from its pollution. As Stone points out, the sum adequate to compensate the latter may well be much less than that required to restore the river to its unpolluted state, thus making it economic, and in terms of the human chauvinist theory, fair and reasonable, to compensate those damaged and continue pollution of the river. In the first case, of course, adequate compensation or restoration for the harm done would have to consist in restoring the river to its unpolluted condition and will not just be paid to the people affected. Compare here Stone's example of compensation for injury to a Greek slave; in the instrumentalist case this will involve compensating the slave's owner for the loss of his slave's working time; in the other, where the slave is regarded as not merely an instrument for his owner, it will compensate the *slave* not the *owner*, for this compensation will also take account of the pain and suffering of the slave, even where this has not affected his working ability. There is a difference not only in the amount of compensation, but to *whom* it is directed. In the case of a natural item damage may be compensated by payment to a trust set up to protect and restore it.

Example 2   The believer in intrinsic values may avoid making unnecessary and excessive noise in the forest, out of respect for the forest and its non-human inhabitants. She will do this even when it is certain that there is no other human around to know the difference. For one to whom the forest and its inhabitants are merely another conventional utility, however, there will be no such constraint. He may avoid unnecessary noise if he thinks it will disturb other humans, but if he is certain none is about to hear him he will feel at liberty to make as much and as loud a noise as he chooses, and this will affect his behaviour. Examples like this cannot be dealt with by the introduction of future humans, since they will be unable to hear the noise in question. To claim that the making of noise in such circumstances is a matter of no importance, and therefore there is no important difference in behaviour, is of course to assess the matter through human chauvinist eyes. So such a claim is **question begging**. From the intrinsic viewpoint it *would* make a difference, and be reflected in practical behavioural difference.

begging the question

Example 3   Consider an aboriginal tribe which holds a particular place to be sacred, and where this sanctity and intrinsic valuableness and beauty is celebrated by a number of beautiful cave paintings. A typically 'progressive' instrumentalist Western view would hold the cave (and perhaps place) to be worth preservation because of its value to the aboriginal people, and because of the artistic merit of the human artefacts, the cave paintings the cave contained. To the 'enlightened' Westerner, if the tribe should cease to exist, and the paintings be destroyed, it would be permissible to destroy the place if this should be in what is judged to be the best interests of human kind, e.g. to get at the uranium underneath. To the aboriginal, the human artefacts – the cave paintings – would be irrelevant, a celebration of the value of the place, but certainly not a surrogate for it, and the obligation to the place would not die because the tribe disappeared or declined. Similarly no ordinary sum of money would be able to compensate for the loss of such place, in the way that it might for something conceived of as a utility or convenience, as having value only because of the benefits it confers on the 'users' of it.

There is an enormous *felt* or *emotive* difference between feeling that a place should be valued or respected for itself, for its perceived beauty and character, and feeling that it should not be defaced because its is valued by one's fellow humans, and provides pleasurable sensations or money or convenience for them. Compare too the differences between feeling that a yellow robin, say, is a fellow creature in many ways akin to oneself, and feeling that it is a nice little yellow and grey, basically clockwork, aesthetic object. These differences in emotional presentation are accompanied by or expressed by an enormous range of behavioural differences, of which the examples given represent only a very small sample. The sort of behaviour *warranted* by each viewpoint and thought *admissible* by it, the concept of what one is free to do, for example, will normally be very different. It is certainly no coincidence that cultures holding to the intrinsic view have normally been far less destructive of nature than the dominant Western human chauvinist culture.

In summary, the claim that there is no *real practical* difference, that the intrinsic value viewpoint is empty verbalization, does not stand up to examination.

The capacity – no doubt exaggerated, but none the less far from negligible – of Western industrial societies to solve their ecological problems (at least to their own pathetically low standards) within a chauvinistic framework does considerably complicate, and obstruct, an alternative more practical argument to the need for a new ethic, *the argument from environmental problems,*

> that in no other way... [than] prepared[ness] to accept a 'new ethic', as distinct even from adding one or two new moral principles to an accepted common... can modern industrial societies solve their ecological problems.

Notes

*From Richard and Val Routley, 'Human chauvinism and environmental ethics', in Mannison, McRobbie and Routley (eds), *Environmental Philosophy*, Department of Philosophy, Research School of Social Sciences, Australian National University, 1980, pp.129–31.

[1] C. Stone (1975) *Should Trees Have Standing? Towards Legal Rights for Natural Objects,* Avon Books.

'The Cultural Approach to Conservation Biology'

Bryan G. Norton

Norton distinguishes between the 'intellectual debate' and the 'strategic debate'.* The intellectual debate is about whether policies directed to conserve non-human species ultimately rest on their value to human beings, or on the recognition that they have value independent of human interests. The strategic debate is about which kind of argument is more likely to succeed in convincing policy makers to act. He reserves judgement on the intellectual debate, though he hopes that eventually philosophers will make out the case for the 'intrinsic value' of species. But he points out that human-centred considerations are clearer and find readier acceptance with policy makers, so are to be preferred in the context of practical debate. However, human-centred considerations go much deeper than is often supposed. Wild species are not of value to us merely as commodities, but as sources of experiences that enrich our lives. If these deeper considerations are recognized they will have, Norton believes, the same practical consequences as the intrinsic value position.

One lazy Saturday afternoon I was walking on the beach on the North end of Longboat Key, Florida – the last unspoiled strip of beach on that once-beautiful island. The currents in Longboat Pass had shifted and were dumping sand in a crescent spit out into the Gulf of Mexico. The new sandbar was forming a tidal lagoon. As I walked along on the sandbar, I came face to face with an eight-year-old girl as she clambered from the lagoon onto the ledge of the sandbar. She was cradling a dozen fresh sand dollars [flat sea-urchins] in her arms. Looking past her, I saw her mother and older sister dredging sand dollars from the shallow lagoon. They walked back and forth, systematically scuffing their feet through the soft sand. As they dislodged the sand dollars, they picked them up and held them for the little girl, who transported and piled them by their powerboat that was beached on the sandbar. A pile of several hundred had accumulated on the sand by the boat.

'You know, they're alive', I said indignantly.

'We can bleach 'em at home and they'll turn white', the little girl informed me. I could hardly argue with that.

'Do you need so many?' I asked.

'My momma makes 'em outta things', she explained.

I pressed my case: 'How many does she need to make things?'

'We can get a nickel apiece for the extras at the craft store', the little girl replied.

Our brief conversation ended, as suddenly as it had begun, in ideological impasse. As I wandered away, muttering to myself, I turned over and over in my mind what I should have said to the little girl. Our discussion on the sand had posed, in microcosm, the problem of environmental values.

I might have talked to the little girl about sustainable yields and tried to get her to worry about whether there would be sand dollars the next time she came to the beach. That's what I was trying to get at when I asked if she needed so many. But, when I asked how many she needed, I'd already granted the utilitarian value of sand dollars. If one is worth a nickel, more will be worth dollars. I didn't want to object to the exploitation of the sand dollars merely on conservationist grounds; I wanted to say more, that the sand dollars are more than mere commodities to be measured in nickels.

I had encountered what David Ehrenfeld has aptly described as the conservationist's dilemma.[1] To give 'economic' arguments in terms of sustainable yields is to admit that species have value as commodities. And it is difficult to rein in exploitation once it is admitted there are profits to be made, for, in our society at least, the value of commodities is described by the adage 'More is better'.

Ehrenfeld has accordingly chosen the other horn of the conservationist's dilemma. He says that, by reason of their long-standing existence in nature, other species have an 'unimpeachable right to continued existence'.[2] This is an appealing position. It expresses the deeply moral intuition I felt when I saw the pile of green disks drying in the Florida sun and evokes the revulsion we feel in response to apartheid and other abominable discriminations against races of humans. Philosophically, however, this approach is beset with enormous problems. Rights have, historically and semantically, been ascribed to individuals. Could I, with a straight face, say to the little girl, 'Put them all back, each and every one of them; they have a right to live'? I'd have felt silly because I knew this industrious family would not be moved by speeches for sand dollar liberation, however eloquent. Worse, I'd have been a hypocrite. These discoid echinoderms surely have no greater rights than the red snapper I had enjoyed for lunch.

Nor is it easy to transfer the concept of individual rights to species and ecosystems. Individual rights surely have something to do with the fact that individual organisms have a 'good of their own'.[3] But what is the corresponding 'good' of a species? Is it good for the species of sand dollars to be left alone in the lagoon or is it better for little girls to exert adaptational pressure so the species will be prepared for greater exploitative challenges in the future? Should we put a fence around the lagoon to keep out all predators, including little girls? Or should we let sand dollars face, as all truly wild species must, selectional pressures?[4]

While references to rights of wild species are appealing and may be rhetorically useful as propaganda, most philosophers now agree that appeals to rights of non-human species do not provide a coherent and adequate basis for protecting biological diversity. Many philosophers have therefore concluded that when environmentalists speak of rights, they really mean that wild species have *intrinsic value* in some broader sense, a sense that does not require that we attribute rights to them.[5] What is important, on this view, is that wild species are valued *for themselves*, and not as *mere instruments* for the fulfilment of human needs and desires. This view is attractive in many ways, but it is extremely difficult to explain clearly. Does it mean that other species had value even before any conscious valuers emerged on the evolutionary scene? Could species be valued by no valuers?[6]

Or does this view that species have intrinsic value mean only that all conscious valuers should be able to perceive it?[7] But what if some people, such as the little girl and her family, fail to see it? Do we simply accuse them metaphorically, of moral blindness? Or can we somehow explain to them what this intrinsic value is and why they should perceive it?[8]

My point in asking all of these questions is not to prove that intrinsic value in other species does not exist. It may. I hope that someday we will be able to show that it does. In asking these questions, and emphasizing their difficulty, I am trying to refocus attention on a related, but importantly different question: Can appeals to intrinsic value in non-human species be made with sufficient clarity and persuasiveness to effect new policies adequate to protect biological diversity before it is too late? With some experts projecting that a fourth of all species could be lost in the next two decades, I fear not. As a philosopher, I can perhaps say in modesty what would appear to be carping criticism if said by someone else: philosophers seldom resolve big issues quickly. We are still, for example, struggling with a number of questions posed by Socrates. It seems unlikely that the issue of whether wild species have intrinsic value will be decided before the question of saving wild nature has become moot. There are, then, two separate debates about environmental values. One debate is *intellectual*, the other is *strategic*. The first debate concerns the *correct moral stance* toward nature. The second debate concerns which moral stance, or rationale, is likely to be *effective* in saving wild species and natural ecosystems.

Important environmentalists have addressed the second debate and taken a pragmatic approach to rationales for environmental policy. For example, Aldo Leopold advocated a biocentric ethical system, hoping to undermine the human arrogance that reduces nature to an instrument for human satisfactions.[9] But he decided, when entering the public policy arena, to rely on human-centred reasons. In one of his early essays on conservation policy, Leopold outlined a non-human-centred outlook on nature, but then said, '...to most men of affairs, this reason is too intangible to either accept or reject as a guide to human conduct.' He proceeded to argue for conservation on the basis of concern for future generations of humans.[10]

Similarly, Rachel Carson's career as a writer began with beautiful books on the sea. There, she used the ecological idea that all things are interrelated and interdependent to question human-centred attitudes and human arrogance. But, when she saw that the wild world she loved was threatened by persistent pesticides, she wrote *Silent Spring*.[11] In that book, she used the same ideas of interconnectedness to argue that spreading persistent pesticides indiscriminately in the environment places *humans* at risk of cancer and other debilitating illnesses. William Butler, who was the Environmental Defense Fund's council when the DDT case was argued in hearings before the Environmental Protection Agency (EPA), told me in an interview that they first presented evidence that wildlife was being killed by DDT, and that it was by no means clear that the case to ban DDT would prevail. But when they introduced into the hearings evidence of human effects, Butler reports that their arguments were attended to, and DDT was banned.[12]

To those who are uncommitted to environmentalism (and this includes many important decision makers), appeals to intrinsic values in nature and to rights of non-humans appear 'soft', 'subjective', and 'speculative'. We can accept this fact of political life, without agreeing with it. Whatever the answer to the intellectual question of whether non human species have intrinsic value, I agree with Leopold, Carson, and Butler that human-oriented reasons carry more weight in current policy debates. Given the urgency of environmental degradation and the irreversibility of losses in biodiversity, it would be equivalent to fiddling while Rome burns to delay action until the achievement of a positive social consensus attributing rights and intrinsic value to non human species.

In the remainder of this chapter, I shall therefore concentrate on the human, cultural reasons to preserve species. I shall emphasize two points about these human reasons. First, these reasons are far broader, deeper, and more powerful than is usually recognized. Both environmentalists and their critics tend to emphasize, when focusing on human reasons for preservation, the commercial and commodity-oriented concerns about saving species.[13] But this approach ignores a vast range of important cultural, aesthetic, and social reasons for a preservationist policy. Second, I would like to emphasize that, at least in the short run, there is hardly any difference in the public policies that would be advocated under a broadly cultural, human-centred value system and the policy advocated by a biocentric value system. Both world views imply that we should do all we can do to save species and representative ecosystems.

Before I explain why I say the cultural and biocentric views have apparently identical policy implications, I must emphasize the breadth of human values that are served by wild nature. To do that, I want to return to the scene on the sandbar. There I was, facing Ehrenfeld's conservationist's dilemma while talking to an eight year-old. I tried the respect-for-life approach as well as the conservation-for-future-use approach. The little girl wasn't buying the right-to-life approach; and the conservationist approach, by admitting that sand dollars are commodities to be exploited, admitted too much. It may be useful to set aside philosophical abstractions for a moment and consider the microcosmic situation on the sandbar strategically. I wanted the little girl to put most of the living sand dollars back. How could I accomplish that end?

If I have the chance again, if I run into another little girl with too many sand dollars, I think I'll become a labour organizer on the beach. I'll ask the little girl if she's having fun. 'Wouldn't you rather build sand castles?', I'd say. Or, better yet, I'd ask her if she'd like to get to know a sand dollar. I'd pick one up and show her its tiny sucker feet and let her feel them knead her hand, almost imperceptibly. I'd explain how, with those tiny feet, the sand dollar pulls itself through the sand by tugging on many individual grains. I'd tell her how the sand dollar picks up particles of sand with its teeth, and digests the tiny diatoms that cling to the particles as they pass through its alimentary canal.

Sand dollars and many other echinoderms, such as sea urchins and starfish, have five sections. The little girl might be surprised to note that they share their pentagonal structure with us, in that we have one head, two arms, and two legs. But I'd point out that the sand dollar's five sections are all the same.

They have evolved a less differentiated nervous system. Their behaviour is consequently less complex than ours, and I hope the little girl will see that different species have evolved different adaptations to deal with quite different situations. The ancestors of sand dollars, beset with many predators in lagoons, invested in armour, rather than mobility. But I'd try to get her to see that our mobility isn't necessarily better; what works depends on the situation.

I hope, by the time we talk about all those things, the little girl will be distracted from her task of bleaching sand dollars for nickels and that she will prefer live sand dollars to dead ones. Ehrenfeld's conservationist's dilemma encourages us to face a bipolar choice: Will we value sand dollars as commodities to be used or will we attribute to them rights and intrinsic value and thereby respect them as worthy of our moral concern? In fact, these are not the only two alternatives, and the dilemma posed is a false one. By focusing on the little girl's attitudes and behaviour, we can see a third alternative: The environmentalist's case for preserving wild nature can be expressed in terms of human culture.

The beach was being used that afternoon not just as an opportunity for exploitation: it was also being used as a schoolroom – the little girl was being taught that the value of beaches is a commodity value. In the process of teaching children that sand dollars are mere commodities to be exploited, we also teach them that children are mere consumers. The reduction of little girls to mere consumers follows inevitably upon the reduction of sand dollars and other wildlife to mere commodities. When all of nature is subdued and made mere commodities in our economy, we will have destroyed our only symbols of freedom. When the commercial world view entirely takes over, sand dollars will be mere commodities, and little girls in search of nickels will be mere consumers. Like other domesticated species, they will obediently seek the products that are glamorized in media advertising. The manipulative culture of capitalistic commerce will have become all-pervasive, and the greatest losers will be children who have lost the ability to wonder at wild, living nature.

And the reduction of children to mere consumers is unfortunate for *human* reasons – it represents a contraction of the child's value system. Whatever we believe about the intrinsic value of sand dollars, we can say that, when the little girl lost her chance to *wonder* at the living world of sand dollars at the bottom of lagoons, she was impoverished. The little girl's experience at the beach that Saturday was merely a manifestation of a broader cultural phenomenon. When little girls look at sand dollars and see nickels, they are expressing the same attitude as developers who look at unspoiled beaches and see condominium sites. The beach is shelled, fished, sand-dollared, and used as a tanning salon. But is it appreciated for its real value? Do we cherish its ability to contrast with, and call into question, our everyday world of commerce and profit-making? Hardly at all. Here, we can apply Roderick Nash's point that recreation and tourism involve a search for contrasts.[14] If all of our beaches are seawalled, boardwalked, and lined with pizza stands, how will they contrast with our roadways?

When we teach little girls to encounter sand dollars as mere opportunities to make nickels, we impoverish childhood experience. And, as that process is repeated throughout our culture, we impoverish our culture. We begin to see nature as a mere storehouse, rather than as the context in which our culture, our struggle to maintain a niche in nature, has developed and will develop. And we forget that our future, as well as our past, depends on our integration into the broader processes of life-building and niche-carving.

The struggle of sand dollars to survive in newly formed lagoons provides a symbol of our struggle to survive as self-determining creatures. The sand dollars must, in the face of hostile and predatory forces in the lagoon, negotiate a niche. In doing so, they create a tiny colony of life, a community that is supported by, and in turn supports other forms of life. While the Darwinian revolution in biological science has undermined many of our older metaphysical, religious, and spiritual beliefs, it has also pointed out a new direction for understanding human life and the place of humans in the great experiment of evolution. Our species has emerged from the same processes that created sand dollars. Our natural history is, in a sense, contemporary with us; every species illustrates an alternative means of sustaining life. Every wild species is a repository of analogies that inform our ongoing struggle to survive. In the same way that we might learn to avoid errors of past cultures by studying cultural history, we can learn to avoid ecological disasters by studying the natural history of other living things.

The little girl was being cheated out of valuable experiences. She exchanged an afternoon of discovering nature for a few nickels. On this point, I'm sure, Ehrenfeld and I are in agreement. But I do not accept the implication that the only alternative to valuing wild species as nickels is to say that they have intrinsic value: they can also be valued as occasions for expanding and uplifting human experience.

If our culture proves incapable of preserving other forms of life in the wild, we will lose our only means to understand the great mystery of life's emergence and diversification. We will doom ourselves and our descendants to ignorance of the roots of our existence. The reduction of human valuing of wild nature to mere commodities, to mere objects to be exploited, doubly undermines human values. First, it narrows and cheapens human experience. The little girl entirely missed the mystery and wonder of living beaches.

Second, that attitude is destroying the possibilities for future children to experience wild beaches and to expand their horizons of valuing. If we do not change this attitude, and the trends it promotes, there will be no more beaches where little girls might learn the wonder and value of living sand dollars. Those trends will have, and already have had, dreadful consequences for our culture. The valuing of solitude, the value of experiencing unmanipulated ecosystems, the value of seeing nature as a larger enterprise than our search for economic gain are all threatened by the attitude that sand dollars are mere commodities.

I've tried, then, to explain why the cultural approach to valuing biological diversity is broad, deep, and powerful. It is broad, because it appeals to the values of diversity, contrast, solitude, and so forth that commercial culture is in danger of forgetting. It is deep because it digs below the shallow tendency of our culture to reduce all things to the mere value they will bring in a marketplace. Finally, it is powerful because it addresses the question: What sort of world do we want our children and grandchildren to experience? If we extinguish wild nature, we will extinguish with it our ability to wonder; we will have extinguished a part of our consciousness. We might, of course, decry the passing of wild nature because we will have failed to protect intrinsic values residing in other species. But we can as well, and less controversially, decry the loss of richness from the human experience.

Now I would like to apply this cultural rationale for saving species to policy issues. What policy would be pursued if one believes in the cultural value of wildlife and natural ecosystems?

I believe it is important to emphasize the *contributory* value of wild species. Economists who try to measure commercial and other economic values for species and environmentalists who emphasize the aesthetic-cultural value of species both tend to under-emphasize the contributory value of species. Species do not exist in isolation. Most species function as important parts of ecosystems and therefore contribute to the support and sustenance of other species.[15] If one values a wild grass because it provides an opportunity to develop a perennial hybrid of corn, or if one values a sighting of a rare whooping crane, one must value not just those species, but the entire fabric of life on which those species depend. Similarly, we cannot place a value on a little girl discovering the wonder of living sand dollars without valuing the beach where sand dollars live. Economists and ecologists cannot tell us how to save economically and aesthetically important species without saving the ecosystems on which they depend. This is especially true of culturally valuable species. A dead sand dollar on a dissecting tray cannot provide the same experience as a living sand dollar with sucker feet kneading a little girl's hand. If we are to save the experience of nature, we must save that experience whole. The species we never notice, like the tiny diatom that nourishes the sand dollar, must be appreciated along with the sand dollar and the red snapper. If we are to save the experiences that enliven and enlighten our culture, then we must save whole ecosystems and all the species that contribute to them. It is difficult to see what believers in the intrinsic value of species would advocate, in addition to this policy.

The debate about policy regarding biological diversity, the debate about what ought to be done, is best seen as a *strategic* debate, largely independent of the *intellectual* debate about whether wild species have intrinsic value. If we recognize the full range of human values served by wild species, we will adopt as a policy goal an attempt to save all wild nature. Admittedly, we will fail in this idealistic goal – the task is too large and our culture has evolved a set of commodity-oriented values that push us inexorably to alter habitats and to threaten wild species. But pious assertions that species, dying out around us, have intrinsic value will make them no less extinct. My point is that a policy of saving as many species as possible is the logical implication of either a non-human-centred value system *or* a human-centred value system which recognizes the full range of human values. It is true that if our culture perceived species as intrinsically valuable, we would do more to save wild species. But it is also true that if our culture perceived the breadth, depth, and power of human-oriented values of species, we would do more to save them. Given this context, the debate about intrinsic values in nature should be seen as an intellectual one and the task of saving species should be addressed strategically. We need not first prove that wild species have intrinsic value and *then* begin working to save them.

An analogy may illustrate this point. Suppose a family must move across country and fit all their belongings in their station wagon. In the end, they find they cannot fit both the television and the large, old family Bible in the space available. One family member suggests they go to the pawn shop and determine which is more valuable and take the commercially valuable item. Another member might be affronted by the treatment of the family Bible, with its record of births and deaths recorded in the hand of patriarchal ancestors, as a mere commodity. This family member might insist the Bible has intrinsic value and should therefore be saved. A debate ensues and the trip is in danger of being delayed. But a wise member of the family cuts through the problem by pointing out that the Bible is valuable as a symbol of the family's struggle and unity and that seeing and touching the ancestral record will be valuable *for the family and its offspring*. If this point is made, that the Bible has irreplaceable value for building the family's character, the question of what to do need not wait upon agreement concerning its intrinsic value. Rather than standing on the sidewalk discussing the intrinsic value of family Bibles, the family should leave the television, pack up the Bible, and discuss intrinsic value en route. Similarly for saving wild species. Given the powerful case for saving species as a cultural need, it makes very little difference to policy whether those species are also attributed intrinsic value.

Cultural attitudes determine the values we express and pursue. If we develop a healthy attitude toward nature and experiences of nature, we will act to save wild species and natural eco-systems. I have tried to emphasize the depth, the breadth, and the power of these attitudes and rationales for saving nature based on them.

I suspect that there is an underlying fear among American conservationists that if conservation goals are based on cultural attitudes, we have no right to work to save wildlife in other lands inhabited by other cultures. If the cultural value of wildlife were limited to American values, this limitation might pose a problem.[16] but all cultures relate to nature and derive important symbols from the unique communities of wildlife that grace their countryside. Further, if we believe in evolutionary theory, all cultures have evolved in a context of natural systems and can learn their place in the natural world by paying attention to their natural heritage.

A possible corollary to the concern about international action to save wildlife is the thought that perhaps we Americans, as citizens of an advanced industrial nation, have no right to impose what we have learned about evolution and the interdependence of living things upon other nations with different ideas. It is correct to say that we have no right to *impose* our knowledge and related attitudes, just as we have no right to impose our commercial attitudes on them, just as we have no right to export our idea that true civilization requires a fast-food restaurant on every corner and a herd of cattle on every hectare of formerly forested tropics. But at the same time, we cannot deny our role as world leaders in cultural opinions, as well as in economic organization. What we can do is act responsibly as leaders of world opinion to make available our science, our understanding of evolution, and the importance of that understanding in achieving a modern, but healthy, attitude toward human culture and its context in natural ecosystems. If we do that, if we develop a healthy attitude toward the natural world at home and share that attitude with people of other cultures, we will have gone a long way toward preserving the natural world and, more than incidentally, a place for a truly human and humane existence in that world.

Notes

* From Bryan G. Norton, 'The cultural approach to conservation biology', in David Western and Mary C. Pearl (eds) *Conservation for the Twenty-first Century*, 1989, pp.241–6.

1 Ehrenfeld, D. (1976). The conservation of non-resources. *Am. Scientist* 64:648–656. Ehrenfeld, D. (1988) 'Why put a value on Biodiversity?' in Biodiversity, ed. E.O. Wilson, pp.212–16, National Academy Press.

2 Ehrenfeld, D. (1988) op. cit.

3 Taylor, P.(1986). *Respect for Nature,* Princeton University Press.

4 Norton, B. G. (1987). *Why Preserve Natural Variety?* Princeton University Press.

5 Callicott, J. B. (1986a). The intrinsic value of non-human species. In: *The Perservation of Species: The Value of Biological Diversity,* ed. B. G. Norton, Princeton University Press.

6 See, for example, Rolston, H. (1986). *Values Gone Wild: Essays in Environmental Ethics.* Prometheus Books, chap.22; Taylor (1986) op. cit.

7 Callicott (1986a) op. cit.

8 Norton (1987) op. cit.

9 Leopold, A. (1949). *Sand County Almanac.* Oxford University Press.

10 Leopold, A. (1923). Some fundamentals in conservation in the Southwest. *Environ. Ethics* (1979) 1:131–141; Norton, B. G. (1986a). Conservation and preservation. A conceptual rehabilitation, *Environ. Ethics* 8:195–220.

11 Carson, R. (1962). *Silent Spring.* Houghton-Mifflin.

12 Butler, W. (1986). Interview with Bryan Norton. April 4, Audubon Society, N.Y.

13 See, for example, Myers, N. (1983a). *A Wealth of Wild Species.* Westview Press; Prescott-Allen, R., and C. Prescott-Allen (1985) *What's wildlife Worth?* Earthscan Publications.

14 Nash, R. (1986). The future of nature tourism. Unpublished remarks. Conservation 2100 Conference, New York Zoological Society and The Rockefeller University, New York.

15 Norton (1987) op. cit.

16 See Regan, T. (1981). The nature and possibility of an environmental ethic. *Environ. Ethics* 3:19–34; Sagoff, M. (1974). On preserving the natural environment. *Yale Law J.* 84:205–267.

'The Environmental Ethic'

Edward O. Wilson

At the conclusion of a long book* tracing the processes by which the diversity of plant and animal species has developed and the causes that now threaten a great extinction, the entomologist Edward O. Wilson undertakes to explain why biodiversity is valuable, why it is important not to accelerate the natural process of extinction. Many other species provide us with things of use such as foodstuffs and medicine, and there is likely to be a wealth of such resources yet to be discovered. Ecosystems provide the conditions for human life, and are fragile. But these 'services' are not the whole story. We need to understand the whole evolutionary history in which we evolved as a species in order to understand ourselves.

The sixth great extinction spasm of geological time is upon us, grace of mankind. Earth has at last acquired a force that can break the crucible of biodiversity. I sensed it with special poignancy that stormy night at Fazenda Dimona, when lightning flashes revealed the rain forest cut open like a cat's eye for laboratory investigation. An undisturbed forest rarely discloses its internal anatomy with such clarity. Its edge is shielded by thick secondary growth or else, along the river bank, the canopy spills down to ground level. The night-time vision was a dying artefact, a last glimpse of savage beauty. A few days later I got ready to leave Fazenda Dimona: gathered my muddied clothes in a bundle, gave my imitation Swiss army knife to the cook as a farewell gift, watched an overflight of Amazonian green parrots one more time, labelled and stored my specimen vials in reinforced boxes, and packed my field notebook next to a dog-eared copy of Ed McBain's police novel *Ice,* which, because I had neglected to bring any other reading matter, was now burned into my memory.

Grinding gears announced the approach of the truck sent to take me and two of the forest workers back to Manaus. In bright sunlight we watched it cross the pastureland, a terrain strewn with fire-blackened stumps and logs, the battlefield my forest had finally lost. On the ride back I tried not to look at the bare fields. Then, abandoning my tourist Portuguese, I turned inward and daydreamed. Four splendid lines of Virgil came to mind, the only ones I ever memorized, where the Sibyl warns Aeneas of the Underworld:

> The way downwards is easy from Avernus.
> Black Dis's door stands open night and day.
> But to retrace your steps to heaven's air,
> There is the trouble, there is the toil ...

For the green prehuman earth is the mystery we were chosen to solve, a guide to the birthplace of our spirit, but it is slipping away. The way back seems harder every year. If there is danger in the human trajectory, it is not so much in the survival of our own species as in the fulfilment of the ultimate irony of organic evolution: that in the instant of achieving self-understanding through the mind of man, life has doomed its most beautiful creations. And thus humanity closes the door to its past.

The creation of that diversity came slow and hard: 3 billion years of evolution to start the profusion of animals that occupy the seas, another 350 million years to assemble the rain forests in which half or more of the species on earth now live. There was a succession of dynasties. Some species split into two or several daughter species, and their daughters split yet again to create swarms of descendants that deployed as plant feeders, carnivores, free swimmers, gliders, sprinters, and burrowers, in countless motley combinations. These ensembles then gave way by partial or total extinction to newer dynasties, and so on to form a gentle upward swell that carried biodiversity to a peak – just before the arrival of humans. Life had stalled on plateaus along the way, and on five occasions it suffered extinction spasms that took 10 million years to repair. But the thrust was upward. Today the diversity of life is greater than it was a 100 million years ago – and far greater than 500 million years before that.

Most dynasties contained a few species that expanded disproportionately to create satrapies of lesser rank. Each species and its descendants, a sliver of the whole, lived an average of hundreds of thousands to millions of years. Longevity varied according to taxonomic group. Echinoderm lineages, for example, persisted longer than those of flowering plants, and both endured longer than those of mammals.

Ninety-nine percent of all the species that ever lived are now extinct. The modern fauna and flora are composed of survivors that somehow managed to dodge and weave through all the radiations and extinctions of geological history. Many contemporary world-dominant groups, such as rats, ranid frogs, nymphalid butterflies, and plants of the aster family Compositae, attained their status not long before the Age of Man. Young or old, all living species are direct descendants of the organisms that lived 3.8 billion years ago. They are living genetic libraries, composed of nucleotide sequences, the equivalent of words and sentences, which record evolutionary events all across that immense span of time. Organisms more complex than bacteria – protists, fungi, plants, animals – contain between 1 and 10 billion nucleotide letters, more than enough in pure information to compose an equivalent of the *Encyclopaedia Britannica*. Each species is the product of mutations and recombinations too complex to be grasped by unaided intuition. It was sculpted and burnished by an astronomical number of events in natural selection, which killed off or otherwise blocked from reproduction the vast majority of its member organisms before they completed their lifespan. Viewed from the perspective of evolutionary time, all other species are our distant kin because we share a remote ancestry. We still use a common vocabulary, the nucleic-acid code, even though it has been sorted into radically different hereditary languages.

Such is the ultimate and cryptic truth of every kind of organism, large and small, every bug and weed. The flower in the crannied wall – it *is* a miracle. If not in the way Tennyson, the Victorian romantic, bespoke the portent of full knowledge (by which 'I should know what God and man is'), then certainly a consequence of all we understand from modern biology. Every kind of organism has reached this moment in time by threading one needle after another, throwing up brilliant artifices to survive and reproduce against nearly impossible odds.

Organisms are all the more remarkable in combination. Pull out the flower from its crannied retreat, shake the soil from the roots into the cupped hand, magnify it for close examination. The black earth is alive with a riot of algae, fungi, nematodes, mites, springtails, enchytraeid worms, thousands of species of bacteria. The handful may be only a tiny fragment of one ecosystem, but because of the genetic codes of its residents it holds more order than can be found on the surfaces of all the planets combined. It is a sample of the living force that runs the earth – and will continue to do so with or without us.

We may think that the world has been completely explored. Almost all the mountains and rivers, it is true, have been named, the coast and geodetic surveys completed, the ocean floor mapped to the deepest trenches, the atmosphere transacted and chemically analysed. The planet is now continuously monitored from space by satellites; and, not least, Antarctica, the last virgin continent, has become a research station and expensive tourist stop. The biosphere, however, remains obscure. Even though some 1.4 million species of organisms have been discovered (in the minimal sense of having specimens collected and formal scientific names attached), the total number alive on earth is somewhere between 10 and 100 million. No one can say with confidence which of these figures is the closer. Of the species given scientific names, fewer than 10 percent have been studied at a level deeper than gross anatomy. The revolution in molecular biology and medicine was achieved with a still smaller fraction, including colon bacteria, corn, fruit flies, Norway rats, rhesus monkeys, and human beings, altogether comprising no more than a hundred species.

Enchanted by the continuous emergence of new technologies and supported by generous funding for medical research, biologists have probed deeply along a narrow sector of the front. Now it is time to expand laterally, to get on with the great Linnean enterprise and finish mapping the biosphere. The most compelling reason for the broadening of goals is that, unlike the rest of science, the study of biodiversity has a time limit. Species are disappearing at an accelerating rate through human action, primarily habitat destruction but also pollution and the introduction of exotic species into residual natural environments. I have said that a fifth or more of the species of plants and animals could vanish or be doomed to early extinction by the year 2020 unless better efforts are made to save them. This estimate comes from the known quantitative relation between the area of habitats and the diversity that habitats can sustain. These area-biodiversity curves are supported by the general but not universal principle that when certain groups of organisms are studied closely, such as snails and fishes and flowering plants, extinction is determined to be widespread. And the corollary: among plant and animal remains in archaeological deposits, we usually find extinct species and races. As the last forests are felled in forest strongholds like the Philippines and Ecuador, the decline of species will accelerate even more. In the world as a whole, extinction rates are already hundreds or thousands of times higher than before the coming of man. They cannot be balanced by new evolution in any period of time that has meaning for the human race.

Why should we care? What difference does it make if some species are extinguished, if even half of all the species on earth disappear? Let me count the ways. New sources of scientific information will be lost. Vast potential biological wealth will be destroyed. Still undeveloped medicines, crops, pharmaceuticals, timber, fibres, pulp, soil-restoring vegetation, petroleum substitutes, and other products and amenities will never come to light. It is fashionable in some quarters to wave aside the small and obscure, the bugs and weeds, forgetting that an obscure moth from Latin America saved Australia's pastureland from overgrowth by cactus, that the rosy periwinkle provided the cure for Hodgkin's disease and childhood lymphocytic leukaemia, that the bark of the Pacific yew offers hope for victims of ovarian and breast cancer, that a chemical from the saliva of leeches dissolves blood clots during surgery, and so on down a roster already grown long and illustrious despite the limited research addressed to it.

In amnesiac revery it is also easy to overlook the services that ecosystems provide humanity. They enrich the soil and create the very air we breathe. Without these amenities, the remaining tenure of the human race would be nasty and brief. The life-sustaining matrix is built of green plants with legions of micro-organisms and mostly small, obscure animals – in other words, weeds and bugs. Such organisms support the world with efficiency because they are so diverse, allowing them to divide labour and swarm over every square metre of the earth's surface. They run the world precisely as we would wish it to be run, because humanity evolved within living communities and our bodily functions are finely adjusted to the idiosyncratic environment already created. Mother Earth, lately called Gaia, is no more than the communality of organisms and the physical environment they maintain with each passing moment, an environment that will destabilize and turn lethal if the organisms are disturbed too much. A near infinity of other mother planets can be envisioned, each with its own fauna and flora, all producing physical environments uncongenial to human life. To disregard the diversity of life is to risk catapulting ourselves into an alien environment. We will have become like the pilot whales that inexplicably beach themselves on New England shores.

Humanity co-evolved with the rest of life on this particular planet; other worlds are not in our genes. Because scientists have yet to put names on most kinds of organisms, and because they entertain only a vague idea of how ecosystems work, it is reckless to suppose that biodiversity can be diminished indefinitely without threatening humanity itself. Field studies show that as biodiversity is reduced, so is the quality of the services provided by ecosystems. Records of stressed ecosystems also demonstrate that the descent can be unpredictably abrupt. As extinction spreads, some of the lost forms prove to be keystone species, whose disappearance brings down other species and triggers a ripple effect through the demographics of the survivors. The loss of a keystone species is like a drill accidentally striking a powerline. It causes lights to go out all over.

These services are important to human welfare. But they cannot form the whole foundation of an enduring environmental ethic. If a price can be put on something, that something can be devalued, sold, and discarded. It is also possible for some to dream that people will go on living comfortably in a biologically impoverished world. They suppose that a prosthetic environment is within the power of technology, that human life can still flourish in a completely humanized world, where medicines would all be synthesized from chemicals off the shelf, food grown from a few dozen domestic crop species, the atmosphere and climate regulated by computer-driven fusion energy, and the earth made over until it becomes a literal spaceship rather than a metaphorical one, with people reading displays and touching buttons on the bridge. Such is the terminus of the philosophy of exemptionalism: do not weep for the past, humanity is a new order of life, let species die if they block progress, scientific and technological genius will find another way. Look up and see the stars awaiting us.

But consider: human advance is determined not by reason alone but by emotions peculiar to our species, aided and tempered by reason. What makes us people and not computers is emotion. We have little grasp of our true nature, of what it is to be human and therefore where our descendants might someday wish we had directed Spaceship Earth. Our troubles, as Vercors said in *You Shall Know Them,* arise from the fact that we do not know what we are and cannot agree on what we want to be. The primary cause of this intellectual failure is ignorance of our origins. We did not arrive on this planet as aliens. Humanity is part of nature, a species that evolved among other species. The more closely we identify ourselves with the rest of life, the more quickly we will be able to discover the sources of human sensibility and acquire the knowledge on which an enduring ethic, a sense of preferred direction, can be built.

The human heritage does not go back only for the conventionally recognized 8000 years or so of recorded history, but for at least 2 million years, to the appearance of the first 'true' human beings, the earliest species composing the genus *Homo.* Across thousands of generations, the emergence of culture must have been profoundly influenced by simultaneous events in genetic evolution, especially those occurring in the anatomy and physiology of the brain. Conversely, genetic evolution must have been guided forcefully by the kinds of selection rising within culture.

Only in the last moment of human history has the delusion arisen that people can flourish apart from the rest of the living world. Preliterate societies were in intimate contact with a bewildering array of life forms. Their minds could only partly adapt to that challenge. But they struggled to understand the most relevant arts, aware that the right responses gave life and fulfilment, the wrong ones sickness, hunger, and death. The imprint of that effort cannot have been erased in a few generations of urban existence. I suggest that it is to be found among the particularities of human nature, among which are these:

- People acquire phobias, abrupt and intractable aversions, to the objects and circumstances that threaten humanity in natural environments:

heights, closed spaces, open spaces, running water, wolves, spiders, snakes. They rarely form phobias to the recently invented contrivances that are far more dangerous, such as guns, knives, automobiles, and electric sockets.

- People are both repelled and fascinated by snakes, even when they have never seen one in nature. In most cultures the serpent is the dominant wild animal of mythical and religious symbolism. Manhattanites dream of them with the same frequency as Zulus. This response appears to be Darwinian in origin. Poisonous snakes have been an important cause of mortality almost everywhere, from Finland to Tasmania, Canada to Patagonia; an untutored alertness in their presence saves lives. We note a kindred response in many primates, including Old World monkeys and chimpanzees: the animals pull back, alert others, watch closely, and follow each potentially dangerous snake until it moves away. For human beings, in a larger metaphorical sense, the mythic, transformed serpent has come to possess both constructive and destructive powers: Ashtoreth of the Canaanites, the demons Fu-Hsi and Nu-kua of the Han Chinese, Mudamma and Manasa of Hindu India, the triple-headed giant Nehebkau of the ancient Egyptians, the serpent of Genesis conferring knowledge and death, and, among the Aztecs, Cihuancoatl, goddess of childbirth and mother of the human race, the rain god Tlaloc, and Quetzalcoatl, the plumed serpent with a human head who reigned as lord of the morning and evening star. Ophidian power spills over into modern life; two serpents entwine the caduceus, first the winged staff of Mercury as messenger of the gods, then the safe-conduct pass of ambassadors and heralds, and today the universal emblem of the medical profession.

- The favoured living place of most peoples is a prominence near water from which parkland can be viewed. On such heights are found the abodes of the powerful and rich, tombs of the great, temples, parliaments, and monuments commemorating tribal glory. The location is today an aesthetic choice and, by the implied freedom to settle there, a symbol of status. In ancient, more practical times the topography provided a place to retreat and a sweeping prospect from which to spot the distant approach of storms and enemy forces. Every animal species selects a habitat in which its members gain a favourable mix of security and food. For most of deep history, human beings lived in tropical and subtropical savannah in East Africa, open country sprinkled with streams and lakes, trees and copses. In similar topography modern peoples choose their residences and design their parks and gardens, if given a free choice. They simulate neither dense jungles, toward which gibbons are drawn, nor dry grasslands, preferred by hamadryas baboons. In their gardens they plant trees that resemble the acacias, sterculias, and other native trees of the African savannahs. The ideal tree crown sought is consistently wider than tall, with spreading lowermost branches close enough to the ground to touch and climb, clothed with compound or needle-shaped leaves.

- Given the means and sufficient leisure, a large portion of the populace backpacks, hunts, fishes, birdwatches, and gardens. In the United States and Canada more people visit zoos and aquariums than attend all professional athletic events combined. They crowd the national parks to view natural landscapes, looking from the tops of prominences out across rugged terrain for a glimpse of tumbling water and animals living free. They travel long distances to stroll along the seashore, for reasons they can't put into words.

These are examples of what I have called *biophilia,* the connections that human beings subconsciously seek with the rest of life. To biophilia can be added the idea of wilderness, all the land and communities of plants and animals still unsullied by human occupation. Into wilderness people travel in search of new life and wonder, and from wilderness they return to the parts of the earth that have been humanized and made physically secure. Wilderness settles peace on the soul because it needs no help; it is beyond human contrivance. Wilderness is a metaphor of unlimited opportunity, rising from the tribal memory of a time when humanity spread across the world, valley to valley, island to island, godstruck, firm in the belief that virgin land went on forever past the horizon.

I cite these common preferences of mind not as proof of an innate human nature but rather to suggest that we think more carefully and turn philosophy to the central questions of human origins in the wild environment. We do not understand ourselves yet and descend farther from heaven's air if we forget how much the natural world means to us. Signals abound that the loss of life's diversity endangers not just the body but the spirit. If that much is true, the changes occurring now will visit harm on all generations to come.

The ethical imperative should therefore be, first of all, prudence. We should judge every scrap of biodiversity as priceless while we learn to use it and come to understand what it means to humanity. We should not knowingly allow any species or race to go extinct. And let us go beyond mere salvage to begin the restoration of natural environments, in order to enlarge wild populations and staunch the haemorrhaging of biological wealth. There can be no purpose more enspiriting than to begin the age of restoration, reweaving the wonderous diversity of life that still surrounds us.

The evidence of swift environmental change calls for an ethic uncoupled from other systems of belief. Those committed by religion to believe that life was put on earth in one divine stroke will recognize that we are destroying the Creation, and those who perceive biodiversity to be the produce of blind evolution will agree. Across the other great philosophical divide, it does not matter whether species have independent rights or, conversely, that moral reasoning is uniquely a human concern. Defenders of both premises seem destined to gravitate toward the same position on conservation.

The stewardship of environment is a domain on the near side of metaphysics where all reflective persons can surely find common ground. For what, in the final analysis, is morality but the command of conscience seasoned by a rational examination of consequences? And what is a fundamental precept but one that serves all generations? An enduring environmental ethic will aim to preserve not only the health and freedom of our species, but access to the world in which the human spirit was born.

Notes

* From Edward O. Wilson, *The Diversity of Life*, Penguin, 1994, pp.327–35.

'Economic Valuation of Environmental Goods'

David Pearce, Anil Markandya and Edward B. Barber

This reading is an extract from *Blueprint for a Green Society** which was a report commissioned by the British government when it discovered the environment. Public policy with regard to development and conservation is based to a great extent on economic grounds, but environmental goods, because they do not 'come to market' are difficult to value in economic terms. In the report the authors explain the need to put an economic value on environmental goods and how this can be done.

...[H]owever sustainable development is interpreted it requires that we raise the political and economic profile of the environment. But there is an implicit bias in the way in which economies work. Many goods and services have prices which can be observed in the marketplace. Environmental goods and services and the general functions which environments serve (e.g. as a waste sink) are not invariably bought and sold in the marketplace. Thus if we leave the allocation of resources to the unfettered market, it will tend to *over-use* the services of natural environments.

This observation ... is a fundamental feature of economic science. In order to ensure a better allocation of resources, one that at least tries to correct the bias implicit in the unfettered marketplace, it is important to have some idea of what the environment is 'worth'. [We have] stressed the importance of a proper *valuation* of the environment as a major feature of sustainable development. This notion offends some conservationists. It is therefore worthwhile explaining the basics of the economic valuation of environmental services.

Economics and environmental values

Care and concern for the environment can be thought of as positive preferences for cleaner air and water, less noise, protection of wildlife, and so on. Economics is about choice, and choice relates to situations in which we have preferences for certain things but in which we cannot choose everything we like because of income limitations. Very simply, given limited resources, the rational thing to do is to choose between our preferences in an effort to get the most satisfaction – or 'welfare', to use the economist's term – we can. If we apply economics to environmental issues, then, we should expect to obtain some insights into the desirability of improving the environment further, taking the social objective of increasing people's overall satisfaction (or welfare) as given. This assumption about the social objective used to derive measures of gains and losses is important.

To be clear, what is being said is that an improvement in environmental quality is also an economic improvement if it increases social satisfaction or welfare.

Such a definition raises a host of questions and problems. For example, whose welfare are we talking about? It could readily be the case that we can improve this generation's welfare but only at the cost of the next generation's. Should we take this into account, and, if so, how? How far into the future should we look – a few generations, hundreds of years, or maybe thousands? Another problem concerns the legitimacy of measuring gains and losses according to how they impinge on human welfare alone. There is an extensive philosophical debate on the moral rights and standing of living creatures other than man: if they are ascribed rights, what relation do these rights have to human rights – are they equal, superior or less? A third problem (there are many more) is that a social objective based on mankind's more immediate well-being need not be consistent with long-run welfare or even human survival: while it is tempting to think that economic systems should contain some in-built mechanisms for sustainability, there is no evidence that they do. Some care needs to be exercised, then, that the use of social objective such as gains in welfare does not dictate or support policies which are inconsistent with the ecological preconditions for existence or, at least, some minimal quality of life.

The preferences for the environment, which show up as gains in welfare to human beings, need to be measured. It may seem odd to speak of 'measuring preferences' but this is exactly what that branch of environmental economics devoted to *benefit measurement* does. A benefit is any gain in welfare (or satisfaction or 'utility'). A cost is any loss in welfare. We are concerned then with the measurement of the benefits from improvements in, or the costs of reductions in, environmental quality. If we prefer clean air, we place a value on it. But since clean air is not bought and sold in the marketplace, at least not directly, money is not directly involved. None the less, the benefit of clean air is an economic benefit – it improves the welfare of people.

In benefit estimation money is used as a measuring rod, a way of measuring preferences. There are very good reasons for supposing that money is a good measure of the gains and losses to people from environmental change. What is important is that money just happens to be a convenient measuring rod. As long as we do not forget that there will be some immeasurable gains and losses, the measurement of gains and losses in money terms will turn out to be revealing and, we shall argue, supportive of environmental values and environmental policy.

Although we limit money to being just a measuring rod, even this limited role for it still causes many people problems. For example, what does it mean to place a money value on the benefit of preserving the Californian condor or the African rhinoceros? The temptation is to say that such creatures are 'beyond price'.

There are, however, two interpretations that might be placed on the idea that something is priceless. The first is that priceless objects are of infinite money value. When art experts speak of priceless works of art, however, they do not mean that they have infinite values. They mean that they are unique and irreplaceable, but that, in auction they would fetch very high prices indeed. A moment's reflection will indicate that no one can or would pay an infinite price for them. So it is with the condor and the rhinoceros: their preservation is worth very large sums of money – many of us would pay substantial sums to see them preserved – but none of us values them at an infinite price. The equation of 'priceless' with 'infinite value' is illicit. The second interpretation is more appealing. This says that there are some things in life which simply cannot be valued in money terms – there is somehow a compartment of our thinking that refuses to place money values on, say, human life. While this is a more reasonable interpretation of phrases such as 'beyond price' care needs to be taken in applying it. We do not act as if human life, for example, is outside our capacity to value things in money terms. We quite explicitly draw boundaries round the kinds of expenditures that we are prepared to make to save life. Thus, while there remains a quite warranted suspicion that the process of money valuation is illicit in some contexts, the reality is that choices have to be made in contexts of scarce resources. Money as a measuring rod is a satisfactory means of proceeding.

Environmental improvements can show up in the form of effects which *direct money values*. Improving a beach or river or wetland area, for example, can increase the number of visitors and, if the area has entrance charges, the revenue from those charges will increase. Reducing air pollution can improve the growth and quality of agricultural crops and there is obviously a direct monetary counterpart to such gains. Reducing sulphur emissions may lower the rate at which buildings or metal structures corrode. The direct market value of such reduced corrosion can be estimated by looking at the prolonged life of the structures and hence the reduced cost of protecting them or replacing them. Slightly less obvious is the effect that improving human health has on the saving of marketed resources. Reductions in respiratory disease from reducing air pollution, for example, will show up in a reduced demand for health care, thus saving on health service costs, and in less days lost from work due to illness. Notice, however, that these gains in rescued resource costs and increased productivity are not adequate measures of the welfare gain. This can only be measured by the value placed on improved health by the person at risk, and, typically, this will bear little relation to the resource costs that are saved...

The above examples indicate some of the ways that we can approach the monetary evaluation of the welfare gains from environmental improvement. But many of the gains will not show up even in such an indirect fashion. Suppose for example that the improved wilderness area is not subject to entrance charges but that because of the improvements more people do visit it. There is no apparent 'market' in the environmental improvement: the gain is not bought and sold by anyone.

It is important to realize that, while the absence of markets or indirect markets makes the process of economic evaluation more difficult, it by no means renders it impossible. Even more important, the absence of a market or indirect market does not mean the economic gains are not present. There are still welfare improvements – people prefer the wilderness area to be improved. This preference has to be measured.

The uses of monetary measures

Why is it important to place monetary measures on environmental gains and losses? There are several reasons.

Preferences for environmental improvement can show up in various ways. We have already noted, for example, that membership of environmental bodies responds to increased awareness. Political lobbies are another mechanism, not unrelated to membership of pro-environment organizations, and the concern of political parties to secure the 'green vote' is another manifestation of the importance of environmentalism. Both expressions of concern capture to some extent the intensity of preference for the environment, but the attraction of placing money values on these preferences is that they measure the *degree* of concern. The way in which this is done is by using, as the means of 'monetization', the willingness of individuals to pay for the environment.

At its simplest, what we seek is some expression of how much people are willing to pay to preserve or improve the environment. Such measures automatically express not just the fact of a preference for the environment, but also the intensity of that preference. Instead of 'one man one vote', then, monetization quite explicitly reflects the depth of feeling contained in each vote.

If, of course, the issue is one of losing an environmental benefit, we may wish to rephrase the problem in terms of individuals' willingness to accept monetary compensation for the loss, rather than their willingness to pay to prevent the loss. This can result in very large implied values of environmental quality. Our first reason for seeking a monetary measure, then, is that it will, to some considerable extent, reflect the strength of feeling for the environmental asset in question.

The second reason arises out of the first: provided the monetary measures that are revealed are sufficiently large, they offer a supportive argument for environmental quality. The usefulness of such arguments in turn arises from the fact that voters, politicians and civil servants are readily used to the meaning of gains and losses that are expressed in pounds or dollars.

To say that a particular species in danger from some development is valued very highly because of the vocal expression of concern is one thing. To support that argument with a monetary expression of that concern makes the case for preservation stronger than if one argument is used alone.

The third reason for wanting to make the effort at monetization is that it may permit comparison with other monetary benefits arising from alternative uses of funds.

The point here is that preserving and improving the environment is never a free option: it costs money and uses up real resources. This is true whether actual expenditures are incurred to preserve a habitat or insulate houses against noise or introduce sulphur emission reductions, or whether the cost of preservation is in terms of some benefit forgone. Preserving a wetlands area, for example, may well be at the cost of agricultural output had the land been drained. If a monetary measure of environmental benefits can be secured, it can be compared to the monetary benefits of the agricultural output. This will help in any analysis of the extent to which it is socially worthwhile to preserve the land. The option with the biggest net benefit – i.e. the excess of benefits over costs – will be the one that is preferred, subject to any other considerations relating, say, to the interest of future generations.

The reasoning above may be formalized. The exercise of comparing the costs and benefits of two or more options of the use of land in the manner discussed is known as cost benefit analysis.

Cost benefit analysis (or CBA for short) makes operational the very simple, and rational, idea that decisions should be based on some weighing up of the advantages and disadvantages of an action.

At the moment, it is important to stress that CBA is not the only way to assist in decisions of the kind under consideration. There are other approaches which may be preferred. But CBA is the only one which explicitly makes the effort to compare like with like using a single measuring rod of benefits and costs, money.

Total economic value

While the terminology is still not agreed, environmental economists have gone some considerable way towards a taxonomy of economic values as they relate to natural environments. Interestingly, this taxonomy embraces some of the concerns of the environmentalist. It begins by distinguishing user values from 'intrinsic' values. User values, or user benefits, derive from the actual use of the environment. An angler, wildfowl hunter, fell walker, ornithologist, all use the natural environment and derive benefit from it. Those who like to view the countryside, directly or through other media such as photograph and film, also 'use' the environment and secure benefit. The values so expressed are economic values in the sense we have defined. Slightly more complex are values expressed through *options* to use the environment, that is, the value of the environment as a potential benefit as opposed to actual present use value. Economists refer to this as *option value*. It is essentially an expression of preference, a willingness to pay, for the preservation of an environment against some probability that the individual will make use of it at a later date. Provided the uncertainty about future use relates to the availability, or 'supply', of the environment, the theory tells us that this option value is *likely* to be positive. In this way we obtain the first part of an overall equation for total economic value (TEV). This equation says:

TOTAL USER VALUE = ACTUAL USE VALUE + OPTION VALUE

Intrinsic values present more problems. They suggest values which are in the real nature of the thing and unassociated with actual use, or even the option to use the thing. 'Intrinsic' value is a value that resides 'in' something *and that is unrelated to human beings altogether*. Put another way if there were no humans, some people would argue that animals, habitats, etc. would still have 'intrinsic' value. There is a separate, but not wholly independent, concept of intrinsic value, namely value that resides 'in' something but which is captured by people through their preferences in the form of non-use value. It is this second definition of intrinsic value that we use. That is, values are taken to be entities that reflect people's preferences, but those values *include* concern for, sympathy with and respect for the rights or welfare of non-human beings. The briefest introspection will confirm that there are such values. A great many people value the remaining stocks of blue, humpback and fin whales. Very few of those people value them in order to maintain the option of seeing them for themselves. What they value is the *existence* of whales, a value unrelated to use, although, to be sure, the vehicle by which they secure the knowledge for that value to exist may well be a film or photograph or the recounted story. The example of the whales can be repeated many thousands of times for other species, threatened or otherwise, and for whole ecosystems such as rainforests, wetlands, lakes, rivers, mountains and so on.

The *existence values* are certainly funny values. It is not very clear how they are best defined. They are not related to vicarious benefit, i.e. securing pleasure because others derive a use value. Vicarious benefit belongs in the class of option values, in this case a willingness to pay to preserve the environment for the benefit of others. Nor are existence values what the literature calls *bequest values*, a willingness to pay to preserve the environment for the benefit of our children and grandchildren. That motive also belongs with option value. Note that if the bequest is for our immediate descendants we shall be fairly confident at guessing the nature of their preferences. If we extend the bequest motive to future generations in general, as many environmentalists would urge us to, we face the difficulty of not knowing their preferences. This kind of uncertainty is different from the uncertainty about availability of the environment in the future which made option value positive. Assuming it is legitimate to include the preferences of as yet unborn individuals uncertainty about future preferences could make option value negative.

Provisionally, we state that:

INTRINSIC VALUE = EXISTENCE VALUE

Thus we can write our formula for total economic value as:

TOTAL ECONOMIC VALUE = ACTUAL USE VALUE + OPTION VALUE + EXISTENCE VALUE

Within this equation we might also state that:

OPTION VALUE = VALUE IN USE (by the individual) + VALUE IN USE BY FUTURE INDIVIDUALS (descendants and future generations) + VALUE IN USE BY OTHERS (vicarious value to the individual)

The context in which we tend to look for total economic values should also not be forgotten ... [I]n many of those contexts three important features are present. The first is *irreversibility*. If the asset in question is not preserved it is likely to be eliminated with little or no chance of regeneration. The second is *uncertainty:* the future is not known, and hence there are potential costs if the asset is eliminated and a future choice is forgone. A dominant form of such uncertainty is our ignorance about how ecosystems work: in sacrificing one asset we do not know what else we are likely to lose. The third feature is *uniqueness*. Some empirical attempts to measure existence values tend to relate to endangered species and unique scenic views. Economic theory tells us that this combination of attributes will dictate preferences which err on the cautious side of exploitation. That is, preservation will be relatively more favoured in comparison to development.

[...]

Contingent valuation

The contingent valuation method (CVM) uses a direct approach – it basically asks people what they are willing to pay for a benefit, and/or what they are willing to receive by way of compensation to tolerate a cost. This process of 'asking' may be either through a direct questionnaire/survey or by experimental techniques in which subjects respond to various stimuli in 'laboratory' conditions. What is sought are the personal valuations of the respondent for increases or decreases in the quantity of some good, contingent upon an hypothetical market. Respondents say what they would be willing to pay or willing to accept *if* a market existed for the good in question. A contingent market is taken to include not just the good itself (an improved view, better water quality, etc.), but also the institutional context in which it would be provided, and the way in which it would be financed.

One major attraction of CVM is that it should, technically, be applicable to all circumstances and thus has two important features:

- it will frequently be the *only* technique of benefit estimation;

- it should be applicable to most contexts of environmental policy.

The aim of the CVM is to elicit valuations – or 'bids' – which are close to those that would be revealed if an actual market existed. The hypothetical market – the questioner, questionnaire and respondent – must therefore be as close as possible to a real market. The respondent must, for example, be familiar with the good in question. If the good is improved scenic visibility, this might be achieved by showing the respondent photographs of the view with and without particular levels of pollution. The respondent must also be familiar with the hypothetical means of payment – say a local tax or direct entry charge – known as the payment *vehicle.*

The questioner suggests the first bid (the 'starting-point bid (price)') and the respondent agrees or denies that he/she would be willing to pay it. An iterative procedure follows: the starting-point price is increased to see if the respondent would still be willing to pay it, and so on until the respondent declares he/she is not willing to pay the extra increment in the bid. The last accepted bid, then, is the maximum willingness to pay (MWTP). The process works in reverse if the aim is to elicit *willingness to accept* (WTA): bids are systematically lowered until the respondent's minimum WTA is reached.

A very large part of the literature on CVM is taken up with discussion about the 'accuracy' of the CVM. Accuracy is not easy to define. But since the basic aim of CVM is to elicit 'real' values, a bid will be accurate if it coincides (within reason) with one that would result if an actual market existed. But since actual markets do not exist *ex hypothesi* (otherwise there would be no reason to use the technique), accuracy must be tested by seeing that:

- the resulting bid is similar to that achieved by other techniques based on surrogate markets (house price approach, wage studies, etc.);

- the resulting bid is similar to one achieved by introducing the kinds of incentives that exist in real markets to reveal preference.

One significant feature of the CVM literature has been its use to elicit the different kinds of valuation that people place on environmental goods. In particular, CVM has suggested that existence values may be very important, as we shall see.

[...]

More on existence value

The introduction indicated that existence value is a value placed on an environmental good and which is *unrelated to any actual or potential use of the good.* At first sight this may seem an odd category of economic value, for, surely, value derives from use? To see how existence values can be positive, consider the many environmental funds and organizations in existence to protect endangered species. The subject of these campaigns could be a readily identifiable and used habitat near to the person supporting the campaign. It is very often a remote environment, however, so much so that it is not realistic to expect the campaigner to use it now, or even in the future. Many people none the less support campaigns to protect tropical forests, to ban the hunting of whales, to protect giant pandas, rhinoceros, and so on. All are consumable vicariously through film and television, but vicarious demand cannot explain the substantial support for such campaigns and activities ... This type of value, unrelated to use, is existence value.

Economists have suggested a number of motives, all of which reduce to some form of *altruism* – caring for other people or other beings:

(i)   *Bequest* motives relate to the idea of willing a supply of natural environments to one's heirs or to future generations in general. It is no different to passing on accumulated personal assets. As noted above, however, we prefer to see bequest motives as part of a *use* value, the user being the heir or future generation. It is possible, of course, to think of a bequest as relating to the satisfaction that we believe will be given to future generations from the mere existence of the asset, but the very notion of bequest tends to imply that the inheritor makes some use of the asset;

(ii) *Gift* motives are very similar but the object of the gift tends to be a current person – a friend, say, or a relative. Once again gift motives are more likely to be for use by the recipient. We do not therefore count the gift motive as explaining existence value – it is one more use value based on altruism.

(iii) *Sympathy* for people or animals. This motive is more relevant to existence value. Sympathy for animals tends to vary by culture and nation, but in a great many nations it is the norm, not the exception. It is consistent with this motive that we are willing to pay to preserve habitats out of sympathy for the sentient beings, including humans, that occupy them.

Much of the literature on existence value stops here. The reason for this is that altruistic motives are familiar to economists. They make economic analysis more complex but, by and large, altruism can be conveniently subsumed in the conventional model of rational economic behaviour. Essentially, it says that the well-being of one individual depends on the well-being of another individual. There may, however, be other motives at work. Existence values may, for example, reflect some judgement about the 'rights' of other non-human beings, or a feeling of 'stewardship' about the global or local environment.

Genuine motives for environmental concern are likely to be many and varied. For current purposes what matters is that economic valuation of environmental gains and losses needs to take account of those motives.

[...]

Conclusions on valuing the environment

It is not essential to be persuaded that the monetary valuations illustrated in this chapter are 'accurate'. Economics is not, and cannot be, a science in the sense of a laboratory subject or an analysis of physical objects. Its laboratory, after all, is human society itself. What does matter is that the implications of the valuation procedures outlined here are understood. These are:

(i) By at least trying to put money values on some aspects of environmental quality we are underlining the fact that environmental services are *not* free. They do have values in the same sense as marketed goods and services have values. The absence of markets must not be allowed to disguise this important fact.

(ii) By trying to value environmental services we are forced into a rational decision-making frame of mind. Quite simply, we are forced to think about the gains and losses, the benefits and costs of what we do. If nothing else, economic valuation has made a great advance in that respect.

(iii) Many things *cannot* be valued in money terms. That is altogether different from saying they are 'priceless' in the sense of having infinite values.

(iv) The fact that we find *positive* values for so many environmental functions means that an economic system which allocates resources according to economic values (i.e. consumer preferences) *must* take account of the positive economic values for environmental quality. Yet the actual values (as opposed to those imputed by the techniques discussed in this chapter) are zero in many cases ...

Notes

* From David Pearce, Anil Markandya and Edward B. Barker, *Blueprint for a Green Economy*, Earthscan Publications Ltd, 1989, pp.51–7, 69–71, 75–7, 80–1.

'A Reply to some Criticisms'

David Pearce

Many environmentalists were hostile to the approach of *Blueprint*. In this Reading* Pearce takes on his critics.

The green economy: a middle way

In *Blueprint* [See Reading 4] my colleagues and I set out what we regard as a reasonably coherent set of policies designed to decouple economic activity and environmental impact.

The issue of valuation

We sought also to argue that environmental conservation is *economically important.* We did not mean by this that conserving the environment results in cash flows, although it may well do. To the economist, economic value arises if someone is made to feel better off in terms of their wants and desires. The feeling of well-being from contemplating a beautiful view is therefore an economic value, as is the feeling of well-being I get from an unblemished glass of Talisker or Gewürtztraminer. Positive economic value – a benefit – arises when people feel better off, and negative economic value – cost – arises when they feel worse off. It is as simple as that. Would that some of our critics took the trouble to investigate the meaning of economic value.

There is, of course, the view that we 'cannot value the environment'. But the meaning of this objection is not always clear, and confusion has arisen because economists have themselves used slipshod language. What economic valuation does is to measure *human preferences* for or against changes in the state of environments. It does not 'value the environment'. Indeed, it is not clear exactly what 'valuing the environment' would mean. In measuring preferences, economists do no more than market researchers do when assessing the market for existing or new products. Few people regard market research as unscientific or invalid.

Once the nature of economic valuation is clear, continued objection must mean one of the following things:

(a) the exercise of seeking measures of individuals' willingness to pay for environmental quality is itself somehow flawed. There are indeed technical problems in validating the measures obtained – i.e. in determining whether they are 'true' valuations or not (see below):

(b) that the fate of environments should not be determined by human wants at all;

(c) that human wants matter, but are not the *only* source of value. For example, there exists something called 'intrinsic' value, value 'in' things rather than 'of' things.

Proposition (a) is not the dominant reason behind the objections to valuation. Proposition (b) is clearly untenable if there is to be any semblance of democracy, and, in any event, would rule out the objectors' preferences as well (unless they can justifiably claim to be speaking uniquely 'on behalf of' the environment in some selfless sense). Proposition (c) appears to explain much of the objection, but it is invalid as an objection to *economic* valuation. Economists do not deny that 'other' values exist. They make no claim to be working with other values, only economic values – i.e. preference-based valuations. Intrinsic and economic values may therefore co-exist. Practical issues do of course arise, since *someone* still has to say what these intrinsic values are and how they trade off against other values (e.g. the rights of trees to exist and the rights of people to a livelihood).

There *are* of course criticisms of actual valuation procedures, and of the legitimacy of some responses, particularly where the valuation exercise relates to environmental assets of which the respondent has little or no direct experience. But as in any social science in which the laboratory is the real world of human behaviour, we cannot expect accuracy in the sense of the physical sciences. Valuations do vary with the degree of information and disinformation in the possession of the respondent, but then so do political preferences and so do decisions to buy goods in the supermarket – just think of eggs and Perrier water. The fear may be that the economist will deliberately bias the results of such a valuation exercise. That is a risk, but it is a risk that can be minimized by proper scientific enquiry and cross-examination.

Accuracy can also be tested in other ways and the literature is replete with such tests.

Let me offer one very real-world reason why valuation matters. In the rich world and poor world, politicians and their advisors are engaged in the activity of trading off environment against economic activity. That is a daily experience. Defending the environment means presenting the arguments in terms of units that politicians understand. For the development option it is simple. It is a matter of jobs, or exports, or simply giving people what they invariably want – a better material standard of living. The environmental case looks weak in terms of those units of importance – it seems to detract from employment, it cannot be exported and it does not result in cash flows. Assembling the case for the environment, then, means assessing what people want. That means looking at opinion polls, hearing views at public inquiries, responding to the environmentalist lobbies, and so on. It can also mean finding measures of public preference for the environment expressed in the same units as the development option – money. The economic valuation exercise appears as another input to the information gathering and decision making process. In short, the problem for the politician is one of deriving evidence that the trade-off of environment for development is worthwhile. I have never suggested that economic valuation is the *only* criterion for making decisions, nor does *Blueprint* say this. But adducing evidence that the environment does matter in economic terms is important, especially as the record of decision-making in the absence of such valuations is hardly encouraging for the environment.

One wonders, for example, what might have happened if the M3 motorway inquiry in the UK had sought a valuation of the option of a tunnel as opposed to a surface road over the South Downs. This was the option finally chosen, which will destroy a significant environmental asset. The extra cost of the tunnel is £92 million, or, say, £7.5 million p.a. as an annuity over 50 years. A valuation exercise could at least have asked whether people were willing to pay this extra to preserve the down.

The valuation issue is important, but it is perhaps worth pointing out that even if valuation is rejected, there remains a powerful case for the rest of the 'middle way' approach to a green economy.

Notes

* From David Pearce, 'Green Economics', *Environmental Values*, vol.1, no 1, Spring 1992, pp.6–8.

'The Tragedy of the Commons'

Garrett Hardin

Hardin tells a story* about a common pasture on which a number of herdsmen graze their cows. It is to the advantage of each herdsman to put an extra cow on the common, but the collective result of their all doing so is the destruction of the common. 'Freedom in a commons brings ruin to all'. Hardin applies this model situation to the problem of population growth, but, as he points out, it serves as the model for a whole range of environmental problems. Since, in his view, appeals to conscience are ineffective or even make things worse, he recommends as the only solution, 'mutual coercion mutually agreed upon'.

At the end of a thoughtful article on the future of nuclear war, J.B. Wiesner and H.F. York concluded that: 'Both sides in the arms race are ... confronted by the dilemma of steadily increasing military power and steadily decreasing national security. *It is our considered professional judgement that this dilemma has no technical solution.* If the great powers continue to look for solutions in the area of science and technology only, the result will be to worsen the situation.'[1]

I would like to focus your attention not on the subject of the article (national security in a nuclear world) but on the kind of conclusion they reached, namely that there is no technical solution to the problem. An implicit and almost universal assumption of discussions published in professional and semi-popular scientific journals is that the problem under discussion has a technical solution. A technical solution may be defined as one that requires a change only in the techniques of the natural sciences, demanding little or nothing in the way of change in human values or ideas of morality.

In our day (though not in earlier times) technical solutions are always welcome. Because of previous failures in prophecy, it takes courage to assert that a desired technical solution is not possible. Wiesner and York exhibited this courage; publishing in a science journal, they insisted that the solution to the problem was not to be found in the natural sciences. They cautiously qualified their statement with the phrase, 'It is our considered professional judgement...' Whether they were right or not is not the concern of the present article. Rather, the concern here is with the important concept of a class of human problems which can be called 'no technical solution problems', and more specifically, with the identification and discussion of one of these.

It is easy to show that the class is not a null class. Recall the game of tick-tack-toe? Consider the problem, 'How can I win the game of tick-tack-toe?' It is well known that I cannot, if I assume (in keeping with the conventions of game theory) that my opponent understands the game perfectly. Put another way, there is no 'technical solution' to the problem. I can win only by giving a radical meaning to the word 'win'. I can hit my opponent over the head; or I can falsify the records. Every way in which I 'win' involves, in some sense, an abandonment of the game, as we intuitively understand it. (I can also, of course, openly abandon the game – refuse to play it. This is what most adults do.)

The class of 'no technical solution problems' has members. My thesis is that the 'population problem', as conventionally conceived, is a member of this class. How it is conventionally conceived needs some comment. It is fair to say that most people who anguish over the population problem are trying to find a way to avoid the evils of over-population without relinquishing any of the privileges they now enjoy. They think that farming the seas or developing new strains of wheat will solve the problem – technologically. I try to show here that the solution they seek cannot be found. The population problem cannot be solved in a technical way, any more than can the problem of winning the game of tick-tack-toe.

What shall we maximize?

Population, as Malthus said, naturally tends to grow 'geometrically', or, as we would now say, exponentially. In a finite world this means that the per-capita share of the world's goods must decrease. Is ours a finite world?

A fair defence can be put forward for the view that the world is infinite; or that we do not know that it is not. But, in terms of the practical problems that we must face in the next few generations with the foreseeable technology, it is clear that we will greatly increase human misery if we do not, during the immediate future, assume that the world available to the terrestrial human population is finite. 'Space' is no escape.[2]

A finite world can support only a finite population; therefore, population growth must eventually equal zero. (The case of perpetual wide fluctuations above and below zero is a trivial variant that need not be discussed.) When this condition is met, what will be the situation of mankind? Specifically, can Bentham's goal of 'the greatest good for the greatest number' be realized?

No – for two reasons, each sufficient by itself. The first is a theoretical one. It is not mathematically possible to maximize for two (or more) variables at the same time. This was clearly stated by von Neumann and Morgenstern,[3] but the principle is implicit in the theory of partial differential equations, dating back at least to D'Alembert (1717–1783).

The second reason springs directly from biological facts. To live, any organism must have a source of energy (for example, food). This energy is utilized for two purposes: mere maintenance and work. For man, maintenance of life requires about 1600 kilocalories a day ('maintenance calories'). Anything that he does over and above merely staying alive will be defined as work, and is supported by 'work calories' which he takes in. Work calories are used not only for what we call work in common speech; they are also required for all forms of enjoyment, from swimming and automobile racing to playing music and writing poetry. If our goal is to maximize population it is obvious what we must do: We must make the work calories per person approach as close to zero as possible. No gourmet meals, no vacations, no sports, no music, no literature, no art ... I think that everyone will grant, without argument or proof, that maximizing population does not maximize goods. Bentham's goal is impossible.

In reaching this conclusion I have made the usual assumption that it is the acquisition of energy that is the problem. The appearance of atomic energy has led some to question this assumption. However, given an infinite source of energy, population growth still produces an inescapable problem. The problem of the acquisition of energy is replaced by the problem of its dissipation, as J.H. Fremlin has so wittily shown.[4] The arithmetic signs in the analysis are, as it were, reversed; but Bentham's goal is unobtainable.

The optimum population is, then, less than the maximum. The difficulty of defining the optimum is enormous; so far as I know, no one has seriously tackled this problem. Reaching an acceptable and stable solution will surely require more than one generation of hard analytical work – and much persuasion.

We want the maximum good per person; but what is good? To one person it is wilderness, to another it is ski lodges for thousands. To one it is estuaries to nourish ducks for hunters to shoot; to another it is factory land. Comparing one good with another is, we usually say, impossible because goods are incommensurable. Incommensurables cannot be compared.

Theoretically this may be true; but in real life incommensurables *are* commensurable. Only a criterion of judgement and a system of weighting are needed. In nature the criterion is survival. Is it better for a species to be small and hideable, or large and powerful? Natural selection commensurates the incommensurables. The compromise achieved depends on a natural weighting of the values of the variables.

Man must imitate this process. There is no doubt that in fact he already does, but unconsciously. It is when the hidden decisions are made explicit that the arguments begin. The problem for the years ahead is to work out an acceptable theory of weighting. Synergistic effects, non-linear variation, and difficulties in discounting the future make the intellectual problem difficult, but not (in principle) insoluble.

Has any cultural group solved this practical problem at the present time, even on an intuitive level? One simple fact proves that none has: there is no prosperous population in the world today that has, and has had for some time, a growth rate of zero. Any people that has intuitively identified its optimum point will soon reach it, after which its growth rate becomes and remains zero.

Of course, a positive growth rate might be taken as evidence that a population is below its optimum. However, by any reasonable standards, the most rapidly growing populations on earth today are (in general) the most miserable. This association (which need not be invariable) casts doubt on the optimistic assumption that the positive growth rate of a population is evidence that it has yet to reach its optimum.

We can make little progress in working toward optimum population size until we explicitly exorcise the spirit of Adam Smith in the field of practical demography. In economic affairs, *The Wealth of Nations* (1776) popularized the 'invisible hand', the idea that an individual who 'intends only his own gain', is, as it were, 'led by an invisible hand to promote ... the public interest'.[5] Adam Smith did not assert that this was invariably true, and perhaps neither did any of his followers. But he contributed to a dominant tendency of thought that has ever since interfered with positive action based on rational analysis, namely, the tendency to assume that decisions reached individually will, in fact, be the best decisions for an entire society. If this assumption is correct it justifies the continuance of our present policy of *laissez-faire* in reproduction. If it is correct we can assume that men will control their individual fecundity so as to produce the optimum population. If the assumption is not correct, we need to re-examine our individual freedoms to see which ones are defensible.

Tragedy of freedom in a commons

The rebuttal to the invisible hand in population control is to be found in a scenario first sketched in a little-known pamphlet in 1833 by a William Foster Lloyd (1794–1852).[6] We may well call it 'the tragedy of the commons', using the word 'tragedy as the philosopher Whitehead used it:[7] 'The essence of dramatic tragedy' is not unhappiness. It resides in the solemnity of the remorseless working of things.' He then goes on to say, 'This inevitableness of destiny can only be illustrated in terms of human life by incidents which in fact involve unhappiness. For it is only by them that the futility of escape can be made evident in the drama.'

The tragedy of the commons develops in this way. Picture a pasture open to all. It is to be expected that each herdsman will try to keep as many cattle as possible on the commons. Such an arrangement may work reasonably satisfactorily for centuries because tribal wars, poaching, and disease keep the numbers of both man and beast well below the carrying capacity of the land. Finally, however, comes the day of reckoning, that is, the day when the long-desired goal of social stability becomes a reality. At this point, the inherent logic of the commons remorselessly generates tragedy.

As a rational being, each herdsman seeks to maximize his gain. Explicitly or implicitly, more or less consciously, he asks, 'What is the utility *to me* of adding one more animal to my herd?' This utility has one negative and one positive component.

1   The positive component is a function of the increment of one animal. Since the herdsman receives all the proceeds from the sale of the additional animal, the positive utility is nearly +1.

2   The negative component is a function of the additional overgrazing created by one more animal. Since, however, the effects of overgrazing are shared by all the herdsmen, the negative utility for any particular decision-making herdsman is only a fraction of –1.

Adding together the component partial utilities, the rational herdsman concludes that the only sensible course for him to pursue is to add another animal to his herd. And another... But this is the conclusion reached by each and every rational herdsman sharing a commons. Therein is the tragedy. Each man is locked into a system that compels him to increase his herd without limit – in a world that is limited. Ruin is the destination toward which all men rush, each pursuing his own best interest in a society that believes in the freedom of the commons. Freedom in a commons brings ruin to all.

Some would say that this is a platitude. Would that it were! In a sense, it was learned thousands of years ago, but natural selection favours the forces of psychological denial.[8] The individual benefits as an individual from his ability to deny the truth even though society as a whole, of which he is a part, suffers. Education can counteract the natural tendency to do the wrong thing, but the inexorable succession of generations requires that the basis for this knowledge be constantly refreshed.

A simple incident that occurred a few years ago in Leominster, Massachusetts, shows how perishable the knowledge is. During the Christmas shopping season the parking meters downtown were covered with plastic bags that bore tags reading: 'Do not open until after Christmas. Free parking courtesy of the mayor and city council.' In other words, facing the prospect of an increased demand for already scarce space, the city fathers re-instituted the system of the commons. (Cynically, we suspect that they gained more votes than they lost by this retrogressive act.)

In an approximate way, the logic of the commons has been understood for a long time, perhaps since the discovery of agriculture or the invention of private property in real estate. But it is understood mostly only in special cases which are not sufficiently generalized. Even at this late date, cattlemen leasing national land on the Western ranges demonstrate no more than an ambivalent understanding, in constantly pressuring federal authorities to increase the head count to the point where overgrazing produces erosion and weed-dominance. Likewise, the oceans of the world continue to suffer from the survival of the philosophy of the commons. Maritime nations still respond automatically to the shibboleth of the 'freedom of the seas.' Professing to believe in the 'inexhaustible resources of the oceans', they bring species after species of fish and whales closer to extinction.[9]

The National Parks present another instance of the working out of the tragedy of the commons. At present, they are open to all, without limit. The parks themselves are limited in extent – there is only one Yosemite Valley – whereas population seems to grow without limit. The values that visitors seek in the parks are steadily eroded. Plainly, we must soon cease to treat the parks as commons or they will be of no value to anyone.

What shall we do? We have several options. We might sell them off as private property. We might keep them as public property, but allocate the right to enter them. The allocation might be on the basis of wealth, by the use of an auction system. It might be by lottery. Or it might be on a first-come, first-served basis, administered to long queues. These, I think, are all objectionable. But we must choose – or acquiesce in the destruction of the commons that we call our National Parks.

Pollution

In a reverse way, the tragedy of the commons reappears in problems of pollution. Here it is not a question of taking something out of the commons, but of putting something in – sewage, or chemical, radioactive, and heat wastes into water; noxious and dangerous fumes into the air; and distracting and unpleasant advertising signs into the line of sight. The calculations of utility are much the same as before. The rational man finds that his share of the cost of the wastes he discharges into the commons is less than the cost of purifying his wastes before releasing them. Since this is true for everyone, we are locked into a system of 'fouling our own nest', so long as we behave only as independent, rational, free-enterprisers.

The tragedy of the commons as a food basket is averted by private property, or something formally like it. But the air and waters surrounding us cannot readily be fenced, and so the tragedy of the commons as a cesspool must be prevented by different means, by coercive laws or taxing devices that make it cheaper for the polluter to treat his pollutants than to discharge them untreated. We have not progressed as far with the solution of this problem as we have with the first. Indeed, our particular concept of private property, which deters us from exhausting the positive resources of the earth, favours pollution. The owner of a factory on the bank of a stream – whose property extends to the middle of the stream – often has difficulty seeing why it is not his natural right to muddy the waters flowing past his door. The law, always behind the times, requires elaborate stitching and fitting to adapt it to this newly perceived aspect of the commons.

The pollution problem is a consequence of population. It did not much matter how a lonely American frontiersman disposed of his waste. 'Flowing water purifies itself every ten miles', my grandfather used to say, and the myth was near enough to the truth when he was a boy, for there were not too many people. But as population became denser, the natural chemical and biological recycling processes became overloaded, calling for a redefinition of property rights.

How to legislate temperance?

Analysis of the pollution problem as a function of population density uncovers a not generally recognized principle of morality, namely: *the morality of an act is a function of the state of the system at the time it is performed.*[10] Using the commons as a cesspool does not harm the general public under frontier conditions, because there is no public; the same behaviour in a metropolis is unbearable. A hundred and fifty years ago a plainsman could kill an American bison, cut out only the tongue for his dinner, and discard the rest of the animal. He was not in any important sense being wasteful. Today, with only a few thousand bison left, we would be appalled at such behaviour.

In passing, it is worth noting that the morality of an act cannot be determined from a photograph. One does not know whether a man killing an elephant or setting fire to the grassland is harming others until one knows the total system in which his act appears. 'One picture is worth a thousand words', said an ancient Chinese; but it may take ten thousand words to validate it. It is as tempting to ecologists as it is to reformers in general to try to persuade others by way of the photographic shortcut. But the essence of an argument cannot be photographed: it must be presented rationally – in words.

That morality is system-sensitive escaped the attention of most codifiers of ethics in the past. 'Thou shalt not...' is the form of traditional ethical directives which make no allowance for particular circumstances. The laws of our society follow the pattern of ancient ethics, and therefore are poorly suited to governing a complex, crowded, changeable world. Our epicyclic solution is to augment statutory law with administrative law. Since it is practically impossible to spell out all the conditions under which it is safe to burn trash in the back yard or to run an automobile without smog-control, by law we delegate the details to bureaus. The result is administrative law, which is rightly feared for an ancient reason – *Quis custodiet ipsos custodes?* – Who shall watch the watchers themselves? John Adams said that we must have a 'government of laws and not men.' Bureau administrators, trying to evaluate the morality of acts in the total system, are singularly liable to corruption, producing a government by men, not laws.

Prohibition is easy to legislate (though not necessarily to enforce); but how do we legislate temperance? Experience indicates that it can be accomplished best through the mediation of administrative law. We limit possibilities unnecessarily if we suppose that the sentiment of *Quis custodiet* denies us the use of administrative law. We should rather retain the phrase as a perpetual reminder of fearful dangers we cannot avoid. The great challenge facing us now is to invent the corrective feedbacks that are needed to keep custodians honest. We must find ways to legitimate the needed authority of both the custodians and the corrective feedbacks.

Freedom to breed is intolerable

The tragedy of the commons is involved in population problems in another way. In a world governed solely by the principle of 'dog eat dog' – if indeed there ever was such a world – how many children a family had would not be a matter of public concern. Parents who bred too exuberantly would leave fewer descendants, not more, because they would be unable to care adequately for their children. David Lack and others have found that such a negative feedback demonstrably controls the fecundity of birds.[11] But men are not birds, and have not acted like them for millenniums, at least.

If each human family were dependent only on its own resources; *if* the children of improvident parents starved to death; *if*, thus, over-breeding brought its own 'punishment' to the germ line – *then* there would be no public interest in controlling the breeding of families. But our society is deeply committed to the welfare state,[12] and hence is confronted with another aspect of the tragedy of the commons.

In a welfare state, how shall we deal with the family, the religion, the race, or the class (or indeed any distinguishable and cohesive group) that adopts overbreeding as a policy to secure its own aggrandizement?[13] To couple the concept of freedom to breed with the belief that everyone born has an equal right to the commons is to lock the world into a tragic course of action.

Unfortunately this is just the course of action that is being pursued by the United Nations. In late 1967, some thirty nations agreed to the following: 'The Universal Declaration of Human Rights describes the family as the natural and fundamental unit of society. It follows that any choice and decision with regard to the size of the family must irrevocably rest with the family itself, and cannot be made by anyone else'.[14]

It is painful to have to deny categorically the validity of this right; denying it, one feels as uncomfortable as a resident of Salem, Massachusetts, who denied the reality of witches in the seventeenth century. At the present time, in liberal quarters, something like a taboo acts to inhibit criticism of the United Nations. There is a feeling that the United Nations is 'our last and best hope', that we shouldn't find fault with it; we shouldn't play into the hands of the arch-conservatives. However, let us not forget what Robert Louis Stevenson said: 'The truth that is suppressed by friends is the readiest weapon of the enemy.' If we love the truth we must openly deny the validity of the Universal Declaration of Human Rights, even though it is promoted by the United Nations. We should also join with Kingsley Davis[15] in attempting to get Planned Parenthood–World Population to see the error of its ways in embracing the same tragic ideal.

Conscience is self-eliminating

It is a mistake to think that we can control the breeding of mankind in the long run by an appeal to conscience. Charles Galton Darwin made this point when he spoke on the centennial of the publication of his grandfather's great book. The argument is straightforward and Darwinian.

People vary. Confronted with appeals to limit breeding, some people will undoubtedly respond to the plea more than others. Those who have more children will produce a larger fraction of the next generation than those with more susceptible consciences. The differences will be accentuated, generation by generation.

In C.G. Darwin's words: 'It may well be that it would take hundreds of generations for the progenitive instinct to develop in this way, but if it should do so, nature would have taken her revenge, and the variety *Homo contracipiens* would become extinct and would be replaced by the variety *Homo progenitivus*'.[16]

The argument assumes that conscience or the desire for children (no matter which) is hereditary – but hereditary only in the most general formal sense. The result will be the same whether the attitude is transmitted through germ cells, or exosomatically, to use A.J. Lotka's term. (If one denies the latter possibility as well as the former, then what's the point of education?) The argument has here been stated in the context of the population problem, but it applies equally well to any instance in which society appeals to an individual exploiting a commons to restrain himself for the general good – by means of his conscience. To make such an appeal is to set up a selective system that works toward the elimination of conscience from the race.

Pathogenic effects of conscience

The long-term disadvantage of an appeal to conscience should be enough to condemn it; but it has serious short-term disadvantages as well. If we ask a man who is exploiting a commons to desist 'in the name of conscience', what are we saying to him? What does he hear? – not only at the moment but also in the wee small hours of the night when, half asleep, he remembers not merely the words we used but also the non-verbal communication cues we gave him unawares? Sooner or later, consciously or subconsciously, he senses that he has received two communications, and that they are contradictory: (1) (intended communication) 'If you don't do as we ask, we will openly condemn you for not acting like a responsible citizen'; (2) (the unintended communication) 'If you *do* behave as we ask, we will secretly condemn you for a simpleton who can be shamed into standing aside while the rest of us exploit the commons.'

Everyman then is caught in what Bateson has called a 'double bind.' Bateson and his co-workers have made a plausible case for viewing the double bind as an important causative factor in the genesis of schizophrenia.[17] The double bind may not always be so damaging, but it always endangers the mental health of anyone to whom it is applied. 'A bad conscience', said Nietzsche, 'is a kind of illness.'

To conjure up a conscience in others is tempting to anyone who wishes to extend his control beyond the legal limits. Leaders at the highest level succumb to this temptation. Has any president during the past generation failed to call on labour unions to moderate voluntarily their demands for higher wages, or to steel companies to honour voluntary guidelines on prices? I can recall none. The rhetoric used on such occasions is designed to produce feelings of guilt in non-cooperators.

For centuries it was assumed without proof that guilt was a valuable, perhaps even an indispensable, ingredient of the civilized life. Now, in this post-Freudian world, we doubt it.

Paul Goodman speaks from the modern point of view when he says: 'No good has ever come from feeling guilty, neither intelligence, policy, nor compassion. The guilty do not pay attention to the object but only to themselves, and not even to their own interests, which might make sense, but to their anxieties'.[18]

One does not have to be a professional psychiatrist to see the consequences of anxiety. We in the Western world are just emerging from a dreadful two centuries-long Dark Ages of Eros that was sustained partly by prohibition laws, but perhaps more effectively by the anxiety-generating mechanisms of education. Alex Comfort has told the story well in *The Anxiety Makers*;[19] it is not a pretty one.

Since proof is difficult, we may even concede that the results of anxiety may sometimes, from certain points of view, be desirable. The larger question we should ask is whether, as a matter of policy, we should ever encourage the use of a technique the tendency (if not the intention) of which is psychologically pathogenic. We hear much talk these days of responsible parenthood; the coupled words are incorporated into the titles of some *organizations* devoted to birth control. Some people have proposed massive propaganda campaigns to instil responsibility into the nation's (or the world's) breeders. But what is the meaning of the word 'conscience'? When we use the word 'responsibility' in the absence of substantial actions are we not trying to browbeat a free man in a commons into acting against his own interest? Responsibility is a verbal counterfeit for a substantial quid pro quo. It is an attempt to get something for nothing.

If the word responsibility is to be used at all, I suggest that it be in the sense Charles Frankel uses it.[20] 'Responsibility', says this philosopher, 'is the product of definite social arrangements.' Notice that Frankel calls for social arrangements not propaganda.

Mutual coercion mutually agreed upon

The social arrangements that produce responsibility are arrangements that create coercion, of some sort. Consider bank robbing. The man who takes money from a bank acts as if the bank were a commons. How do we prevent such action? Certainly not by trying to control his behaviour solely by a verbal appeal to his sense of responsibility. Rather than rely on propaganda we follow Frankel's lead and insist that a bank is not a commons; we seek the definite social arrangements that will keep it from becoming a commons. That we thereby infringe on the freedom of would-be robbers we neither deny nor regret.

The morality of bank robbing is particularly easy to understand because we accept complete prohibition of this activity. We are willing to say 'Thou shalt not rob banks', without providing for exceptions. But temperance also can be created by coercion. Taxing is a good coercive device. To keep downtown shoppers temperate in their use of parking space we introduce parking meters for short periods, and traffic fines for longer ones. We need not actually forbid a citizen to park as long as he wants to; we need merely make it increasingly expensive for him to do so. Not prohibition, but carefully biased options are what we offer him. A Madison Avenue man might call this persuasion; I prefer the greater candour of the word 'coercion'.

'Coercion' is a dirty word to most liberals now, but it need not forever be so. As with the four-letter words, its dirtiness can be cleansed away by exposure to the light, by saying it over and over without apology or embarrassment. To many, the word 'coercion' implies arbitrary decisions of distant and irresponsible bureaucrats; but this is not a necessary part of its meaning. The only kind of coercion I recommend is mutual coercion, mutually agreed upon by the majority of the people affected.

To say that we mutually agree to coercion is not to say that we are required to enjoy it, or even to pretend we enjoy it. Who enjoys taxes? We all grumble about them. But we accept compulsory taxes because we recognize that voluntary taxes would favour the conscienceless. We institute and (grumblingly) support taxes and other coercive devices to escape the horror of the commons.

An alternative to the commons need not be perfectly just to be preferable. With real estate and other material goods, the alternative we have chosen is the institution of private property coupled with legal inheritance. Is this system perfectly just? As a genetically trained biologist I deny that it is. It seems to me that, if there are to be differences in individual inheritance, legal possession should be perfectly correlated with biological inheritance – that those who are biologically more fit to be the custodians of property and power should legally inherit more. But genetic recombination continually makes a mockery of the doctrine of 'like father, like son' implicit in our laws of legal inheritance. An idiot can inherit millions, and a trust fund can keep his estate intact. We must admit that our legal system of private property plus inheritance is unjust but we put up with it because we are not convinced, at the moment, that anyone has invented a better system. The alternative of the commons is too horrifying to contemplate. Injustice is preferable to total ruin.

It is one of the peculiarities of the warfare between reform and the status quo that it is thoughtlessly governed by a double standard. Whenever a reform measure is proposed it is often defeated when its opponents triumphantly discover a flaw in it. As Kingsley Davis has pointed out,[21] worshipers of the status quo sometimes imply that no reform is possible without unanimous agreement, an implication contrary to historical fact. As nearly as I can make out, automatic rejection of proposed reforms is based on one of two unconscious assumptions: (1) that the status quo is perfect; or (2) that the choice we face is between reform and no action; if the proposed reform is imperfect, we presumably should take no action at all, while we wait for a perfect proposal.

But we can never do nothing. That which we have done for thousands of years is also action. It also produces evils. Once we are aware that the status quo is action, we can then compare its discoverable advantages and disadvantages with the predicted advantages and disadvantages of the proposed reform, discounting as best we can for our lack of experience. On the basis of such a comparison, we can make a rational decision which will not involve the unworkable assumption that only perfect systems are tolerable.

Recognition of necessity

Perhaps the simplest summary of this analysis of man's population problems is this: the commons, if justifiable at all, is justifiable only under conditions of low-population density. As the human population has increased, the commons has had to be abandoned in one aspect after another.

First we abandoned the commons in food gathering, enclosing farmland and restricting pastures and hunting and fishing areas. These restrictions are still not complete throughout the world.

Somewhat late we saw that the commons as a place for waste disposal would also have to be abandoned. Restrictions on the disposal of domestic sewage are widely accepted in the Western world; we are still struggling to close the commons to pollution by automobiles, factories, insecticide sprayers, fertilizing operations, and atomic energy installations.

In a still more embryonic state is our recognition of the evils of the commons in matters of pleasure. There is almost no restriction on the propagation of sound waves in the public medium. The shopping public is assaulted with mindless music, without its consent. Our government has paid out billions of dollars to create a supersonic transport which would disturb 50,000 people for every one person whisked from coast to coast 3 hours faster. Advertisers muddy the airwaves of radio and television and pollute the view of travellers. We are a long way from outlawing the commons in matters of pleasure. Is this because our Puritan inheritance makes us view pleasure as something of a sin, and pain (that is, the pollution of advertising) as the sign of virtue?

Every new enclosure of the commons involves the infringement of somebody's personal liberty. Infringements made in the distant past are accepted because no contemporary complains of a loss. It is the newly proposed infringements that we vigorously oppose; cries of 'rights' and 'freedom' fill the air. But what does 'freedom' mean? When men mutually agreed to pass laws against robbing, mankind become more free, not less so. Individuals locked into the logic of the commons are free only to bring on universal ruin; once they see the necessity of mutual coercion, they become free to pursue other goals. I believe it was Hegel who said, 'Freedom is the recognition of necessity.'

The most important aspect of necessity that we must now recognize, is the necessity of abandoning the commons in breeding. No technical solution can rescue us from the misery of overpopulation. Freedom to breed will bring ruin to all. At the moment, to avoid hard decisions many of us are tempted to propagandize for conscience and responsible parenthood. The temptation must be resisted, because an appeal to independently acting consciences selects for the disappearance of all conscience in the long run, and an increase in anxiety in the short.

The only way we can preserve and nurture other and more precious freedoms is by relinquishing the freedom to breed, and that very soon.

'Freedom is the recognition of necessity' – and it is the role of education to reveal to all the necessity of abandoning, the freedom to breed. Only so, can we put an end to this aspect of the tragedy of the commons.

Notes

* From Garrett Hardin, 'The Tragedy of the Commons', *Science*, 162, 1968, pp.1243–8; reprinted in *Managing the Commons*, Garrett Hardin and John Baden (eds), W.H. Freeman and Co.,1977.

[1] J.B. Wiesner and H.F. York, *Scientific American*, 211, no 4, 27, 1964.

[2] G. Hardin, *Journal of Heredity*, 50,68,1959; S. von Hoerner, *Science*, 137, 18, 1962.

[3] J. von Neumann and O. Morgenstern, *Theory of Games and Economic Behaviour*, Princeton University Press, 1947, p.11.

[4] J.H. Fremlin, *New Scientist*, No. 415 (1964), p.285.

[5] A. Smith, *The Wealth of Nations*, Modern Library, 1937, p.423.

[6] W.F. Lloyd, *Two Lectures on the Checks to Population*, Oxford Univiversity Press, 1833, reprinted (in part) in *Population, Evolution, and Birth Control*, G. Hardin (ed.), Freeman, 1964, p.37.

[7] A.N. Whitehead, *Science and the Modern World*, Mentor, 1948, p.17.

[8] G. Hardin (ed.) *Population, Evolution, and Birth Control*, Freeman, 1964, p.56.

[9] S. McVay, *Scientific American*, 216, no. 8, 13, 1966.

[10] J. Fletcher, *Situation Ethics*, Westminster, 1966.

[11] D. Lack, *The Natural Regulation of Animal Numbers*, Clarendon Press, 1954.

[12] H. Girvetz, *From Wealth to Welfare*, Stanford Univiversity Press, 1950.

[13] G. Hardin, *Perspec. Biol. Med.*, 6, 366, 1963.

[14] U. Thant, *International Planned Parenthood News*, no. 168, February 1968, p.3.

[15] K. Davis, *Science*, 158, 730, 1967.

[16] S. Tax (ed.), *Evolution after Darwin*, University of Chicago Press, 1960, vol. 2, p.469.

[17] G. Bateson, D.D. Jackson, J. Haley and J. Weakland, *Behavioural Science*, 1, 251, 1956.

[18] P. Goodman, *New York Review of Books*, 10 (8), 22, 23 May 1968.

[19] A. Comfort, *The Anxiety Makers*, Nelson, 1967.

[20] C. Frankel, *The Case for Modern Man*, Harper, 1955, p.203.

[21] J.D. Roslansky, *Genetics and the Future of Man*, Appleton-Century-Crofts, 1966, p.177.

'Game Theory Analysis'

J.L. Mackie

In the book from which this reading is taken,* Mackie argues that morality is subjective: it does not rest on values that have any foundation in reality and that we can be said to discover. But morality does exist among the members of a society as a set of practices which have come to be mutually agreed upon to perform a function that all have an interest in, the protection of their basic interests. The basic morality that is agreed upon consists of constraints on injuring others, on unfair competition, on theft, on failing to honour agreements and so on. The feature of human beings that makes such constraints necessary also makes it difficult to make them operative: the fact that we have limited sympathies – our natural concern for the interests of others is strong in the case of a quite restricted circle, beyond which it weakens progressively as our relations with others become less close. In this reading Mackie draws on models from the mathematical study of game theory to illuminate the problem posed by limited sympathies and what is needed in a solution.

The natural starting point is what is known as the Prisoners' Dilemma; but its significance and its connections are brought out better by one of the other variants of the story. Two soldiers, Tom and Dan, are manning two nearby strong-posts in an attempt to hold up an enemy advance. If both remain at their posts, they have a fairly good chance of holding off the enemy until relief arrives, and so of both surviving. If they both run away, the enemy will break through immediately, and the chance of either of them surviving is markedly less. But if one stays at his post while the other runs away, the one who runs will have an even better chance of survival than each will have if both remain, while the one who stays will have an even worse chance than each will have if they both run. Suppose that these facts are known to both men, and each calculates in a thoroughly rational way with a view simply to his own survival. Tom reasons: if Dan remains at his post, I shall have a better chance of surviving if I run than if I stay; but also if Dan runs away I shall have a better chance if I run than if I stay; so whatever Dan is going to do, I would be well advised to run. Since the situation is symmetrical, Dan's reasoning is exactly similar. So both will run. And yet they would have had a better chance of survival, that is, of achieving the very end they are, by hypothesis, aiming at, if both had remained at their posts.

At first sight this may seem to be a paradox; but in fact there is nothing paradoxical about it. Why should it be surprising if two men, making separate, uncoordinated choices of action, aimed, however rationally, at separate, private goals, should fail to achieve them, or that they would have a better chance of each achieving his private goal if only they could co-ordinate their choices of action? But how can they do this? The best result for each is that the other should somehow be induced to stay while he runs away; but since this is asymmetrical it could be achieved only by some kind of trickery or exploitation. The best symmetrical result, and therefore the best that could be achieved by any device which both could freely accept, is that both should stay. But how can this be achieved? What they need is something that will literally or metaphorically tie their actions together. If they both know that the only options open are that both should stay or both should run, then, calculating rationally but selfishly as before, both will stay. But what will serve to tie their actions together? Suppose that they make a bargain; each says 'I will remain at my post if you remain at yours.' But still, if they are rational egoists, each will have the same motive for breaking this agreement that he originally had for running away before there was an agreement. If each can see the other, and each knows that the other will know the moment he abandons his post, will this make him more likely to keep the agreement? It may, if Tom believes that Dan is more likely to break the agreement if he sees Tom breaking it, and more likely to keep it as long as he knows that Tom is keeping it, and vice versa; but as yet, on the assumptions so far introduced, neither has any reason to believe this.

On the other hand, it would be effective, and in the supposed situation rational, for both men to agree to be literally chained to their posts. It would be rational for each to accept this loss of his own freedom of choice provided that his comrade's freedom was similarly taken away. Almost equally effective would be some external discipline, if each knew that any man who ran away would be severely punished. But what is important for our purposes is that there can be psychological substitutes for physical chains and external penalties. Military traditions of honour and loyalty to comrades can serve as invisible chains. The stigma of cowardice, with the disgrace and shame associated with it, can be as effective as external penalties. Also, given the hypothetical situation, it is rational to prefer to be encumbered with these psychological fetters, provided that one's comrades are so too. If you have to fight, it is better, even from a purely selfish point of view, to be a member of a disciplined unit with good morale than a member of a rabble.

But it is also clear that if Tom and Dan have a general tradition of keeping agreements, they will be able to achieve much the same result. They will then be able to make a bargain that each will remain at his post, and the agreement-keeping tradition will then hold each man there. Moreover, since it is a bargain, each will feel bound to keep it only so long as the other does, and each will know that the other feels this; and then if each can see whether the other is remaining at his post, each will have a further motive for doing so himself, namely the knowledge that by remaining he encourages his comrade to remain. It is true that in practice a general agreement-keeping tradition is likely to be rather less effective, in situations of extreme danger (such as our hypothetical one) than more specialized military traditions of honour and loyalty; but it has the advantage of being more flexible; it can be applied to support the making and keeping of all sorts of useful bargains. Hume was quite right in saying that a man is the more useful, both to himself and to others, the greater degree of probity and honour he is endowed with.

The particular example we have used here to illustrate this form of two-person game has the advantage of being both dramatic and realistic, but it has the disadvantage that it does not lend itself to repeated trials by the same two players. Let us think of some other example, where even if Tom, say, comes off badly at the first trial he will still survive to play with Dan again. Let us assume that each man has only a weak agreement-keeping tendency, and that neither can see, on any one occasion, whether the other is keeping the bargain until he himself is committed either to keeping it or to breaking it. Let us make the further reasonable assumptions that if both men keep the agreement on one occasion, each is more likely to keep it next time, whereas if either or both men break the agreement on one occasion, each is less likely to keep it next time, that all these tendencies are known to both men, and that each time Tom and Dan play this game they know that they will have to play it again with one another. These assumptions alter the form of the game, and bring it about that if, on any one occasion, Dan is going to keep the agreement, it will be to Tom's selfish advantage, with a view to the future, to do so too, though if Dan is going to break the agreement this time, it will be to Tom's advantage also to break it. And of course the situation is still symmetrical. Self-interest no longer unambiguously urges each man to break the agreement on any one occasion: consequently only a fairly weak agreement-keeping tendency will be needed to tip the balance. Fairly obvious and natural assumptions lead to a similar conclusion if we extend the game in another direction as well, and assume that there are more than two players. It will be to each man's selfish advantage to keep the agreement if most of the others are going to keep it and to try to enforce it, though not if most of the others are going to break it. This is, of course; the pattern of relationships that Hobbes envisaged; again in any situation of this sort only a fairly weak agreement-keeping tendency is needed to tip the balance, because it does not have to overcome any clear, one-sided counsel of self-interest. But the balance still needs to be tipped; no rational calculation of self-interest alone will even now clearly direct each man to keep the agreement.

It would be irrelevant to our purpose to go far into the endless variety of types of situation that can be studied by the theory of games, but one complication at least must be mentioned. In our examples so far both the initial situations and the agreements considered have been symmetrical, but of course they need not be so. Even if Tom and Dan are initially placed alike, there may be several possible agreements between them, each of which is better for each man singly than the results of failure to agree or of failure to keep the agreement, but some of which are in various degrees more advantageous to Tom than to Dan, and vice versa. In these circumstances the man who is, or gives the appearance of being, the more reluctant to make, or to adhere to, an agreement is likely to get more advantageous terms. Though complete intransigence in either party is disastrous for both, incomplete relative intransigence is differentially advantageous to its possessor. This holds, as I have said, even if the initial situation is symmetrical; but if one party has less to lose by failure to agree, or less to gain from a stable agreement, further possibilities of unequal agreements arise. Rational bargaining can result in exploitation. Beneficial though the invisible chains of which we have spoken are, they may not be an unmixed blessing.

There can be no doubt that many real-life situations contain, as at least part of their causally relevant structure, patterns of relationship of which various simple 'games' are an illuminating description. An international arms race is one obvious example: another is the situation where inflation can be slowed down only if different trade unions can agree to limit their demands for wage increases. One merit of such simplified analyses is that they show dramatically how the combined outcome of several intentional actions, even of well-informed and rational agents, may be something that no one of the agents involved has intended or would intend. Even purely descriptive social sciences have as a large part of their subject matter, as Popper has neatly put it, the unintended effects of intentional actions. But from our point of view the game theory approach merely reinforces the lessons that we have extracted from the arguments of Protagoras, Hobbes, Hume, and Warnock. The main moral is the practical value of the notion of obligation, of an invisible and indeed fictitious tie or bond, whether this takes the form of a general requirement to keep whatever agreements one makes or of various specific duties like those of military honour or of loyalty to comrades or to an organization.

One moral that we might be inclined to draw from the game theory analyses is that prudence is not enough, that the rational calculation of long-term self-interest is not sufficient in itself to lead men to make mutually beneficial agreements or, once made, to keep them. But here some caution is needed. This is true of the particular 'games' we have described. But nothing in the game theory analyses rules out the possibility of what Hobbes suggests, agreement backed by a coercive device (the sovereign), where the motives of the sovereign himself, those who obey him, and those whose support constitutes his power, are exclusively prudential. It is indeed hard to see how such a construction could be brought into existence by the operation of selfish motives, however rationally directed; but it is not so hard to see how once in existence it could be maintained by such motives alone. The real weakness of the Hobbesian solution lies not in anything that the game theory models show, but in what, just by being models, they leave out. Real situations always incorporate, along with the skeletal structure of some fairly simple game, other forces and tendencies whose strength varies through time. The Hobbesian solution is, as I have said, like a house of cards – each bit is held up by others – and it is inflexible in the same way. A structure is more likely to be able to bend in response to changing forces without collapsing if it is held together by ties of which some are less conditional than those of prudence.

Notes

* From J.L. Mackie, *Ethics: Inventing Right and Wrong*, Penguin, 1977, pp.115–20.

'Science, Wonder and Lust of the Eyes'

John O'Neill

In his book *Ecology, Policy and Politics** O'Neill opposes two approaches to environmental decision making which he takes to be the dominant ones, on the one hand the position that holds that environmental problems can be accommodated within existing procedures of public decision making, one of whose main methods is cost benefit analysis. and on the other hand the 'deep green' approach popular with many environmental philosophers and green activists. He argues against the former that the standard economic assessment of environmental goods values them in the wrong way and against the latter that there is no incompatibility between a concern for human well-being and the recognition of, and care for, the intrinsic (non-instrumental) value of the non-human world. The Reading is part of the chapter in which he focuses on the way in which science and the arts contribute to well-being through the appreciation of the intrinsic value of the non-human world.

Science, value and human well-being

Why is science of value in itself? The standard answer refers to the intrinsic value of knowledge. But in what does the value of knowledge consist? One answer is that offered by Aristotle:

> In all natural things there is something wonderful. And just as Heraclitus is said to have spoken to his visitors, who were waiting to meet him but stopped as they were approaching when they saw him warming himself at the oven – he kept telling them to come in and not worry, 'for there are gods here too' – so we should approach the inquiry about each animal without aversion knowing that in all of them there is something natural and beautiful.[1]

The value of knowledge lies in the contemplation of that which is wonderful and beautiful. Such contemplation extends our own well-being since it realizes our characteristic human capacities. There is a relationship between our capacity to appreciate the value of the natural world and human well-being.

This Aristotelian position is developed further by Marx in his remarks on the 'humanization of the senses' in the *Economic and Philosophical Manuscripts.*[2] Both art and science humanize the senses in that they allow humans to respond to the *qualities* that objects possess. We respond in a disinterested fashion – and it is a characteristic feature of humans that they can thus respond to objects. In contrast, our senses are dehumanized when we respond to objects only as items that satisfy narrowly conceived interests:

> *Sense* which is a prisoner of crude practical need has only a *restricted* sense. For a man who is starving the human form of food does not exist, only its abstract form exists; it could just as well be present in its crudest form, and it would be hard to say how this way of eating differs from that of *animals.* The man who is burdened with worries and needs has no *sense* for the finest of plays; the dealer in minerals sees only the commercial value, and not the beauty and peculiar nature of the minerals; he lacks a mineralogical sense; thus the objectification of the human essence, in a theoretical as well as a practical respect, is necessary both in order to make man's *senses human* and to create an appropriate *human sense* for the whole of the wealth of humanity and nature.[3]

Those who can respond to objects only in terms of how far they impinge on narrowly utilitarian or commercial interests fail to develop their specifically human capacities of perception. The farmer who sees the world simply in terms of production yields sees not a rat, a kestrel or a wolf but different kinds of vermin. He sees not a plant with its specific properties and qualities, but a weed. The developer sees not a wood or forest, but an obstacle to a highway. She sees not a landscape or a habitat, but space for buildings. Hence Leopold's contrast: 'The swoop of the hawk... is perceived by one as the drama of evolution. To another it is only a threat to a full frying pan.'[4] A person driven by narrowly utilitarian and commercial interests responds not to the, 'beauty and peculiar nature' of objects, to 'the whole wealth of... nature' but to the world as an object for the satisfaction of a narrow range of interests.

On this interpretation, Marx's remarks on the humanization of the senses parallel his comments on production. Humans, he argues, are distinguished by being able to produce free from needs:

> [Animals] produce only when immediate physical need compels them to do so, while man produces even when he is free of such need ... Animals produce only

according to the standards and needs of the species to which they belong, while man is capable of producing according to the standards of every species and applying to each object its inherent standard; hence man also produces in accordance with the laws of beauty.[5]

Capitalism dehumanizes in that one produces under compulsion. Our activity is not an end in itself, but a means to another end. Similar remarks might apply to perception. Where other animals can see only in terms of the satisfaction of their own needs, humans are able to perceive in a disinterested fashion. They can respond to the qualities of the objects, freed from the compulsion of need. They exhibit this capacity in science and aesthetic contemplation. Just as capitalism dehumanizes in production, so it also dehumanizes in perception – for it does not allow the individual to develop and exercise this specifically *human* capacity to respond to the world. Communism on this account humanizes the senses just as it *humanizes* productive capacities. That is, it allows us to develop our characteristically human capacities to see.

The Marx that emerges on this interpretation is far more open to the virtues of the contemplative life, far less focused on productive activities as such. He is much more Aristotelian in his account of the good life.[6] Whatever the truth or falsity of this view as an interpretation of Marx – and I think there are difficulties with it – it has considerable merit as a position in its own right. A response to the objects of the non-human world for their own qualities forms part of a life in which human capacities are developed. It is a component of human well-being.

It is in these terms that the specific virtues produced by certain forms of scientific education can be understood. Scientific education involves not simply the apprehension of a set of facts, but also the development of particular intellectual skills and virtues, and capacities of perception. The trained ecologist, be she amateur or professional, is able to see, hear and even smell in a way that a person who lacks such training cannot. The senses are opened to the objects around them. A scientific education can allow the observer to see what is there and to respond to it in a disinterested way. At *this* level, at the level of the development of human capacities, there is a relationship between a scientific training and ethical values. A scientific training *can* issue not only in the traditional intellectual excellencies – in the capacity to distinguish good from bad arguments, a willingness to subject work to the critical scrutiny of others and so on – but also in the capacity to perceive and feel wonder at the natural world. For that reason the ecologist may be able to make not merely good judgements about the make-up of different ecosystems, but also good judgements about their *value*. At the level of the development of habits and capacities there is a relation between science and value. The practice of science develops not just intellectual virtues but also ethical virtues. It is through the sciences, the arts and kindred practices that an appreciation of the intrinsic value of the natural world is developed. It gives grounds for accepting the authoritative status of *some* evaluative claims made by the practising ecologist.

The lust of the eyes

The virtues developed by the sciences and the arts can be better understood if contrasted with a vice. [Elsewhere] I [have] suggested that to take knowledge to be above and independent of other goods involves a failure to recognize what is good about knowledge. The 'humanization of the senses' involves the growth in the capacity for contemplation of objects free from the compulsion of need. One is able to display a disinterested openness to the object – to discover and perceive *its* properties, its 'beauty and peculiar qualities'. It is for this reason that the theoretical practices of science and art have value and a special place in the relation of humans to the natural world.

This relationship of knowledge and object can however be inverted. Knowledge may not issue in a disinterested openness to the object, but rather an object is sought to satisfy the desire to know. Consider the following infamous passage from Claude Bernard:

> The physiologist ... is a man of science, absorbed by the scientific idea which he pursues: he no longer hears the cry of animals, he no longer sees the blood that flows, he sees only his idea and perceives only organisms concealing problems which he intends to solve.[7]

The problem here is not simply Bernard's insensitivity to the *pain* he causes the animal, but his insensitivity *per se*. Consider the following passage from John Fowles:

> I came on my first Military orchid, a species I had long wanted to encounter but hitherto had never seen outside a book. I fell on my knees, before it in a way that all botanists will know. I identified, to be quite certain, with Professors Clapham, Tutin, and Warburg in hand (the standard British *Flora*), I measured, I photographed, I worked out where I was on the map, for future reference. I was excited, very happy, one always remembers one's 'first' of rarer species. Yet five minutes after my wife had finally ... torn me away, I suffered a strange feeling. I realized I had not actually *seen* the three plants in the little colony we had found.[8]

A significant feature of Bernard's and Fowles's accounts of their scientific encounters with the natural world lies in the way that they are characterized in terms of blindness and deafness. Bernard does not see the blood or hear the screams; Fowles comes away with the realization that he has not seen the orchid. Both have a similar view of the goals of science. What moves the scientist for Bernard is the problems for which the organism provides the solution. The organism has value only as a means to the satisfaction of the scientist's curiosity. Fowles similarly characterizes his early interest in natural history in these terms:

> I spent all my younger life as a more or less orthodox amateur naturalist...
> treating nature as some sort of intellectual puzzle, or game, in which to name
> names and explain behaviours... constituted all the pleasures and the prizes.[9]

Organisms become merely means to satisfy the scientist's curiosity – the pleasures of curiosity become the end. For Bernard, this occurs in the course of a celebration of science, for Fowles of a critique. Thus for Fowles, both science and art are just other ways in which nature is reduced to a means to satisfy human interests.

Science, as described by Bernard and Fowles, exhibits and develops not virtues but a vice, a vice to which Augustine refers in the *confessions* by the memorable phrase 'the lust of the eyes'. Augustine characterizes it thus:

> A certain vain desire and curiosity, not of taking delights in the body, but of
> making experiment with the body's aid, and cloaked under the name of learning
> and knowledge. Because this is the appetite to know, and the eyes are the chief
> of the senses we use for attaining knowledge, it is called in Scripture the lust of
> the eyes.[10]

Where the lust of the flesh goes after the beautiful, the lust of the eyes involves 'curiosity for the sake of experiment [which] can go after quite contrary things... through a pure itch to experience and find out'.[11] It is exhibited, says Augustine, in the freak show and the desire to see a mangled corpse.[12] In the modern world tourism often provides it with its occasion: an American tourist in Tibet remarked to me after returning from the spectacle of a 'sky burial' – in which the dead are cut up and fed to vultures – that what he really wanted to see now was a public execution. The same phenomenon is revealed in a more polite form in the scientist as described by Bernard and Fowles.

What is wrong with the 'lust of the eyes'? At one level, it displays an absence of the virtues of temperance and practical wisdom in their classical senses. The term 'lust' is appropriate: the person thus affected pursues one good – knowledge – unrestrained by other goods. The consequence can be a quite self-regarding vice – an obsessiveness exhibited for example by Weizenbaum's 'compulsive programmer'[13] whose life is spent in solitude before a computer terminal and who gives up other goods – those of human companionship. It is also, however, often other-regarding – witness vivisection described by Shaw.[14] The lack of limits described by Shaw is at this level a symptom of intemperance. However, it also involves the failure to understand the proper relation of pleasures and their object, and relatedly of the value of knowledge. Augustine's parallel between the lust of the eyes and the lust of the flesh is, in this regard, an illuminating one.

Consider the latter. To see a friend or lover merely as a means to pleasure – sensual or non-sensual – is not to love or befriend at all. It fails to appreciate the goods of friendship and love. We do not befriend and love another merely for the pleasure it brings us. Both friendship and love involve concern for others for their own sake. Pleasure supervenes on a happy relation with the other person. For example, we take pleasure from helping friends, we do not help friends to get pleasure.

Correspondingly, the real nature of the object of the relationship matters: a surrogate will not do. The person whose relation to others is driven by 'the lust of the flesh', for whom the psychological state of pleasure in itself was the object of desire, has not understood the value of his relations with others. The value of the relation to others would be purely instrumental, and the specific nature of the object, indeed its reality, would not matter.[15] Similar points apply to knowledge: it involves a 'lust of the eyes' to see an object merely as a means to rid oneself of the itch of curiosity – to gain the 'pleasures' of knowing. Such an instrumental attitude indicates a failure to understand what is valuable about knowledge. We know in order to be able to see and appreciate 'the beauty and peculiar qualities' of the object. One does not seek knowledge of objects to get pleasure, one gets pleasure in knowing about them.

It is in these terms, also, that we are able to understand the limits that the pursuit of knowledge itself imposes on the means to and objects of knowledge, and to grasp the nature of the mistake to which Shaw draws attention. A proper understanding of the goods of scientific knowledge imposes limits on the *means* to discovery. An ecologist who was willing to destroy an environment to know about it, who saw nothing but land that 'conceals from him the problem he is seeking to solve', would not have understood the goods of knowledge.[16] If knowledge is sought because it yields appreciation of the object, then means of discovery which destroy that which is of value or render one blind to its qualities are ruled out. One must sometimes be content with a mystery. There are internal limits to what one will do in order to know.

Likewise, there are limits to what forms an object of knowledge. One does not simply seek objects in order to know. Knowledge is driven by the desire to understand the object. It recognizes a difference between those qualities and objects that form important and significant subjects of knowledge and those that do not. The taste of boiled baby, to use Shaw's macabre example, would not form a significant object of knowledge. A child's capacity to learn and develop would.

Notes

* From John O'Neill, *Ecology and Politics: Human Well-being and the Natural World*, Routledge, 1993, pp.159–65.

[1] Aristotle (1972 edn) *De Partibus Animalium I*, D. Balme (trans.), Clarendon Press, Book 1 Chapter 5, 645a 16ff.

[2] Marx's early work can be given an ecologically benign reading in these terms but I am not sure how far such a benign reading can be sustained...

[3] Marx (1844) *Economic and Philosophical Manuscripts*, in *Early Writings*, L. Colletti (ed.), Penguin, 1974.

[4] Leopold, A. (1989) *A Sand County Almanac*, Oxford University Press, p.173. Hence his claim that 'recreational development is a job not of building roads into lovely country, but of building receptivity into the still unlovely human mind' (ibid., p.177): one could then see what is wonderful in 'the weed in the city lot' as well as in the large redwood.

[5] Marx, op. cit., p.329. For criticism of Marx's claims about animals, see Benton, T. (1988) 'Humanism = speciesism: Marx on Humans and Animals', *Radical Philosophy*, 50, 4–18.

[6] Marx's position has other Aristotelian features, in particular with respect to leisure, *schole*. Generally, persons can live a fully human life only if they have some part of their life free of necessity (see Aristotle (1985) *Nicomachean Ethics*, T. Irwin (trans.), Hackett, 1177b 4ff.; (1948) *Politics*, E. Barker (trans.), Oxford University Press, 1333a 30ff., 1334a 11ff.), a point that Marx famously makes in *Capital* vol. III (Marx (1972) *Capital*, vol. III, Lawrence & Wishart, p.820). It is only that one has the luxury of being able to contemplate in a disinterested fashion.

[7] Bernard, C. (1957) *Introduction to the Study of Experimental Medicine*, H. Green (trans.), Dover, p.103.

[8] Fowles, J. (1979) 'Seeing nature whole', *Harper's Magazine*, 259, p.61.

[9] Ibid., p.51.

[10] Augustine (1944) *Confessions*, F. Sheed (trans.), Sheed & Ward, p.197. For a recent discussion of Augustine's theme, see Clarke, S. (1990) *A Parliament of Souls*, Clarendon Press, pp.96–102.

[11] Augustine, op. cit., p.198.

[12] Compare Plato (1974) *The Republic*, D. Lee (trans.), Penguin, Book IV, 439–40, in which Plato employs the example of the desire o look upon corpses to illustrate desires in a state of disorder and the role of *thumos*, spirit, in taking the side of reason to bring order to them.

[13] Weizenbaum, J. (1976) *Computer Power and Human Reason*, Freeman, Chapter 4.

[14] [The quotation from Shaw that O'Neill refers to is: 'The vivisector-scoundrel has no limits... No matter how much he knows there is always, as Newton confessed, an infinitude of things still unknown, many of them still discoverable by experiment. When he has discovered what boiled baby tastes like, and what effect it has on the digestion, he has still to ascertain the gustatory and metabolic peculiarities of roast baby and fried baby, with, in each case, the exact age at which the baby should, to produce such and such results, be boiled, roast, fried, or fricasseed.' (G.B. Shaw (1927) reply to H.G. Wells, *The Sunday Express*, August; reprinted in J. Wynne-Tyson (ed.) (1990) *The Extended Circle*, Sphere.)]

[15] See Lodge, D. (1984) *Small World*, Penguin, pp.324–6.

[16] Consider, for example, the Spartina archipelago experiments in which, to test the MacArthur–Wilson equilibrium theory of insular biogeography six islands were 'defaunated... with methyl bromide gas' (Rey, J. (1984) 'Experimental tests of island biogeographic theory', in D. Strong, D. Simberloff, L. Abele and A. Thistle (eds) *Ecological Communities: Conceptual Issues and Evidence*, Princeton University Press, p.102).

'Neither Use nor Ornament: a Consumers' Guide to Care'

Jane Howarth

Jane Howarth discusses* the contrast between valuing things for the use we can make of them and valuing them for themselves. She describes the cherishing of special things as an example of the latter and draws an analogy between cherishing, and the concept of care used by the phenomenologist Martin Heidegger to characterize a basic human relationship to the non–human world. Phenomenology is a method of philosophical investigation. It aims to describe the 'lived-world' – the world as we act in it prior to any theorising about it. A central thesis of phenomenology is that subjects and objects are essentially inter–related. In exploring 'value' – or, to emphasize the relatedness, 'valuing' – phenomenologically, one should look for the activities (of the subject) involved in valuing and the features (of the object) which valuing brings to light.

Introduction

There has been much debate about whether the environment has intrinsic or instrumental value, value in itself or value as a means to our, and possibly other creatures', ends. There is further debate about whether a proper respect for the environment requires that we recognize that it has intrinsic value or worth. There is also debate on the meta-level about whether the intrinsic value of something depends upon, or is independent of, our interests. Those debates are not ones with which I shall explicitly engage.

What I shall look at is human-centred values. There are commonly thought to be two kinds of these: instrumental and non-instrumental. Things with instrumental value include consumables, raw materials and, literally, instruments, equipment, whether natural or artefactual. Such things serve as means to our ends, they serve our purposes, we use them to satisfy our wants or needs. This class includes luxuries of the kind we consume or use, such as quail's eggs or dish-washers which we consume or use but do not need. Things with non-instrumental value are things in which we have an interest, but which we do not *use*. We rather enjoy having them around, we contemplate them, they have value for us because of the way they are, the specific properties they have, we value them 'for themselves'.

If an object has instrumental value, its value does not depend upon its specific categorical properties but rather upon its disposition or capacity to fulfil a function or serve a purpose. Anything which serves the purpose equally well will have the same value, can replace the original without loss of value. So, if the instrumental value of an oak tree is to provide shelter from the rain, then a bus shelter may serve equally well, different though its actual properties are. Similarly, the heavy, blunt weapon or the light hand gun, arsenic or a landmine, different though they are in themselves, may serve equally well as instruments of death.

The crucial feature of non-instrumental value, in contrast, is that the object has value because of the specific properties it has. A change to those properties would affect, or at least require a re-assessment of, its value. To value an oak tree for what it is or to recognize its non-instrumental value is to recognize that replacement by a horse chestnut or a bus shelter, would involve a loss of value, though it might, if the replacement had value, also involve a gain.

Instrumental value, then, is a disposition. It depends upon the thing's actual properties, but alternatives are possible. Non-instrumental value, in contrast, depends more closely on the actual properties of the thing. It follows from this, and we can take this as a criterion of instrumental value that something with only this sort of value is, in principle, replaceable, without loss of value, by a qualitatively different thing. The criterion of non-instrumental value, in contrast, is that the object with such value is not replaceable, except perhaps by something exactly similar.

It is, of course, possible that an instrument or consumable may be so specifically geared to its particular use, that there is in fact no adequate replacement. For certain purposes, the surgeon's scalpel or Parmesan cheese may fall into that category. Equally, it seems possible that something valued for itself, for the way it is, is so common that replacement by exactly similar ones is very easy. There are an awful lot of near identical mass produced ornaments, or red roses, hence one can order a dozen by phone. It would be neurotic or irrational to find deciding between numerically different ones a problem once one had decided that they were exactly similar. One might have difficulty in ensuring that they *were* exactly similar; but, once that decision is made, which one to prefer or purchase is not a sensible issue. If two or more things appear just the same, how could their ornamental values differ?

Clearly this is not straightforwardly a distinction between *kinds* of objects. It is rather a distinction between two kinds of ways of valuing or appreciating something. One can value a picture purely as a doorstop, or an investment, a river purely as a source of fish. Alternatively, one can appreciate an instrument, a spinning wheel or grand piano, purely as an object of contemplation, a fashionable ornament.

Part 1

If different ways in which we value objects are distinguished with reference to conditions of replaceability, then clearly there is a third kind of human-centred value. This is where things are valued, but are not replaceable at all. Such things are not replaceable without loss of value even by exactly similar things, 'dead ringers': and this is not because there happen to be no dead ringers, but because, even if there were, they would not be valued.

If this seems odd, look at examples. In Chapter 7 of *Environmental Ethics*,[1] Des Jardins gives the example of a shopkeeper who has kept the first dollar bill he ever took in his shop. He would not, Des Jardins says, accept two fifty-cent coins in exchange. My point, however, is that he would not accept another dollar bill in exchange. Even if the dollar bills were completely indistinguishable, bore exactly the same marks of wear and tear, it is the original one which he values. He will not, of course, be able to detect the difference. Suppose he were offered two bills side by side, one of which was the original, and asked which one he valued more. He cannot pick the valued one out; but he can 'tell' the difference between them, *say* what it is: he values the one, whichever it is, which he has kept all these years. Someone could effect the switch without his knowledge, but that would be to impose a loss upon him, and the loss does not lie only in the deception. Like infidelity, the deception is an additional injury. Whether the shopkeeper knows or not, he has lost his treasured first dollar bill. This we might call 'cherishing' or 'treasuring' things: they have 'sentimental' value.

Such value can attach either to instruments or to non-instruments. Consider a chef's favourite knife, a cricketer's bat, a musician's 'cello. Cherished things with non-instrumental value might include one's childhood teddy bear, one's wedding ring, gifts, souvenirs, one's own paintings. A replica is an extremely inadequate replacement. All these are artefacts. So, a replica could be produced. If, and this is precisely the case I am considering, it really was a dead ringer, signs of wear and tear included, even the cherisher could not tell the difference, could be fooled into thinking the replacement was the original one. It seems clear, that to trick someone in this way is to impose a loss upon them. If they discovered the switch, they would surely feel a loss; and the loss lies not in the discovery, but in the substitution.

In what does this irreplaceability of cherished objects consist? There is characteristic behaviour: objects which one cherishes one takes care of, uses with care, regrets their destruction, etc. But cherishing cannot be characterized in terms of behaviour. One would, if one did not know, treat the dead ringer in just the same way, and one might treat non-cherished objects in that way.

The difference between the cherished object and the dead ringer lies in the past interactions between the cherishing subject and the object. All the cases I have considered involve essentially the past, one *comes* to cherish, to value, such things. That one cherishes and what one cherishes is a significant fact about one: it would, or should, get into one's autobiography. Cherished objects often come to show signs of one's interactions with them. The torn ear on the teddy bear, the thinning of the knife-blade from countless sharpenings, the moulding of the handle resulting from the frequent grasping by a particular hand. Those marks of wear on one's own treasured possessions were made by oneself over the years. These features are implicit in one's valuing the thing, they make up what the thing means to one. Actual physical marks are not necessary: the thing still has special significance because of those past interactions. Of course any actual marks could be replicated, though the cherishing subject might be harder to fool than the replicators can cater for. However, when they are replicated, the signs of wear are no longer signs of that subject's past interactions with the object. They might put one in mind of those interactions; but the replica object is not the object one has in mind.

What gives these things their specific value for a subject is past interactions between the subject and the object. Hence, in order to understand the value the thing has, why it is irreplaceable, one needs to understand how it came to be valued.

I have introduced the notion of cherishing via examples which I trust are not contentious, that is, it is uncontentious that there are cases of the kind I have described. Cherishing, I have claimed, has three aspects: what one cherishes, one takes care of; what one cherishes is irreplaceable; and there is a history of past interactions with the cherished object.

It looks as if cherishing is too rare a human practice to be of much significance for environmental philosophy. Attachments to cherished objects are very particular ones, and there are not very many of them. It is hard to see how this unusual sort of case can have any serious implications for how we are to care for the planet, though the planet is, as far as we know, irreplaceable and we all have past interactions with it or some parts of it. Furthermore, this kind of valuing looks unpromising environmentally. Such working attachment, for example, to the land may be a feature of certain cultures – bio-regionalism may be based on it; but, since such attachment tends to exclude others from one's land, it seems clear that there is not now enough land for everyone to be attached to it in that way. Cherishing would seem to involve the need for close interaction with the environment. But that is likely to have an adverse effect on the environment, certainly it would be bad news for wilderness.

I have focused on cherishing not in order to recommend wholesale destruction of wilderness: but to throw light on *a*, possibly *the*, fundamental notion in phenomenology, the interrelatedness of subjects and objects in the lived-world.[2] This, I believe, does have significance for environmental philosophy. In Heidegger's work, this is the notion of Care.[3] Heidegger believed that Care, which I hope to show has points in common with cherishing, is our fundamental relation with, among other things, our environment. One point it might seem not to share with cherishing is the element of anxiety. However, while anxiety is not part of the meaning of cherishing, it does naturally attend it: we are anxious that what we cherish should not be threatened, lost or destroyed.

I am not aiming to do full justice to Heidegger's notion of Care. In this section, I shall indicate links between it and other fundamental notions in Heidegger's philosophy. The rest of my paper will seek some measure of fairly free interpretation of Heidegger's notion and an application of it to the concepts of instrumental and non-instrumental value.

One difference between cherishing and Heidegger's notion of Care is that Care is much more widespread. It is, according to Heidegger, present in all our dealings with the world of objects; though it is 'covered up' by modern life and modern philosophy. The proper task of philosophy, according to Heidegger, is to uncover it. It is also clear that Heidegger thought it an ill of modern life that it covers up Care. So the scope of application of Care and cherishing are different: but, I believe, the concepts have similarities. Indeed, it may be that such cherishing as occurs in modern life is the precise point at which, Heidegger would claim, Care is not covered up.

What similarities are there between cherishing and Care? All three elements of cherishing are present in Heidegger's notion of Care. First, the behavioural element is surely there: the practical consequence of uncovering Care would be that we would *take* care of things. Second, what we cherish is irreplaceable, one cherishes the particular object. Appreciation of the irreplaceability, the particularity, of things is, I believe, part of what Heidegger means by Care, part of what is largely covered up by modern life. He recommends that we should 'let things show themselves'. One thing which would be revealed would be that all things that 'show' themselves are in fact particular things: that is the character of the world and of our ways of encountering it. This is part of what Heidegger meant when he bemoaned our loss of Being behind meaning. We have lost sight of the particularity of things, we concentrate on the *kinds* of things they are and not on the particular things they are.

A related feature which Heidegger believes would be 'revealed' would be the raw materials out of which things are made. Regarded as raw materials, the objects we consume, use or contemplate are not so obviously replaceable. In some sense, everything, regarded as raw material, is irreplaceable: once you've burnt that particular shovel full of coal, that's it; you cannot burn *it* again, you have to find some other particular pieces of coal. In this, perhaps peculiar, sense, everything is irreplaceable. We can replace it with some more of the same which will suit our needs equally well, but once that particular hunk of raw material is used up, *it* cannot be replaced. We regard *things* as replaceable because we are interested in their role in satisfying our needs. But, *in themselves*, though they can be replaced by other things, they cannot, once used up, literally be put back in place.

The third common feature of cherishing and Care is that, just as cherishing involves past interactions, so does Care. These are covered up; but they are still implicit in our ability to operate in the world. Heidegger holds that our way of being is Dasein, or 'being there'. We are 'thrown' into our place in the world and we become as we are because of where we are. Our skills and our perceptions are moulded by our environment. We are an 'openness' to the world, and it should be a source of wonder that the world is amenable to our perceiving, it is significant to us and we have learnt to act in it. We become the subjects we are and objects have the significance they have because of our past encounters with the world in which we live.

According to Heidegger, if we were to recognize these two features of our encounters with the world: their particular character and their history, then we would take care of the world, be mindful of it, mind it in the sense of looking after it, as we do with objects we cherish.

Of course, there is a difference between cherishing and Care. It is part of our adaptability that we do not need to stick with any given set of particular objects. That is a crucial difference between cherishing and Care. I am not claiming that we need to cherish everything in my original sense. What I am claiming is that we might look at how we value things and how we come to value things with a view to revealing how we fundamentally relate to our environment and how this is covered up, how this cover up involves both our losing sight of the true significance of objects and our becoming alienated subjects, and how the cover up maybe exacerbates the environmental crisis.

Part 2

How does modern life cover up Care? Heidegger could find some measure of support for his claim from familiar criticisms of modern Western society. The criticism, rightly or wrongly, is that it is a society of mass consumption and selfish individualism. Cherishing is bad for business! This would certainly support the claim that modern society *lacks* Care. It leaves it open as to whether Care is absent or merely covered up. Many would want to draw a more radical contrast than would Heidegger between our careless culture and more mindful ones in which caring for the environment is or was the norm.

Leaving aside that issue for the moment, there would seem to be some plausibility to the claim that Care is not an obvious feature of modern culture.

Perhaps the most obvious place where Care is covered up or absent is in our culture's favoured decision-making procedure: cost benefit analysis. The underlying principle is that the correct policy to pursue is the one which has the greatest balance of benefits over costs. In order to assess which one that is, all benefits and costs need to be presented in numerical, strictly monetary, terms. Many attacks have been made on this way of determining policy. In an environmental context, the challenge is that there is no clear way of presenting environmental damage as a cost compared with the obvious financial benefit of, for example, developing a shopping complex. Further, it is argued that, even if environmental costs could be precisely measured, it is unlikely that they would often win the day. In this context, the criticism is of the underlying assumption that everything is replaceable, specifically, saleable, all things have their price. But what one cares for or cherishes is not of that sort. Modern society recognizes that some areas of life are not amenable to this kind of analysis: even the staunchest proponent of cost benefit analysis would not, undisguisedly at least, invite people to evaluate their grandmothers in this way. However, the natural world, the only one we have, the only one which makes sense to us and where our lives make sense is regarded as being adequately represented in financial terms.

Phenomenology claims, not only that modern life, but that modern philosophy 'covers up' Care. Very briefly, the phenomenological critique of orthodox philosophy is that philosophers, at least since Descartes and Locke, have accepted from physics a world of objects defined in terms of their primary, measurable, qualities and having powers to produce perceptual effects on conscious subjects. Subjects are rational and conscious individuals, and are logically distinct from objects. This ontology invites the question whether value is in the object or in the subject. It also invites the answer that, if values are in the object, they are so only in a peculiar, unreal non-primary way, as tertiary properties or 'projections' of subjects. Values are hence thought to originate in subjects.

The phenomenological critique would claim that this is the wrong question to ask about values. The modern world view essentially problematizes values, raises about them questions which are unanswerable because they presuppose a framework which, from the beginning, has no proper place for values. The subject and the object are defined in a particular way, independent of each other, this rules out of court the very area of enquiry which, according to phenomenology, is the area where values arise: the essential relationships, interactions, between subjects and objects.

The phenomenological enterprise is, then, to uncover and explore activities, in this context, the activity of valuing, which is held, in Heidegger's case, to underlie or be involved in all other interactions between us and the world. Such an enquiry will provide the basis of, rather than being dependent upon, an account of what subjects and objects 'really' are.

Part 3

In the case of values, then, phenomenology recommends that we should look first at the activity of valuing, rather than at the object and the subject to ask where value lies. It also holds that the character of the subject and of the object is dependent on the activity of valuing, not prior to it. What is involved in valuing something as an instrument? In the typical case, and phenomenology recommends that we proceed from the typical case, this will involve actually using the object, or at least being able to use it, to satisfy one's aims, ends, purposes. What is involved in using something as an instrument? Crucially, one must have the appropriate skills or habits. These skills have to be learnt, the habits acquired. So, using an instrument essentially has a past. And this past makes us the particular subjects we are and gives objects their significance, they call forth our skills and habits.

This, it seems, though, is not the whole story about valuing. Not all useful things are valued in any ordinary sense of value. Ask the average restaurant diner if they value their knife. The response will likely be: well it's nice to have something to cut the food with but what's so special about this knife? Compare that with the lone explorer, or the master chef. They clearly value their knives in a way which goes beyond just using them.

To value consumables or raw materials involves not just using them, but using them well, making good use of them, using them economically, sparingly, not wasting them. To value instruments involves not just using them but using them skilfully, for the purpose for which they are intended, taking care of them, using them carefully, treating them well, not destructively, mindlessly or brutally. It involves a willingness to learn to use them properly, so as to get the best out of them, not to break them. To overload the washing machine, neglect to service the car, or kick the television, indicates a lack of valuing these instruments.

We also have notions of good and bad habits of use. We admire in others and take pride in ourselves when we use things well. We admire, not only skilful human subjects, but animals for their efficiency, adaptedness, economy of movement.

Similarly for contemplation. The contemplating subject has to learn skills of contemplating nature. These are of two sorts. First, one has to learn to notice what is there to be seen. These may be a matter of 'scientific' distinctions or aesthetic ones. Contemplation involves appreciating detail: but also appreciating drama. Also, typically, one needs to learn to negotiate one's way through the natural environment, or even learn survival skills in a harsh environment in order to be able to appreciate it.

But such activities are not the whole of valuing what we contemplate. We have all seen the thirteen-year-old child staring in blank apathy at the scene which so entrances its parents, kicking the ground and wondering what the point of it all is. It is, in a sense, contemplating; but not valuing.

To value what one contemplates is not just to contemplate it. There is, I want to claim, such a thing as contemplating well. This involves bringing knowledge, skills of observation, discrimination, sensitivity to what one contemplates and is a richer experience for that. One aspect of contemplating nature well would involve awareness that what one contemplates has a past, and awareness of that past is a vital factor in one's contemplation. The age of the sea, the cliffs, the rocks, the trees, impinge on one's awareness of them, are an essential part of that awareness. Much of nature is redolent with its past, it has a certain significance. The phenomenological thesis is that these significances are not over and above the primary and secondary qualities, but are what we notice first, a necessary condition of the world being a world of objects for us, making sense to us. They are what the scientist abstracts from, not what the aesthete projects onto the world.

Just as it is argued that the age of a work of art, the culture in which it was created, matters, forms an essential part of one's appreciation of it, and constitutes what the work is, so, the phenomenologist would argue, for the natural world. It is first and foremost our home, it makes sense to us and our lives make sense in it. These significances are an essential part of what we contemplate, what our interest is in having such a world to contemplate. There is a vast difference between contemplating nature as nature and contemplating it as made. A mined and restored landscape, like the dead ringer of the cherished object, is a fake. One may not be able to detect the difference but the way one is contemplating it is wrong, one is misled by the signs of age. One is not contemplating the thing one is perceiving.

So, just as valuing instruments involves using them well, so valuing objects of contemplation involves contemplating them well.

Does this conform with Heidegger's notion of Care? Care involves not just certain sorts of behaviour, taking care, but also it allows the thing to show itself, and it involves past interactions between the subject and the thing which contribute to making the subject what it is.

In the case of valuing instruments, does using well allow the thing to show itself? There are two ways in which one might think that it does. To use an instrument skilfully is to reveal what that instrument can do, what it is good for, what it was intended for, its fittedness for use. Second, and this obviously relates to Heidegger's emphasis on raw materials, using many instruments well involves respecting the character of the raw materials out of which they are made. Driving well involves respecting the limitations of the car, as well as displaying its capacities, both as the machine it is, and as made of metal parts liable to overheat, fracture etc.

Using well also has a past. One must have acquired the appropriate skills and habits. And skills and habits of using well are extra to just being able to use somehow or other. The craftsman must learn to respect his or her raw materials, know their capacities and develop skills of working with them. In the experienced craftsman, this is, as we say, 'second nature'. The craftsman gets a 'feel' for the wood. It goes against the grain, of both wood and craftsman, to work it badly. Skills are, in Merleau-Ponty's terms, 'sedimented' in the body. Misuse of tools or raw materials just is not a possibility, and not just because of pride in performance, but because the inexpert, clumsy habits have gone, they are no longer part of the subject's repertoire. Further, one is the particular subject one is because of those skills and habits. They are sedimented in one. In certain situations, they are activated, one just acts.

Contemplation also is surely very much to do with letting the thing show itself, getting to the heart of it. Literature and art seek to do this, even if writers and artists disagree about what the heart is. Even Petrarch, who, notoriously, stopped himself from contemplating nature, did so because he had the Platonic notion that the actual world was a distraction from contemplating ideal reality. The goal of contemplation is the true nature, the significance, of what is contemplated. This, again, is what is wrong with mining and restoring a tract of land to look just the same as it originally did. One who contemplates it, bringing to it the belief that it is untouched nature, is deceived, for it is not.

As to the subject, clearly there are skills and habits of contemplation. These clearly serve to constitute the subject, and the need to be acquired in the presence of the sort of thing contemplated. A skilled observer of nature must have a history of observing nature. He or she must have acquired knowledge and sensitivity.

So, we do have a notion of valuing which is comparable to Heidegger's notion of Care. Value resides not in the object nor in the subject but in interactions between them in which the objects show their significance and the subjects can exercise their abilities, realize their dispositions, be or become themselves.

Postscript

I have discussed only human-centred value, how we value things as objects to use or to contemplate. I have suggested that this might have implications for how we treat or ought to treat our natural environment. But these are surely not the only ways in which we value nature. The true aims of nature preservation or conservation are not *just* to ensure that nature is there for our future use of contemplation; they involve a deeper respect for nature as it is and not merely how it seems to us in the light of our interests. This deeper respect, it might be thought, can have no possible phenomenological basis, since it goes against the central tenet of phenomenology: the essential relatedness of human subjects and the world of objects. Phenomenology can speak only of objects as they show themselves to us and not as they really are; but only by respecting nature as it really is will we be able to come to relate to it properly.

The charge deserves fuller treatment than I can give it here. However, it does seem to me to be misguided. One thing phenomenology teaches us is that how nature shows itself to us is just that: how it shows itself to *us*. We have a point of view on the world but it is just our viewpoint. This might be taken as grounds for humility in contrast with the seemingly more arrogant claim to know what nature is *really* like.

Second, one important way in which nature shows itself to us, if we allow it to, is as being independent of us, as having a life of its own, as having its own way to go, what Merleau-Ponty called its 'aseity'. How nature shows itself in this way would need to be explored in more detail: but *one* way is in its capacity, especially over time, to surprise us. Anything which has this sort of independence is surely a candidate for respect and also for disrespect or violation. Again, what would count as respect and what violation would need detailed work to determine. It may be that we have rather stronger 'intuitions' about examples of disrespect: wanton destruction of life, pollution of habitats. The task of phenomenology would, then, be to tease out what it is about these examples which makes them examples of disrespect for nature. We might thereby come to a fuller account of what respecting nature, valuing it as recognizably independent of us, involves.

Phenomenological method does not preclude the acknowledgement and exploration of characteristics and values which are independent of us. What it does require is that these characteristics and values show themselves to us in some way. In defence of that stance, it is hard to see how any practicable recommendations as to how we should act could follow from the existence of value, in nature or elsewhere, which was undetectable by us.

Notes

* From Jane Howarth, 'Neither use nor ornament: a consumers' guide to Care', Thingmount Working Paper 96–05, Department of Philosophy, University of Lancaster, 1996.

[1] Joseph R. Des Jardins, *Environmental Ethics: An Introduction to Environmental Philosophy*, Wadsworth Publishing Co., 1992.

[2] The notion of the 'lived-world' is central in Edmund Husserl, *The Crisis of European Sciences and Transcendental Phenomenology*, David Carr (trans.), Northwestern University Press, 1970 and in Merleau-Ponty, *Phenomenology of Perception*, Colin Smith (trans.), Routledge & Kegan Paul, 1962. It is our fundamental way of experiencing and acting in the world prior to our reflecting upon it or theorizing about it.

[3] Martin Heidegger, *Being and Time*, John Macquarrie and Edward Robinson (trans.), Basil Blackwell, 1980. See also Martin Heidegger, *Basic Writings*, David Farrell Krell (ed.), Routledge, 1993, especially 'Building Dwelling and Thinking' and 'The Origin of the Work of Art'.

'Respect for Nature'

Paul W. Taylor

Taylor's book, *Respect for nature: a theory of environmental ethics,* elaborates a theory that has three components. There is, first, a belief system, the biocentric outlook on nature, acceptance of which involves awareness of ourselves as biological entities. This belief system supports, secondly, the basic moral attitude of respect for nature. Then, thirdly, the attitude entails the adoption of certain rules of conduct. The first extract in the Reading* summarizes the main elements of the belief system and indicates the way in which it supports the moral attitude of respect. The second, longer extract explains two concepts that have to be understood in order to grasp what the attitude of respect for nature is: the concept of the good of a being and the concept of inherent worth.

The biocentric outlook on nature

The belief-system constitutes a philosophical world view concerning the order of nature and the place of humans in it. I call this world view 'the biocentric outlook on nature'. When one conceives of oneself, one's relation to other living things, and the whole set of natural ecosystems on our planet in terms of this outlook, one identifies oneself as a member of the Earth's community of Life. This does not entail a denial of one's personhood. Rather, it is a way of understanding one's true self to include one's biological nature as well as one's personhood. From the perspective of the biocentric outlook, one sees one's membership in the Earth's Community of Life as providing a common bond with all the different species of animals and plants that have evolved over the ages. One becomes aware that, like all other living things on our planet, one's very existence depends on the fundamental soundness and integrity of the biological system of nature. When one looks at this domain of life in its totality, one sees it to be a complex and unified web of interdependent parts.

The biocentric outlook on nature also includes a certain way of perceiving and understanding each individual organism. Each is seen to be a teleological (goal-oriented) centre of life, pursuing its own good in its own unique way. This, of course, does not mean that they all seek their good as a conscious end or purpose, the realization of which is their intended aim. Consciousness may not be present at all, and even when it is present the organism need not be thought of as intentionally taking steps to achieve goals it sets for itself. Rather, a living thing is conceived as a unified system of organized activity, the constant tendency of which is to preserve its existence by protecting and promoting its well-being.

Finally, to view the place of humans in the natural world from the perspective of the biocentric outlook is to reject the idea of human superiority over other living things. Humans are not thought of as carrying on a higher grade of existence when compared with the so-called 'lower' orders of life. The biocentric outlook precludes a hierarchical view of nature. To accept that outlook and view the living world in its terms is to commit oneself to the principle of species-impartiality. No bias in favour of some over others is acceptable. This impartiality applies to the human species just as it does to non-human species.

These are the implications of accepting the biocentric outlook .... [W]e shall simply assume its justifiability and consider how its acceptance supports and makes intelligible a moral agent's adopting the attitude of respect for nature. It can be seen from the foregoing account that insofar as one conceives of one's relation to the whole system of nature through the conceptual framework of the biocentric outlook, one will look at members of non-human species as one looks at members of one's own species. Each living thing, human and non-human alike, will be viewed as an entity pursuing its own good in its own way according to its species specific nature. (For humans this will include not only an autonomous, self-directed pursuing of one's good, but also the self-created conception of what one's true good is.) No living thing will be considered inherently superior or inferior to any other, since the biocentric outlook entails species-impartiality. All are then judged to be equally deserving of moral concern and consideration.

Now, for a moral agent to be disposed to give equal consideration to all wild living things and to judge the good of each to be worthy of being preserved and protected as an end in itself and for the sake of the being whose good it is means that every wild living thing is seen to be the appropriate object of the attitude of respect. Given the acceptance of the biocentric outlook, the attitude of respect will be adopted as the only suitable or morally fitting attitude to have toward the Earth's wild creatures. One who takes the attitude of respect toward the individual organisms, species-populations, and biotic communities of the Earth's natural ecosystems regards those entities and groups of entities as possessing inherent worth, in the sense that *their value of worth does not depend on their being valued for their usefulness in furthering human ends* (or the ends of any other species). When such an attitude is adopted as one's ultimate moral attitude, I shall speak of that person as having *respect for nature*.

[...]

The concept of the good of a being

Some entities in the universe are such that we can meaningfully speak of their having a good of their own, while other entities are of a kind that makes such a judgement nonsense. We may think, for example, that a parent is furthering the good of a child by going on a camping trip with it. Our thinking this may be true or it may be false, depending on whether the child's good is actually furthered. But whether true or false, the idea of furthering the good of a child is an intelligible notion. The concept of entity-having-a-good-of-its-own includes in its range of application human children. Suppose, however, that someone tells us that we can further the good of a pile of sand by, say, erecting a shelter over it so that it does not get wet in the rain. We might be puzzled about what the person could mean. Perhaps we would interpret the statement to mean that, since wet sand is no good for a certain purpose, it should be kept dry. In that case it is not the sand's own good that would be furthered, but the purpose for which it is to be used. Presumably this would be some human purpose, so that if any being's good is furthered by keeping the sand dry, it is the good of those who have this purpose as one of their ends. Concerning the pile of sand itself, however, it is neither true nor false that keeping it dry furthers its good. The sand has no good of its own. It is not the sort of thing that can be included in the range of application of the concept, entity-that-has-a-good-of-its-own.

One way to know whether something belongs to the class of entities that have a good is to see whether it makes sense to speak of what is good or bad *for* the thing in question. If we can say, truly or falsely, that something is good for an entity or bad for it, without reference to any *other* entity, then the entity has a good of its own. Thus we speak of someone's doing physical exercise daily as being good for him or her. There is no need to refer to any other person or thing to understand our meaning. On the other hand, if we say that keeping a machine well-oiled is good for it we must refer to the purpose for which the machine is used in order to support our claim. As was the case with the pile of sand, this purpose is not attributable to the machine itself, but to those who made it or who now use it. It is not the machine's own good that is being furthered by being kept well-oiled, but the good of certain humans for whom the machine is a means to their ends.

Just as we speak of what is good for an entity, so we speak of what does an entity good. Concerning an elderly couple who have moved to a warm climate, we might say things like, 'The change was good for them' or 'it did them a lot of good.'[1]

It is easy to see how the good of a being is connected with what is good for it and with what does it good. What is good for a being or what does it good is something that promotes or protects its good. Correspondingly, what is bad for a being is something damaging or detrimental to its good. These ideas can equally well be expressed in terms of benefit and harm. To benefit a being is to bring about or to preserve a condition that is favourable to it, or to avoid, get rid of, or prevent from occurring a condition that is unfavourable to it. To harm it is either to bring about a condition unfavourable to it or to destroy or take away a condition favourable to it. The terms 'favourable' and 'unfavourable' apply to something whose well-being can be furthered or damaged, and this can meaningfully be said only of an entity that has a good of its own. Indeed, an entity's well-being can ordinarily be taken as synonymous with its good.

To promote a being's good is either to bring about a state of affairs not yet realized in its existence that is conducive to its good, or to get rid of a condition in its existence that is detrimental to its good. Protecting an entity's good can be done in any number of ways; by avoiding causing it harm (that is, by refraining from doing what would be contrary to its good), by preventing the loss of something needed for the preservation of its good, and by keeping it safe from danger, thereby enabling it to escape harm that might otherwise come to it. All these ways of promoting and protecting a being's good are, by definition, beneficial to it.

In the light of these considerations, what sorts of entities have a good of their own? At first we might think that they are entities that can be said to *have interests* in the sense of having ends and seeking means to achieve their ends. Since piles of sand, stones, puddles of water, and the like do not pursue ends, they have no interests. Not having any interests, they cannot be benefited by having their interests furthered, nor harmed by having their interests frustrated. Nothing gives them either satisfaction or dissatisfaction. It would perhaps be odd to hold that they are indifferent to everything that happens to them or to say that nothing matters to them, for we ordinarily speak this way about people who are in special circumstances (such as being in a severe state of depression), and we are thus contrasting their present state of mind with their normal condition. But inanimate objects are never in a condition where things that happen to them *do* matter to them.

Although having interests is a characteristic of at least some entities that have a good of their own, is it true of all such entities? It seems that this is not so. There are some entities that have a good of their own but cannot, strictly speaking, be described as having interests. They have a good of their own because it makes sense to speak of their being benefited or harmed. Things that happen to them can be judged, from their standpoint, to be favourable or unfavourable to them. Yet they are not beings that consciously aim at ends or take means to achieve such ends. They do not have interests because they are not interested in, do not care about, what happens to them. They can experience neither satisfaction nor dissatisfaction, neither fulfilment nor frustration. Such entities are all those living things that lack consciousness or, if conscious, lack the ability to make choices among alternatives confronting them. They include all forms of plant life and the simpler forms of animal life.

To understand more clearly how it is possible for a being to have a good of its own and yet not have interests, it will be useful to distinguish between an entity having an interest in something and something being in an entity's interest. Something can be in a being's interest and so benefit it, but the being itself might have no interest in it. Indeed, it might not even be the kind of entity that can have interests at all. In order to know whether something is (truly) in X's interests, we do not find out whether X has an interest in it. We inquire whether the thing in question will in fact further X's overall well-being. We ask, 'Does this promote or protect the good of X?' This is an objective matter because it is not determined by the beliefs, desires, feelings, or conscious interests of X.

It is clear that what an entity has an interest in obtaining or doing may not be in its (overall, best, long-range) interest to have or do. In human life this is the basis for the classic distinction between one's apparent good and one's true good. One's apparent good is whatever one values because one *believes* it to be conducive to the realization of one's good. One's true good is whatever *in fact* contributes to the realization of one's good. It is in this way that people often make mistakes in their subjective values. They place value on things that later turn out to be contrary to, or at least not to be instrumental to, their own true good. They aim at ends they come to judge worthless when achieved. What is subjectively valued by them is not objectively valuable to them. Their apparent good does not always coincide with their true good.

In addition to the idea of what people value, then, there is also the idea of what contributes to the realization of their overall good. In order to refer to the objective value concept of a human person's good, I shall use the term 'the Human Good', letting the term 'human values' designate whatever people value subjectively.

What is the Human Good? Philosophers have struggled with this question since the time of Socrates. Many different answers have been proposed. We might think of these various answers as *particular conceptions* of the Human Good, as distinct from the *general concept* of it. Other particular conceptions are found in the ways of life of different cultures and in the value systems of individuals.

The general concept has a number of approximate synonyms, such as 'human flourishing', 'self-actualization', and 'true happiness.' Our grasp of the concept, however, is not helped by simply equating it with one of these terms, since their meaning is as obscure and indeterminate as the idea of 'the good of humans' itself. Perhaps the clearest way to define it is to say that it is the kind of life one *would* place supreme value on if one were fully rational, autonomous, and enlightened. No one's valuation is ever actually made under these conditions. They define an ideal choice of a whole way of life made under the most favourable circumstances. We can say, however, that to the extent a given choice approximates these ideal conditions, to that extent the individual who makes the choice gains a more adequate and clearer understanding of his or her true good. As the person's rationality, autonomy, and factual knowledge increase, the choice of the kind of life most worth living; becomes less subject to revision or abandonment, and the individual in question becomes less subject to regret and disillusionment. Under these conditions the system of valued ends that one considers to be worth pursuing as ultimate goals in life is more likely to constitute one's true good than one's apparent good only.[2]

What about non-human animals? Can we say that the idea of entity-having-a-good-of-its-own also applies to them? With regard to *subjective* value concepts, it is always possible, of course, to raise questions about the behavioural criteria used in applying subjective value concepts to such creatures. One can doubt whether an animal finds anything to be good or bad, desirable or undesirable, worth seeking or worth avoiding. But whatever may be our questions and doubts in this area, they need not bother us as far as developing an adequate life-centred system of environmental ethics is concerned. Disputes about the applicability of *subjective* value concepts to non-human animals are simply not relevant to the ethics of respect for nature. It is the *objective* value concept of a being's good which is presupposed by that theory, not the various subjective concepts that have been mentioned. Once we make the distinction between the two sorts of value concepts, it is no longer necessary to be concerned with the questionable applicability of the subjective ones. For the theory of respect for nature only assumes that animals are beings to which it is correct to apply the objective concept of entity-having-a-good-of-its-own. It is, indeed, one of the fundamental principles of the theory that *all animals, however dissimilar to humans they may be, are beings that have a good of their own.* A second principle, equally fundamental, is that *all plants are likewise beings that have a good of their own.* The reasoning behind both principles will now be set forth.

Consider any doubtful case regarding the applicability of subjective value concepts to an entity. Concerning a butterfly, for example, we may hesitate to speak of its interests or preferences, and we would probably deny outright that it values anything in the sense of considering it good or desirable. But once we come to understand its life cycle and know the environmental conditions it needs to survive in a healthy state, we have no difficulty in speaking about what is beneficial to it and what might be harmful to it. A butterfly that develops through the egg, larva, and pupa stages of its life in a normal manner, and then emerges as a healthy adult that carries on its existence under favourable environmental conditions, might well be said to thrive and prosper. It fares well, successfully adapting to its physical surroundings and maintaining the normal biological functions of its species throughout its entire span of life. When all these things are true of it, we are warranted in concluding that the good of this particular insect has been fully realized. It has lived at a high level of well-being. From the perspective of the butterfly's world, it has had a good life.

Even when we consider such simple animal organisms as one-celled protozoa, it makes perfectly good sense to a biologically informed person to speak of what benefits or harms them, what environmental changes are to their advantage or disadvantage, and what physical circumstances are favourable or unfavourable to them. The more knowledge we gain concerning these organisms, the better are we able to make sound judgement about what is in their interest or contrary to their interest, what promotes their welfare or what is detrimental to their welfare.

We can now understand how it is possible for a human being *to take an animal's standpoint* and, without a trace of anthropomorphism, make a factually informed and objective judgement regarding what is desirable or undesirable *from that standpoint.* This is of considerable importance since... being willing to take the standpoint of non-human living things and to make informed, objective judgements from that standpoint is one of the central elements of the ethics of respect of nature. Once we acknowledge that it is meaningful to speak about what is good or bad for an organism as seen from the standpoint of its own good, we humans can make value judgements from the perspective of the organism's life, even if the organism itself can neither make nor understand those judgements. Furthermore, we can conceive of ourselves as having a duty to give consideration to its good and to see to it that it does not suffer harm as the result of our own conduct. None of these ways of thinking and acting with regard to it presupposes that the organism values anything subjectively or even has an interest in what we may do for it.

All of the foregoing considerations hold true of plants as well as animals. Once we separate the objective value concept of a being's good from subjective value concepts, there is no problem about understanding what it means to benefit or harm a plant, to be concerned about its good, and to act benevolently toward it. We can intentionally act with the aim of helping a plant to grow and thrive, and we can do this because we have genuine concern for its well-being. As moral agents we might think of ourselves as under an obligation not to destroy or injure a plant. We can also take the standpoint of a plant and judge what happens to it as being good or bad from its standpoint. To do this would involve our using as the standard of evaluation the preservation or promotion of the plant's own good. Anyone who has ever taken care of flowers, shrubs, or trees will know what these things mean.

Nothing in the above ways of responding to and dealing with plants implies that they have interests in the sense of having conscious aims and desires. We can deny that subjective value concepts apply to vegetative life and yet hold that plants do have a good of their own, which can be furthered or damaged by our treatment of them.

The particular conditions that make up the *content* of an animal's or plant's good will depend on the kind of animal or plant it is. What furthers the well-being of one species of organism will not necessarily further that of another, and indeed may be harmful to it. In order to know what a particular organism's good consists in, as well as what is good or bad for it, it is necessary to know its species-specific characteristics. These characteristics include the cellular structure of the organism, the internal functioning of its various parts, and its external relations to other organisms and to the physical-chemical aspects of its environment. Unless we learn how the organism develops, grows, and sustains its life according to the laws of its species-specific nature, we cannot fully understand what promotes the realization of its good or what is detrimental to its good.

[...]

The concept of inherent worth

To have the attitude of respect for nature is to regard the wild plants and animals of the Earth's natural ecosystems as possessing inherent worth. That such creatures have inherent worth may be considered the fundamental value-presupposition of the attitude of respect. The same point can be made concerning the attitude of respect for persons in human ethics. Unless we deem persons to be possessors of inherent worth (as distinct from considering them only in terms of their merits, or their instrumental value as contributors to some social goal, or their personal likableness), we will not have respect for them simply in virtue of their being persons. And when we do regard them as having inherent worth we deem them appropriate objects of the attitude of respect and so take that attitude toward them. What is of special interest here is that it is possible to take the same attitude toward non-human living things because it makes sense to regard them as possessors of inherent worth...

The concept of inherent worth must not be confused with the concept of the good of a being. To bring out the difference between them, consider the logical gap between the fact that a being has a good of its own (an is-statement) and the claim that it should or should not be treated in a certain way (an ought-statement). One can acknowledge that an animal or plant has a good of its own and yet, consistently with this acknowledgement, deny that moral agents have a duty to promote or protect its good or even to refrain from harming it. One does not contradict oneself by saying, 'Yes, I know that this action of mine will adversely affect the good of living things, but nevertheless there is no reason why I shouldn't do it'. There may in truth be a reason against doing the act, and that reason may be the fact that the act will be detrimental to the good of living things, but we cannot just assert this to be the case on the ground that the living things in question have a good of their own.

If the fact that an entity has a good of its own does not logically entail that moral agents ought or ought not to treat it in a certain way, the problem arises: What relationship holds (if any) between an entity's having a good and the claim its good makes upon moral agents? I shall argue that, if a moral agent is to recognize or acknowledge such a claim, the entity in question must not only be thought of as having a good of its own; it must also be regarded as having inherent worth. When so regarded, the entity is considered to be worthy of respect on the part of all moral agents. The attitude of respect is itself then seen to be the only suitable, appropriate, or fitting attitude to take toward the entity. In taking that attitude, one commits oneself to following, as one's own moral norm, the principle that living things ought not to be harmed or interfered with in nature, other things being equal.

Notes

* From Paul W. Taylor, *Respect for Nature: A Theory of Environmental Ethics*, Princeton University Press, 1986, pp.44–6, 60–72.

[1] The connections between the good *of* a being, what is good *for* a being, and doing good *to* a being are derived from G.H. von Wright, *The Varieties of Goodness*, Humanities Press, 1963. The general concept of the Human Good (the good of a human being as such) was central to the ethical thought of both Plato and Aristotle.

[2] This 'enlightened preference' view of the Human Good is analysed with care by G.H. von Wright (*ibid.*, Chapter 5). A similar view is the 'rational plan of life' definition of the good of a human individual propounded by John Rawls. See John Rawls, *A Theory of Justice*, Harvard University Press, 1971, sections 63 and 64. In Part II of his book *Impartial Reason,* Stephen Darwall has shown how this way of conceiving the Human Good is relevant to the logical structure of practical reason.

'Nature'

John Stuart Mill

Mill's essay,* 'Nature', one of the few undoubted classics of environmental philosophy, was originally published as one of *Three essays on religion*. Mill wanted to refute the view that the workings of nature can provide good reasons for believing in the existence of a benevolent creator. He also considered that a religion-based view of the goodness of nature was an obstacle to necessary attempts to improve nature. In this Reading, Mill makes a distinction between two different senses of the word 'nature', and argues that in neither sense is it rational to take nature as a guide to be followed by human beings.

1   Nature, natural, and the group of words derived from them, or allied to them in etymology, have at all times filled a great place in the thoughts and taken a strong hold on the feelings of mankind. That they should have done so is not surprising, when we consider what the words, in their primitive and most obvious signification, represent; but it is unfortunate that a set of terms which play so great a part in moral and metaphysical speculation, should have acquired many meanings different from the primary one, yet sufficiently allied to it to admit of confusion. The words have thus become entangled in so many foreign associations, mostly of a very powerful and tenacious character, that they have come to excite, and to be the symbols of, feelings which their original meaning will by no means justify; and which have made them one of the most copious sources of false taste, false philosophy, false morality, and even bad law.

[...]

2   According to the Platonic method which is still the best type of such investigations, the first thing to be done with so vague a term is to ascertain precisely what it means. It is also a rule of the same method, that the meaning of an abstraction is best sought for in the concrete – of an universal in the

particular. Adopting this course with the word Nature, the first question must be, what is meant by the 'nature' of a particular object: as of fire, of water. Or of some individual plant or animal? Evidently the *ensemble* or aggregate of its powers or properties: the modes in which it acts on other things (counting among those things the senses of the observer) and the modes in which other things act upon it; to which, in the case of a sentient being, must be added, its own capacities of feeling, or being conscious. The Nature of the thing means all this; means its entire capacity of exhibiting phenomena. And since the phenomena which a thing exhibits, however much they vary in different circumstances, are always the same in the same circumstances, they admit of being described in general forms of words, which are called the *laws* of the thing's nature. Thus it is a law of the nature of water that under the mean pressure of the atmosphere at the level of the sea, it boils at $212°$ Fahrenheit.

3   As the nature of any given thing is the aggregate of its powers and properties, so Nature in the abstract is the aggregate of the powers and properties of all things. Nature means the sum of all phenomena, together with the causes which produce them; including not only all that happens, but all that is capable of happening; the unused capabilities of causes being as much a part of the idea of Nature, as those which take effect. Since all phenomena which have been sufficiently examined are found to take place with regularity, each having certain fixed conditions, positive and negative, on the occurrence of which it invariably happens; mankind have been able to ascertain, either by direct observation or by reasoning processes grounded on it, the conditions of the occurrence of many phenomena; and the progress of science mainly consists in ascertaining those conditions. When discovered they can be expressed in general propositions, which are called laws of the particular phenomenon, and also, more generally, Laws of Nature. Thus, the truth that all material objects tend towards one another with a force directly as their masses and inversely as the square of their distance, is a law of Nature. The proposition that air and food are necessary to animal life, if it be as we have good reason to believe, true without exception, is also a law of nature, though the phenomenon of which it is the law is special, and not, like gravitation, universal.

4   Nature, then, in this its simplest acceptation, is a collective name for all facts, actual and possible: or (to speak more accurately) a name for the mode, partly known to us and partly unknown, in which all things take place. For the word suggests, not so much the multitudinous detail of the phenomena, as the conception which might be formed of their manner of existence as a mental whole, by a mind possessing a complete knowledge of them: to which

conception it is the aim of science to raise itself, by successive steps of generalization from experience.

5   Such, then, is a correct definition of the word Nature. But this definition corresponds only to one of the senses of that ambiguous term. It is evidently inapplicable to some of the modes in which the word is familiarly employed. For example, it entirely conflicts with the common form of speech by which Nature is opposed to Art, and natural to artificial. For the sense of the word Nature which has just been defined, and which is the true scientific sense, Art is as much Nature as anything else; and everything which is artificial is natural – Art has no independent powers of its own: Art is but the employment of the powers of Nature for an end. Phenomena produced by human agency, no less than those which as far as we are concerned are spontaneous, depend on the properties of the elementary forces, or of the elementary substances and their compounds. The united powers of the whole human race could not create a new property of matter in general, or of any one of its species. We can only take advantage for our purposes of the properties which we find. A ship floats by the same laws of specific gravity and equilibrium, as a tree uprooted by the wind and blown into the water. The corn which men raise for food, grows and produces its grain by the same laws of vegetation by which the wild rose and the mountain strawberry bring forth their flowers and fruit. A house stands and holds together by the natural properties, the weight and cohesion of the materials which compose it: a steam engine works by the natural expansive force of steam, exerting a pressure upon one part of a system of arrangements, which pressure, by the mechanical properties of the lever, is transferred from that to another part where it raises the weight or removes the obstacle brought into connection with it. In these and all other artificial operations the office of man is, as has often been remarked, a very limited one; it consists in moving things into certain places. We move objects, and by doing this, bring some things into contact which were separate, or separate others which were in contact: and by this simple change of place, natural forces previously dormant are called into action, and produce the desired effect. Even the volition which designs, the intelligence which contrives, and the muscular force which executes these movements, are themselves powers of Nature.

6   It thus appears that we must recognize at least two principal meanings in the word Nature. In one sense, it means all the powers existing in either the outer or the inner world and everything which takes place by means of those powers. In another sense, it means, not everything which happens, but only what takes place without the agency, or without the voluntary and intentional agency, of man. This distinction is far from exhausting the ambiguities of the

word; but it is the key to most of those on which important consequences depend.

7   Such, then, being the two principal senses of the word Nature; in which of these is it taken, or is it taken in either, when the word and its derivatives are used to convey ideas of commendation, approval, and even moral obligation?

8   It has conveyed such ideas in all ages. *Naturam sequi* was the fundamental principle of morals in many of the most admired schools of philosophy. Among the ancients, especially in the declining period of ancient intellect and thought, it was the test to which all ethical doctrines were brought. The Stoics and the Epicureans, however irreconcilable in the rest of their systems, agreed in holding themselves bound to prove that their respective maxims of conduct were the dictates of nature... But though perhaps no one could now be found who like the institutional writers of former times, adopts the so-called Law of Nature as the foundation of ethics, and endeavours consistently to reason from it, the word and its cognates must still be counted among those which carry great weight in moral argumentation. That any mode of thinking, feeling, or acting, is 'according to nature' is usually accepted as a strong argument for its goodness. If it can be said with any plausibility that 'nature enjoins' anything, the propriety of obeying the injunction is by most people considered to be made out: and conversely, the imputation of being contrary to nature, is thought to bar the door against any pretension on the part of the thing so designated, to be tolerated or excused; and the word unnatural has not ceased to be one of the most vituperative epithets in the language. Those who deal in these expressions, may avoid making themselves responsible for any fundamental theorem respecting the standard of moral obligation, but they do not the less imply such a theorem, and one which must be the same in substance with that on which the more logical thinkers of a more laborious age grounded their systematic treatises on Natural Law.

9   Is it necessary to recognize in these forms of speech, another distinct meaning of the word Nature? Or can they be connected, by any rational bond of union, with either of the two meanings already treated of? At first it may seem that we have no option but to admit another ambiguity in the term. All inquiries are either into what is, or into what ought to be: science and history belonging to the first division, art, morals and politics to the second. But the two senses of the word Nature first pointed out, agree in referring only to what is. In the first meaning, Nature is a collective name for everything which is. In the second, it is a name for everything which is of itself, without voluntary human intervention. But the employment of the word Nature as a term of ethics seems to disclose a third meaning, in which Nature does not stand for

what is, but for what ought to be; or for the rule of standard of what ought to be. A little consideration, however, will show that this is not a case of ambiguity; there is not here a third sense of the word. Those who set up Nature as a standard of action do not intend a merely bearable proposition; they do not mean that the standard, whatever it be, should be *called* Nature; they think they are giving some information as to what the standard of action really is. Those who say that we ought to act according to Nature do not mean the mere identical proposition that we ought to do what we ought to do. They think that the word Nature affords some external criterion of what we should do; and if they lay down as a rule for what ought to be, a word which in its proper signification denotes what is, they do so because they have a notion, either clearly or confusedly, that what is, constitutes the rule and standard of what ought to be.

10   The examination of this notion, is the object of the present Essay. It is proposed to inquire into the truth of the doctrines which make Nature a test of right and wrong, good and evil, or which in any mode or degree attach merit or approval to following, imitating, or obeying Nature. To this inquiry the foregoing discussion respecting the meaning of terms, was an indispensable introduction. Language is as it were the atmosphere of philosophical investigation, which must be made transparent before anything can be seen through it in the true figure and position ...

11   When it is asserted, or implied, that Nature, or the laws of Nature, should be conformed to, is the Nature which is meant, Nature in the first sense of the term, meaning all which is – the powers and properties of all things? But in this signification, there is no need of a recommendation to act according to nature, since it is what nobody can possibly help doing, and equally whether he acts well or ill. There is no mode of acting which is not conformable to Nature in this sense of the term, and all modes of acting are so in exactly the same degree. Every action is the exertion of some natural power, and its effects of all sorts are so many phenomena of nature, produced by the powers and properties of some of the objects of nature, in exact obedience to some laws or laws of nature. When I voluntarily use my organs to take in food, the act, and its consequences, take place according to laws of nature: if instead of food I swallow poison, the case is exactly the same. To bid people conform to the laws of nature when they have no power but what the laws of nature give them – when it is a physical impossibility for them to do the smallest thing otherwise than through some law of nature, is an absurdity. The thing they need to be told is, what particular law of nature they should make use of in a particular case. When, for example, a person is crossing a river by a narrow bridge to

which there is no parapet, he will do well to regulate his proceedings by the laws of equilibrium in moving bodies, instead of conforming only to the law of gravitation, and falling into the river.

12   Yet, idle as it is to exhort people to do what they cannot avoid doing, and absurd as it is to prescribe as a rule of right conduct what agrees exactly as well with wrong; nevertheless a rational rule of conduct *may* be constructed out of the relation which it ought to bear to the laws of nature in this widest acceptation of the term. Man necessarily obeys the laws of nature, or in other words the properties of things, but he does not necessarily *guide* himself by them. Though all conduct is in conformity to laws of nature, all conduct is not grounded on knowledge of them, and intelligently directed to the attainment of purposes by means of them. Though we cannot emancipate ourselves from the laws of nature as a whole, we can escape from any particular law of nature, if we are able to withdraw ourselves from the circumstances in which it acts. Though we can do nothing except through laws of nature, we can use one law to counteract another. According to Bacon's maxim, we can obey nature in such a manner as to command it.[1] Every alteration of circumstances alters more or less the laws of nature under which we act; and by every choice which we make either of ends or of means, we place ourselves to a greater or less extent under one set of laws of nature instead of another. If, therefore, the useless precept to follow nature were changed into a precept to study nature; to know and take heed of the properties of the things we have to deal with, so far as these properties are capable of forwarding or obstructing any given purpose; we should have arrived at the first principle of all intelligent action, or rather at the definition of intelligent action itself. And a confused notion of this true principle, is, I doubt not, in the minds of many of those who set up the unmeaning doctrine which superficially resembles it. They perceive that the essential difference between wise and foolish conduct consists in attending, or not attending, to the particular laws of nature on which some important result depends. And they think, that a person who attends to a law of nature in order to shape his conduct by it, may be said to obey it, while a person who practically disregards it, and acts as if no such law existed, may be said to disobey it: the circumstance being overlooked, that what is thus called disobedience to a law of nature is obedience to some other or perhaps to the very law itself. For example, a person who goes into a powder magazine either not knowing, or carelessly omitting to think of, the explosive force of gunpowder, is likely to do some act which will cause him to be blown to atoms in obedience to the very law which he has disregarded.

13   But however much of its authority the 'Naturam sequi' doctrine may owe to its being confounded with the rational precept 'Naturam observare', its favourers and promoters unquestionably intend much more by it than that precept. To acquire knowledge of the properties of things, and make use of the knowledge for guidance, is a rule of prudence, for the adaptation of means to ends; for giving effect to our wishes and intentions whatever they may be. But the maxim of obedience to Nature, or conformity to Nature, is held up not as a simply prudential but as an ethical maxim; and by those who talk of *jus nature,* even as a law, fit to be administered by tribunals and enforced by sanctions. Right action, must mean something more and other than merely intelligent action: yet no precept beyond this last, can be connected with the word Nature in the wider and more philosophical of its acceptations. We must try it therefore in the other sense, that in which Nature stands distinguished from Art, and denotes, not the whole course of the phenomena which come under our observation, but only their spontaneous course.

14   Let us then consider whether we can attach any meaning to the supposed practical maxim of following Nature, in this second sense of the word, in which Nature stands for that which takes place without human intervention. In Nature as thus understood, is the spontaneous course of things when left to themselves, the rule to be followed in endeavouring to adapt things to our use? But it is evident at once that the maxim, taken in this sense, is not merely, as it is in the other sense, superfluous and unmeaning, but palpably absurd and self-contradictory. For while human action cannot help conforming to Nature in the one meaning of the term, the very aim and object of action is to alter and improve Nature in the other meaning. If the natural course of things were perfectly right and satisfactory, to act at all would be a gratuitous meddling, which as it could not make things better, must make them worse. Or if action at all could be justified, it would only be when in direct obedience to instincts, since these might perhaps be accounted part of the spontaneous order of Nature; but to do anything with forethought and purpose, would be a violation of that perfect order. If the artificial is not better than the natural, to what end are all the arts of life? To dig, to plough, to build, to wear clothes, are direct infringements of the injunction to follow nature.

15   Accordingly it would be said by every one, even of those most under the influence of the feelings which prompt the injunction, that to apply it to such cases as those just spoken of, would be to push it too far. Everybody professes to approve and admire many great triumphs of Art over Nature: the junction by bridges of shores which Nature had made separate, the draining of Nature's marshes, the excavation of her wells, the dragging to light of what she has

buried at immense depths in the earth; the turning away of her thunderbolts by lightning rods, of her inundations by embankments, of her ocean by breakwaters. But to commend these and similar feats, is to acknowledge that the ways of Nature are to be conquered, not obeyed: that her powers are often towards man in the position of enemies, from whom he must wrest, by force and ingenuity, what little he can for his own use, and deserves to be applauded when that little is rather more than might be expected from his physical weakness in comparison to those gigantic powers. All praise of Civilization, or Art, or Contrivance, is so much dispraise of Nature; an admission of imperfection, which it is man's business, and merit, to be always endeavouring to correct or mitigate.

16   The consciousness that whatever man does to improve his condition is in so much a censure and a thwarting of the spontaneous order of Nature, has in all ages caused new and unprecedented attempts at improvement to be generally at first under a shade of religious suspicion; as being in any case uncomplimentary, and very probably offensive to the powerful beings (or, when polytheism gave place to monotheism, to the all-powerful Being) supposed to govern the various phenomena of the universe, and of whose will the course of nature was conceived to be the expression. Any attempt to mould natural phenomena to the convenience of mankind might easily appear an interference with the government of those superior beings: and though life could not have been maintained, much less made pleasant, without perpetual interferences of the kind, each new one was doubtless made with fear and trembling, until experience had shown that it could be ventured on without drawing down the vengeance of the Gods. The sagacity of priests showed them a way to reconcile the impunity of particular infringements with the maintenance of the general dread of encroaching on the divine administration. This was effected by representing each of the principal human inventions as the gift and favour of some God. The old religions also afforded many resources for consulting the Gods, and obtaining their express permission for what would otherwise have appeared a breach of their prerogative. When oracles had ceased, any religion which recognized a revelation afforded expedients for the same purpose. The Catholic religion had the resource of an infallible Church, authorized to declare what exertions of human spontaneity were permitted or forbidden; and in default of this, the case was always open to argument from the Bible whether any particular practice had expressly or by implication been sanctioned. The notion remained that this liberty to control Nature was conceded to man only by special indulgence, and as far as required by his necessities; and there was always a tendency, though a diminishing one, to regard any attempt to exercise power over nature, beyond a certain degree,

and a certain admitted range, as an impious effort to usurp divine power, and dare more than was permitted to man. The lines of Horace in which the familiar arts of shipbuilding and navigation are reprobated as *vetitum nefas*,[2] indicate even in that sceptical age a still unexhausted vein of the old sentiment. The intensity of the corresponding feeling in the middle ages is not a precise parallel, on account of the superstition about dealing with evil spirits with which it was complicated: but the imputation of prying into the secrets of the Almighty long remained a powerful weapon of attack against unpopular inquirers into nature; and the charge of presumptuously attempting to defeat the designs of Providence, still retains enough of its original force to be thrown in as a make-weight along with other objections when there is a desire to find fault with any new exertion of human forethought and contrivance. No one, indeed, asserts it to be the intention of the Creator that the spontaneous order of the creation should not be altered, or even that it should not be altered in any new way. But there still exists a vague notion that though it is very proper to control this or the other natural phenomenon, the general scheme of nature is a model for us to imitate: that with more or less liberty in details, we should on the whole be guided by the spirit and general conception of nature's own ways: that they are God's work, and as such perfect; that man cannot rival their unapproachable excellence, and can best show his skill and piety by attempting, in however imperfect a way, to reproduce their likeness; and that if not the whole, yet some particular parts of the spontaneous order of nature, selected according to the speaker's predilections, are in a peculiar sense, manifestations of the Creator's will; a sort of finger posts pointing out the direction which things in general, and therefore our voluntary actions, are intended to take. Feelings of this sort, though repressed on ordinary occasions by the contrary current of life, are ready to break out whenever custom is silent, and the native prompting of the mind have nothing opposed to them but reason: and appeals are continually made to them by rhetoricians, with the effect, if not of convincing opponents, at least of making those who already hold the opinion which the rhetorician desires to recommend, better satisfied with it. For in the present day it probably seldom happens that any one is persuaded to approve any course of action because it appears to him to bear an analogy to the divine government of the world, though the argument tells on him with great force, and is felt by him to be a great support, in behalf of anything which he is already inclined to approve.

17   If this notion of imitating the ways of Providence as manifested in Nature, is seldom expressed plainly and downrightly as a maxim of general application, it also is seldom directly contradicted. Those who find it on their path, prefer to turn the obstacle rather than to attack it, being often themselves

not free from the feeling, and in any case afraid of incurring the charge of impiety by saying anything which might be held to disparage the works of the Creator's power. They therefore, for the most part, rather endeavour to show, that they have as much right to the religious argument as their opponents, and that if the course they recommend seems to conflict with some part of the ways of Providence, there is some other part with which it agrees better than what is contended for on the other side. In this mode of dealing with the great *a priori* fallacies, the progress of improvement clears away particular errors while the causes of errors are still left standing, and very little weakened by each conflict: yet by a long series of such partial victories precedents are accumulated, to which an appeal may be made against these powerful prepossessions, and which afford a growing hope that the misplaced feeling, after having so often learnt to recede, may some day be compelled to an unconditional surrender. For however offensive the proposition may appear to many religious persons, they should be willing to look in the face the undeniable fact, that the order of nature, insofar as unmodified by man, is such as no being, whose attributes are justice and benevolence, would have made, with the intention that his rational creatures should follow it as an example. If made wholly by such a Being, and not partly by beings of very different qualities, it could only be as a designedly imperfect work, which man, in his limited sphere, is to exercise justice and benevolence in amending. The best persons have always held it to be the essence of religion, that the paramount duty of man upon earth is to amend himself: but all except monkish quietists have annexed to this in their inmost minds (though seldom willing to enunciate the obligation with the same clearness) the additional religious duty of amending the world, and not solely the human part of it but the material; the order of physical nature.

18   In considering this subject it is necessary to divest ourselves of certain preconceptions which may justly be called natural prejudices, being grounded on feelings which, in themselves natural and inevitable, intrude into matters with which they ought to have no concern. One of these feelings is the astonishment, rising into awe, which is inspired (even independently of all religious sentiment) by any of the greater natural phenomena. A hurricane; a mountain precipice; the desert; the ocean, either agitated or at rest; the solar system, and the great cosmic forces which hold it together; the boundless firmament, and to an educated mind any single star; excite feelings which make all human enterprises and powers appear so insignificant, that to a mind thus occupied it seems insufferable presumption in so puny a creature as man to look critically on things so far above him, or dare to measure himself against the grandeur of the universe. But a little interrogation of our own consciousness will suffice to convince us, that what makes these phenomena

so impressive is simply their vastness. The enormous extension in space and time, or the enormous power they exemplify, constitutes their sublimity; a feeling in all cases, more allied to terror than to any moral emotion. And though the vast scale of these phenomena may well excite wonder, and sets at defiance all idea of rivalry, the feeling it inspires is of a totally different character from admiration of excellence. Those in whom awe produces admiration may be aesthetically developed, but they are morally uncultivated. It is one of the endowments of the imaginative part of our mental nature that conceptions of greatness and power, vividly realized, produce a feeling which though in its higher degrees closely bordering on pain, we prefer to most of what are accounted pleasures. But we are quite equally capable of experiencing this feeling towards maleficent power; and we never experience it so strongly towards most of the powers of the universe, as when we have most present to our consciousness a vivid sense of their capacity of inflicting evil. Because these natural powers have what we cannot imitate, enormous might, and overawe us by that one attribute, it would be a great error to infer that their other attributes are such as we ought to emulate, or that we should be justified in using our small powers after the example which Nature sets us with her vast forces.

19   For, how stands the fact? That next to the greatness of these cosmic forces, the quality which most forcibly strikes every one who does not avert his eyes from it, is their perfect and absolute recklessness. They go straight to their end, without regarding what or whom they crush on the road. Optimists, in their attempts to prove that 'whatever is, is right',[3] are obliged to maintain, not that Nature ever turns one step from her path to avoid trampling us into destruction, but that it would be very unreasonable in us to expect that she should. Pope's 'Shall gravitation cease when you go by?'[4] may be a just rebuke to any one who should be so silly as to expect common human morality from nature. But if the question were between two men, instead of between a man and a natural phenomenon, that triumphant apostrophe would be thought a rare piece of impudence. A man who should persist in hurling stones or firing cannon when another man 'goes by', and having killed him should urge a similar plea in exculpation, would very deservedly be found guilty of murder.

20   In sober truth, nearly all the things which men are hanged or imprisoned for doing to one another, are nature's every day performances. Killing, the most criminal act recognized by human laws, Nature does once to every being that lives; and in a large proportion of cases, after protracted tortures such as only the greatest monsters whom we read of every purposely inflicted on their living fellow-creatures. If, by an arbitrary reservation, we refuse to account

anything murder but what abridges a certain term supposed to be allotted to human life, nature also does this to all but a small percentage of lives, and does it in all the modes, violent or insidious, in which the worst human beings take the lives of one another. Nature impales men, breaks them as if on the wheel, casts them to be devoured by wild beasts, burns them to death, crushes them with stones like the first Christian martyr, starves them with hunger, freezes them with cold, poisons them by the quick or slow venom of her exhalations, and has hundreds of other hideous deaths in reserve, such as the ingenious cruelty of a Nabis or a Domitian never surpassed. All this, Nature does with the most supercilious disregard both of mercy and of justice, emptying her shafts upon the best and noblest indifferently with the meanest and worst; upon those who are engaged in the highest and worthiest enterprises, and often as the direct consequence of the noblest acts; and it might almost be imagined as a punishment for them. She mows down those on whose existence hangs the well-being of a whole people, perhaps the prospects of the human race for generations to come, with as little compunction as those whose death is a relief to themselves, or a blessing to those under their noxious influence. Such are Nature's dealings with life. Even when she does not intend to kill, she inflicts the same tortures in apparent wantonness. In the clumsy provision which she has made for that perpetual renewal of animal life, rendered necessary by the prompt termination she puts to it in every individual instance, no human being ever comes into the world but another human being is literally stretched on the rack for hours or days, not infrequently issuing in death. Next to taking life (equal to it according to a high authority) is taking the means by which we live; and Nature does this too on the largest scale and with the most callous indifference. A single hurricane destroys the hopes of a season; a flight of locusts, or an inundation, desolates a district; a trifling chemical change in an edible root, starves a million of people. The waves of the sea, like banditti seize and appropriate the wealth of the rich and the little all of the poor with the same accompaniments of stripping, wounding, and killing as their human antitypes. Everything in short, which the worst men commit either against life or property is perpetrated on a larger scale by natural agents. Nature has Noyades more fatal than those of Carrier; her explosions of fire damp are as destructive as human artillery; her plague and cholera far surpass the poison cups of the Borgias. Even the love of 'order' which is thought to be a following of the ways of Nature, is in fact a contradiction of them. All which people are accustomed to deprecate as 'disorder' and its consequences, is precisely a counterpart of Nature's ways. Anarchy and the Reign of Terror are overmatched in injustice, ruin, and death, by a hurricane and a pestilence.

21   But, it is said, all these things are for wise and good ends. On this I must first remark that whether they are so or not, is altogether beside the point. Supposing it true that contrary to appearances these horrors when perpetrated by Nature, promote good ends, still as no one believes that good ends would be promoted by our following the example, the course of Nature cannot be a proper model for us to imitate. Either it is right that we should kill because nature kills; torture because nature tortures; ruin and devastate because nature does the like; or we ought not to consider at all what nature does, but what it is good to do. If there is such a thing as a *reductio ad absurdum,* this surely amounts to one. If it is a sufficient reason for doing one thing, that nature does it, why not another thing? If not all things, why anything? The physical government of the world being full of the things which when done by men are deemed the greatest enormities, it cannot be religious or moral in us to guide our actions by the analogy of the course of nature. The proposition remains true, whatever occult quality of producing good may reside in those facts of nature which to our perceptions are most noxious, and which no one considers it other than a crime to produce artificially.

[...]

22   There is however one particular element in the construction of the world, which to minds on the look-out for special indication of the Creator's will, has appeared, not without plausibility, peculiarly fitted to afford them; viz. the active impulses of human and other animated beings. One can imagine such persons arguing that when the Author of Nature only made circumstances, he may not have meant to indicate the manner in which his rational creatures were to adjust themselves to those circumstances; but that when he implanted positive stimuli in the creatures themselves, stirring them up to a particular kind of action, it is impossible to doubt that he intended that sort of action to be practised by them. This reasoning, followed out consistently, would lead to the conclusion that the Deity intended, and approves, whatever human beings do; since all that they do being the consequence of some of the impulses with which their Creator must have endowed them, all must equally be considered as done in obedience to his will. As this practical conclusion was shrunk from, it was necessary to draw a distinction, and to pronounce that not the whole, but only parts of the active nature of mankind point to a special intention of the Creator in respect to their conduct. These parts it seemed natural to suppose, must be those in which the Creator's hand is manifested rather than the man's own: and hence the frequent antithesis between man as God made him, and man as he has made himself. Since what is done with deliberation seems more the man's own act, and he is held more completely responsible for it than for

what he does from sudden impulse, the considerate part of human conduct is apt to be set down as man's share in the business, and the inconsiderate as God's. The result is the vein of sentiment so common in the modern world (though unknown to the philosophic ancients) which exalts instinct at the expense of reason; an aberration rendered still more mischievous by the opinion commonly held in conjunction with it, that every, or almost every, feeling or impulse which acts promptly without waiting to ask questions, is an instinct. Thus almost every variety of unreflecting and uncalculating impulse receives a kind of consecration, except those which, though unreflecting at the moment, owe their origin to previous habits of reflection: these, being evidently not instinctive, do not meet with the favour accorded to the rest; so that all unreflecting impulses are invested with authority over reason, except the only ones which are most probably right. I do not mean, of course, that this mode of judgement is even pretended to be consistently carried out: life could not go on if it were not admitted that impulses must be controlled, and that reason ought to govern our actions. The pretension is not to drive Reason from the helm but rather to bind her by articles to steer only in a particular way. Instinct is not to govern, but reason is to practise some vague and unassignable amount of deference to Instinct. Though the impression in favour of instinct as being a peculiar manifestation of the divine purposes, has not been cast into the form of a consistent general theory, it remains a standing prejudice, capable of being stirred up into hostility to reason in any case in which the dictate of the rational faculty has not acquired the authority of prescription.

23   I shall not here enter into the difficult psychological question, what are, or are not instincts: the subject would require a volume to itself. Without touching upon any disputed theoretical points, it is possible to judge how little worthy is the instinctive part of human nature to be held up as its chief excellence – as the part in which the hand of infinite goodness and wisdom is peculiarly visible. Allowing everything to be an instinct which anybody has ever asserted to be one, it remains true that nearly every respectable attribute of humanity is the result not of instinct, but of a victory over instinct; and that there is hardly anything valuable in the natural man except capacities – a whole world of possibilities, all of them dependent upon eminently artificial discipline for being realized.

24   It is only in a highly artificialized condition of human nature that the notion grew up, or, I believe, ever could have grown up, that goodness was natural: because only after a long course of artificial education did good sentiments become so habitual, and so predominant over bad, as to arise

unprompted when occasion called for them. In the times when mankind were nearer to their natural state, cultivated observers regarded the natural man as a sort of wild animal, distinguished chiefly by being craftier than the other beasts of the field; and all worth of character was deemed the result of a sort of taming; a phrase often applied by the ancient philosophers to the appropriate discipline of human beings. The truth is that there is hardly a single point of excellence belonging to human character, which is not decidedly repugnant to the untutored feelings of human nature.

[...]

25   If it be said, that there must be the germs of all these virtues in human nature, otherwise mankind would be incapable of acquiring them, I am ready, with a certain amount of explanation, to admit the fact. But the weeds that dispute the ground with these beneficent germs, are themselves not germs but rankly luxuriant growths, and would, in all but some one case in a thousand, entirely stifle and destroy the former, were it not so strongly the interest of mankind to cherish the good germs in one another, that they always do so, in as far as their degree of intelligence (in this as in other respects still very imperfect) allows. It is through such fostering, commenced early, and not counteracted by unfavourable influences, that, in some happily circumstanced specimens of the human race, the most elevated sentiments of which humanity is capable become a second nature, stronger than the first and not so much subduing the original nature as merging it into itself. Even those gifted organizations which have attained the like excellence by self-culture, owe it essentially to the same cause; for what self-culture would be possible without aid from the general sentiment of mankind delivered through books, and from the contemplation of exalted characters real or ideal? This artificially created or at least artificially perfected nature of the best and noblest human beings, is the only nature which it is ever commendable to follow. It is almost superfluous to say that even this cannot be erected into a standard of conduct, since it is itself the fruit of a training and culture the choice of which, if rational and not accidental, must have been determined by a standard already chosen.

26   This brief survey is amply sufficient to prove that the duty of man is the same in respect to his own nature as in respect to the nature of all other things, namely not to follow but to amend it.

[...]

27   It will be useful to sum up in a few words the leading conclusions of this Essay.

28   The word Nature has two principal meanings: it either denotes the entire system of things, with the aggregate of all their properties, or it denoted things as they would be, apart from human intervention.

29   In the first of these senses, the doctrine that man ought to follow nature is unmeaning; since man has no power to do anything else than follow nature; all his actions are done through, and in obedience to, some one or many of nature's physical or mental laws.

30   In the other sense of the term, the doctrine that man ought to follow nature, or in other words, ought to make the spontaneous course of things the model of his voluntary actions, is equally irrational and immoral.

31   Irrational, because all human action whatever, consists in altering, and all useful action in improving, the spontaneous course of nature:

32   Immoral, because the course of natural phenomena being replete with everything which when committed by human beings is most worthy of abhorrence, any one who endeavoured in his actions to imitate the natural course of things would be universally seen and acknowledged to be the wickedest of men.

33   The scheme of Nature regarded in its whole extent, cannot have had, for its sole or even principal object, the good of human or other sentient beings. What good it brings to them, is mostly the result of their own exertions. Whatsoever, in nature, gives indication of beneficent design, proves this beneficence to be armed only with limited power; and the duty of man is to co-operate with the beneficent powers, not by imitating but by perpetually striving to amend the course of nature – and bringing that part of it over which we can exercise control, more nearly into conformity with a high standard of justice and goodness.

Notes

* From John Stuart Mill, 'Nature', *Collected Works*, University of Toronto Press, 1963–77, vol. 10, pp.371–86, 391–3, 401–2.

1 *Novum Organium, Works*, vol. IV, p.47.

2 Horace, *Carmina I*, iii, II.25–6; in *Opera*, p.9.

3 Alexander Pope, *Essay on Man*, Epistle I, 1.294; in *Works*. New edn., Joseph Warton, et al. (eds), Priestley, 1822–25, vol. III, p.47.

4 *Ibid.*, Epistle IV, 1.128; vol. III, p.134.

'Can and ought we to follow Nature?'

Holmes Rolston III

Whereas Mill could find no sense in which it is both possible and morally right to follow nature, Holmes Rolston,* while not disagreeing with Mill's main contentions, finds senses of 'following nature' that Mill neglected. He questions Mill's view of nature as hostile and his belief that nature is of no assistance to us in achieving a good life.

Following nature in a tutorial sense

In positing a tutorial sense in which human conduct may follow nature, I admit that I can only give witness and invite the sharing of a gestalt, rather than provide a reasoned conceptual argument. I find I can increasingly 'draw a moral' from reflecting over nature – that is, gain a lesson in living. Nature has a 'leading capacity'; it prods thoughts that educate us, that lead us out (*educo*) to know who and where we are, and what our vocation is. Take what we call natural symbols – *light and fire, water or rock, morning and evening, life and death, waking and sleeping, the warmth of summer and the cold of winter, the flowers of spring and the fruits of fall, rain and rivers, seeds and growth, earth and sky.* How readily we put these material phenomena to 'metaphorical' or 'spiritual' use, as when we speak of life's 'stormy weather', of strength of character 'like a rock', or insecurity 'like shifting sand', or the 'dark cloud with the silver lining', or of our 'roots' in a homeland. Like a river, life flows on with persistence in change. How marvellously Lanier could sing of the watery marshes of Glynn – and the darky, of Old Man River! How profound are the psychological forces upon us of the grey and misty sky, the balmy spring day, the colours we call bright or sombre, the quiet of a snowfall, the honking of a skein of wild geese, or the times of natural passage – birth, puberty, marriage, death! How the height of the mountains 'elevates' us, and the depths of the sea stimulates 'deep' thoughts within!

Folk wisdom is routinely cast in this natural idiom. The sage in Proverbs admonishes the sluggard to consider the ways of the ant and be wise. The farmer urges, 'Work, for the night comes, when man's work is done.' 'Make hay while the sun shines.' The Psalmist notices how much we are like grass which flourishes but is soon gone, and those who understand the 'seasonal' character of life are the better able to rejoice in the turning of the seasons and to do everything well in its time. Jesus asks us in our search for the goods of life, to note the natural beauty of the lilies of the field, which the affected glory of Solomon could not surpass, and he points out birds to us, who, although hardly lazy, are not anxious or worried about tomorrow. *'What you sow, you reap.'* *'Into each life some rain must fall.'* *'All sunshine makes a desert.'* *'By their fruits shall you know them.'* *'The early bird gets the worm.'* *'Time and tide wait for no man.'* *'The loveliest rose has yet its thorns.'* *'The north wind made the Vikings.'* *'The tree stands that bends with the wind.'* *'White ants pick a carcass cleaner than a lion.'* *'Every mile is two in winter.'* *'If winter comes, can spring be far behind?'* It is no accident that our major religious seasons are naturally scheduled: Christmas comes at the winter solstice, Easter with the bursting forth of spring, and Thanksgiving with the harvest. Encounter with nature integrates me, protects me from pride, gives a sense of proportion and place, teaches me what to expect, and what to be content with, establishes other value than my own, and releases feelings in my spirit that I cherish and do not find elsewhere.

Living well is the catching of certain natural rhythms. Those so inclined can reduce a great deal of this to prudence, to the natural conditions of value; we may be particularly prone to do this because nature gives us no ethical guidance in our interhuman affairs. But human conduct must also be an appropriate form of life toward our environment, toward what the world offers us. Some will call this mere efficiency, but for some of us it is a kind of wisdom for which prudence and efficiency are words that are too weak. For we do not merely accept the limits that nature thrusts upon us, but endorse an essential goodness, a sufficiency in the natural fabric of life which encompasses both our natural talents and the constitution of the world in which, with our natural equipment, we must conduct ourselves. What I call a larger moral virtue, excellence of character, comes in large part, although by no means in the whole, from this natural attunement; and here I find a natural ethic in the somewhat old-fashioned sense of a way of life – a life style that should 'follow nature', that is, be properly sensitive to its flow through us and its bearing on our habits of life. A very significant portion of the *meaning* of life consists in our finding, expressing, and endorsing its naturalness. Otherwise, life lacks propriety.

We have enormous amounts of nature programmed into us. The protoplasm that flows within us has flowed naturally for over a billion years. Our internal human nature has evolved in response to external nature for a million years. Our genetic programming – which largely determines what we are, making each of us so alike and yet so different – is entirely natural. It is difficult to think that we do not possess a good natural fit in the wellsprings of our behaviour. Our cultural and our agentive life must be, and, so far as it is optional, ought to be consistent with that fit – freeing us no doubt for the cities we build, permitting our rural adaptations, and yet in the end further fitting us for life within our overarching natural environment. We are not, in the language of geographers, environmentally determined, for we have exciting options, and these increase with the advance of culture. But we are inescapably environmentally grounded as surely as we are mortal. This *is* the case, and hence our optional conduct *ought* to be commensurately natural; and, if we can transpose that from a grudging prudential *ought* to a glad moral *ought*, we shall be the happier and the wiser for finding 'our place under the sun.' Life moves, we are saying, not so much against nature as with it, and that remains true even of cultured human life which never really escapes its organic origins and surroundings. Our ethical life *ought* to maintain for us a good natural fit in both an efficient and a moral sense. This is what Merson means when he commends moral conduct as conformity to the laws of nature. There is in this communion with nature an ethic for life, and that is why exposure to natural wilderness is as necessary for a true education as is the university.

Someone may complain, and perhaps fiercely, that in this ethic nature only serves as an occasion for the construction of human virtues; that the natural wisdom we have cited shows only the virtues that develop *in us* when we confront nature; and that thus there is no following of nature, but rather a resistance to it, a studied surmounting in which we succeed despite nature. But this anthropocentric account is too one-sided. Evolution and ecology have taught us that every kind of life is what is not autonomously but because of a natural fit. We are what I call *environmental reciprocals* indebted to our environment for what we have become in ways that are as complementary as they are oppositional. Nature is, I think, not sufficient to produce all these virtues in us, and that allows for our own integrity and creativity – but nature is necessary for them. Admittedly, we must attain these virtues before we find and establish natural symbols for them – we must undergo the natural course in order to understand it – but I do not think that this ethical strength is merely and simply inside us. It is surely relational, at a minimum, arising out of the encounter between humans and nature. At the maximum, we are realizing and expressing in this strong and good life which we live something of the strength and goodness which nature has bequeathed us.

Nature is often enigmatic. Human life is complex. Each contains many times and seasons. The danger here is that any secretly desired conduct can somehow be construed as natural and found virtuous. Nature gives us little help concerning how we are to behave toward one another. In these matters we are free to do as we please, although nature has endowed us with reason and conscience out of which ethics may be constructed. Especially suspicious are arguments that assign human roles to nature, as is sometimes done with women or blacks, for we easily confuse the natural with the culturally conventional.

There may also be cases where we learn what is bad from nature. In rare cases, we may unwisely elect to follow some process in nature that in itself is indefensible – as some say the bloodthirsty conduct of the weasel is. I do not wish to defend the course of nature in every particular, but most of these cases involve learning something bad – an ethic of selfishness, a dog-eat-dog attitude, or a might-makes-right life style – by inappropriately projecting into moral interhuman conduct, and thereby making bad, what is quite appropriate at some lower, non-moral level – for example, the principle of the survival of the fittest or the self-interest programmed into the lower life forms. We cannot assume that the way things work at lower, non-moral levels is the way that they ought to work at human, moral levels, for the appearance of the capacity for moral deliberation makes a difference. This is what is correct about the *is–ought* distinction. Our moral conduct exceeds nature and we must deliberate with an ethic based on reason and conscience which supplants instinct. It is our conduct or mores insofar as it fits us to our environment – our ethic of bearing toward the natural world, not toward other persons – that I refer to in the tutorial sense, and which I here defend. Moreover, I call this conduct moral too in the sense that it contributes to our wisdom and our excellence of character.

In catching these natural rhythms, we must judiciously blend what I call *natural resistance* and *natural conductance*. Part of nature opposes life, increases entropy, kills, rots, destroys. Human life, like all other life, must struggle against its environment, and I much admire the human conquest of nature. However, I take this dominion to be something to which we are naturally impelled and for which we are naturally well-equipped. Furthermore, this struggle can be resorbed into a natural conductance, for nature has both generated us and provided us with life – support – and she has stimulated us into culture by her resistance. Nature is not all ferocity and indifference. She is also the bosom out of which we have come, and she remains our life partner, a realm of otherness for which we have the deepest need. I resist nature, and readily for my purposes amend and repair it. I fight disease and death, cold and hunger – and yet somehow come to feel that wildness is not only, nor finally, the pressing night. Rather, wildness with me and in me kindles fires against the night.

I am forced, of course, to concede that there are gaps in this account of nature. I do not find nature meaningful everywhere, or beautiful, or valuable, or educational; and I am moved to horror by malaria, intestinal parasites, and genetic deformities. My concept of the good is not coextensive with the natural, but it does greatly overlap it; and I find my estimates steadily enlarging that overlap. I even find myself stimulated positively in wrestling with nature's deceits. They stir me with a creative discontent, and, when I go nature one better, I often look back and reflect that nature wasn't half bad. I notice that my advanced life depends on nature's capacity to kill and to rot, and to make a recycling and pyramidal use of resources. Nature is not first and foremost the bringer of disease and death, but of life, and with that we touch the Latin root, *natus*. When nature slays, she takes only the life she gave, as no murderer can; and she gathers even that life back to herself by reproduction and by re-enfolding organic resources and genetic materials, and produces new life out of it.

Environmental life, including human life, is nursed in struggle; and to me it is increasingly inconceivable that it could, or should, be otherwise. If nature is good, it must be both an assisting and a resisting reality. We cannot succeed unless it can defeat us. My reply, then, to G.L. Dickinson's lament over the kicking and pushing in nature is that, although I do not imitate it, certainly not in human ethics, I would not eliminate it if I could, not at least until I have come to see how life could be better stimulated, and nobler human character produced without it. Nature is a vast scene of birth and death, springtime and harvest, permanence and change, of budding, flowering, fruiting, and withering away, of processive unfolding, of pain and pleasure, of success and failure, of ugliness giving way to beauty and beauty to ugliness. From the contemplation of it we get a feeling for life's transient beauty sustained over chaos. There is as it were a music to it all, and not the least when in a minor key. Even the religious urges within us, though they may promise a hereafter, are likely to advise us that we must for now rest content with the world we have been given. Though we are required to spend our life in struggle, yet we are able to cherish the good Earth and to accept the kind of universe in which we find ourselves. It is no coincidence that the ecological perspective often approaches a religious dimension in trying to help us see the beauty, integrity, and stability of nature within and behind its seeming indifference, ferocity, and evils.

Dickinson's portrait can give an account of only half of nature, natural resistance, and even that is an enigmatic account of human life set oddly, set for martyrdom, in a hostile world. He can give no account of natural conductance; indeed, he cannot even see it, and thus he has mistakenly taken the half for the whole. But the account that I am seeking contains both elements, and not merely as a nonsensical mixture of goods and evils – each absurd in relation to the other. A world in which there is an absurd mixture of helps and hurts is little better than a world of steady hostility. Neither could tutor us. What one needs is a nature where the evils are tributary to the goods, or, in my language of philosophical ecology, where natural resistance is embraced within and made intelligible by natural conductance. It is not death, but life, including human life as it fits this planetary environment, which is the principal mystery that has come out of nature. For several billion years, the ongoing development and persistence of that life, culminating in human life, have been the principal features of eco-nature behind which the element of struggle must be contained as a sub-theme. Our conduct morally ought to fit this natural conductance. Life follows nature because nature follows life.

I do endorse in principle, though not without reservations, the constitution of the ecosystem. I do not make any long-range claims about the invariable, absolute law of evolution, about who is guiding the ship, or about the overall record of cosmic nature. There is beauty, stability, and integrity in the evolutionary ecosystem that we happen to have. There is a natural, an earthen, trend to life, although we cannot know it as a universal law. We ought to preserve and to value this nature, if only because it is the only nature that we know in any complexity and detail. If and when we find ourselves in some other nature, of a sort in which we earthlings can still maintain our sanity, we can then revise our ethic appropriately. In the meantime, however, we can at least sometimes 'seek nature's guidance' in a tutorial sense almost as one might seek guidance from the Bible, or Socrates, or Shakespeare, even though nature, of course, does not 'write' or 'speak.' None of us lives to the fullest who does not study the natural order, and, more than that, none of us is wise who does not ultimately make his or her peace with it.

When Mill faces the prospect of an unending expansion of the urban and rural environments, his attitude toward nature shifts, and, rather surprisingly, we find him among the defenders of nature. Suppose, God forbid, he writes, that we were brought by our industry to some future 'World with nothing left to the spontaneous activity of nature; with every rood of land brought into cultivation, which is capable of growing food for human beings; every flowery waste or natural pasture ploughed up, all quadrupeds or birds which are not domesticated for man's use exterminated as his rivals for food, every hedgerow or superfluous tree rooted out, and scarcely a place left where a wild shrub or flower could grow without being eradicated as a weed in the name of improved agriculture.' Such a world without 'natural beauty and grandeur', Mill asserts, 'is not good for man.' Wild nature 'is the cradle of thoughts and aspirations which are not only good for the individual but which society could ill do without.'[1] Thus, in the end, we must enlist even this celebrated opponent of our morally following nature among those who wish to follow nature in our axiological sense.

For a closing statement on the tutorial sense of following nature, however, we do better to consult a poet rather than an ecologist or an ethicist. 'I came from the wilderness', remembers Carl Sandburg as he invites us to reflect on the wilderness – how it tries to hold on to us and how, in our tutorial sense, we ought not to be separated from it:

> There is an eagle in me and mockingbird... and the eagle flies among the Rocky Mountains of my dreams and fights among the Sierra crags of what I want ... and the mockingbird warbles in the early forenoon before the dew is gone, warbles in the underbrush of my Chattanoogas of hope, gushes over the blue Ozark foothills of my wishes – And I got the eagle and the mockingbird from the wilderness.[2]

Notes

* From Holmes Rolston III, 'Can and ought we to follow nature?', *Environmental Ethics*, 1, 1979; reprinted in Rolston's *Philosophy Gone Wild*, Prometheus Books, 1989, pp.46–52.

[1] John Stuart Mill, *Principles of Political Economy*, in *Collected Works*, vol. 3:p.756. Mill also records that reading Wordsworth's poetry reawoke in him a love of nature after his analytic bent of mind had caused a crisis in his mental history. See John Stuart Mill, *Autobiography*, Houghton Miffin, 1969, pp.88–90.

[2] Carl Sandburg, 'Wilderness', in *Complete Poems*, Harcourt, Brace, Jovanovich, 1970, p.100. Ellipses in original.

'Identification, Oneness, Wholeness, and Self-realization'

Arne Naess

Naess, the Norwegian philosopher whose ideas are the main inspiration of the deep ecology movement, describes, in this extract from his book *Economy, Community and Lifestyle,** how wide identification with non–human forms of life can lead to a concern for their welfare equal to our concern for our own.

Identification and alienation; ideas of oneness and wholeness

In the heading of this section four terms are brought together. Perhaps four contrasting terms should also be kept in mind: alienation, plurality, fragmentarity, and Self-abnegation. The interrelations of these terms may perhaps contribute to the clarification of ecosophy. Let an example introduce the issue.

In a glass veranda with one wall open away from the sun a bunch of children are playing with an insect spray. Insects are trapped flying against the wall pointing towards the sun. Spraying makes them dramatically fall to the floor. Amusing? A grown-up appears, picks up an insect, looks at it with care, and utters dreamingly: 'perhaps those animals might, like you, prefer to live rather than to die?' The point is grasped, the children for a moment see and experience spontaneously and immediately the insects as themselves, not only as something different but in an important sense like themselves. An instance of momentary identification! Perhaps it has no effect in the long run, or perhaps one of the children slightly changes an attitude toward small fellow creatures.

Before the intervention the children saw the movements of half-dead insects but presumably did not react. From the point of view of ecosophy they were alienated in a particular sense of the word, namely being indifferent to something that with normal upbringing would have caused empathy based on identification. Indifference, rather than feelings of strangeness, apartness, aloofness, is of prime importance in the situation.

So much about insects. But what about identification with mountains? The more usual terms are here 'personalizing', 'animism', 'anthropomorphism'. For thousands of years, and in various cultures, mountains have been venerated for their equanimity, greatness, aloofness, and majesty. The process of identification is the prerequisite for feeling the *lack* of greatness, equanimity in one's empirical self. One 'sees oneself in the other', but it is not the empirical self, but the self one would aspire to have. Given adverse conditions a mountain will stand for threat and terror, an adversary to be overcome. The so-called conquest of mountains relieves the threat.

The term 'identification' is used in many ways and the way it is used in the story may be rare and difficult to make clear except through many instances, positive and negative.

The relationship between identification and the narrower process of *solidarity* is such that every deep and lasting state of solidarity presupposes wide identification. The essential sense of common interests is comprehended spontaneously *and is internalized.* This leads to the *dependency of A's Self-realization upon B's.* When *B* seeks just treatment *A* supports the claim. *A* assumes a common stance upon the basis of an identification with *B. A may* also assume a common stance upon the basis of abstract ideas of moral justice, combined with a minimum of identification, but under hard and long-lasting trials the resulting solidarity cannot be expected to hold. The same applies to *loyalty.* When solidarity and loyalty are solidly anchored in identification, they are not experienced as moral demands; they come of themselves.

Continental European critique of western industrial society stresses the alienation caused by a kind of technology that reduces everything to mere objects of manipulation. *Verdinglichtung!* Not only animals are thus treated, workers tend to be mere factors – mostly causing trouble – in the production process. Big finance tends to enhance this trend. What is produced and how it is produced is irrelevant, what counts is profitable sale. Comparing the alienation process in various cultures one might often find technologies involving cruelty and vast indifference to suffering. What is expected today is that societies are rich enough to afford the gradual elimination of alienation.

From the identification process stems unity, and since the unity is of a gestalt character, the wholeness is attained. Very abstract and vague! But it offers a framework for a total view, or better, a central perspective.

The above seems to point in the direction of philosophical mysticism, but the fourth term, self-realization, breaks in and reinstates the central position of the individual – even if the capital 'S' is used to express something beyond narrow selves. The widening and deepening of the individual selves *somehow* never makes them into one 'mass'. Or into an organism in which every cell is programmed so as to let the organism function as one single, integrated being. How to work out this in a fairly precise way I do not know. It is a meagre consolation that I do not find that others have been able to do this in their contemplation of the pair unity–plurality. 'In unity diversity!', yes, but how? As a vague postulate it has a specific function within a total view, however imperfectly.

Identification and self-realization

Death of individuals and extinction of species are indispensable parts of evolution. So is the killing of one individual or species by another, even if non-organic environmental causes predominate. But evolution also shows the rise of mutual aid, and mature human beings cannot but work toward a state of affairs a little more like what their phantasy suggests could come in the very long run.

The maxim 'live and let live' suggests a class-free society in the entire ecosphere, a democracy in which we can speak about justice, not only with regard to human beings, but also for animals, plants and landscapes. This presumes a great emphasis upon the interconnectedness of everything and that our *egos* are fragments – not isolatable parts. We, as egos, have an extremely limited power and position within the whole, but it is sufficient for the unfolding of our potential, something vastly more comprehensive than the potential of our egos. So we are more than our egos, and are not fragments, hardly small and powerless. By identifying with greater wholes, we partake in the creation and maintenance of this whole. *We thereby share in its greatness.* New dimensions of satisfaction are revealed. The egos develop into selves of greater and greater dimension, proportional to the extent and depth of our processes of identification.

The conceptually simplest and historically speaking most ancient access to such an ecosophy is perhaps the one which analyses *dissimilar conceptions* of the 'self'. The first years of life, the self is not much broader than the ego – the narrow selfish centre which serves to satisfy the simplest biological needs. It is then best to eat the whole cake *alone*. About the age of seven, and until puberty, a socialization takes place which extends the self appreciably: the self comes to comprise one's family and closest friends.

The intensity of identification with other life depends upon milieu, culture and economic conditions. The ecosophical outlook is developed through an identification so deep that one's *own self* is no longer adequately delimited by the personal ego or the organism. One experiences oneself to be a genuine part of all life. Each living being is understood as a goal in itself, *in principle* on an equal footing with one's own ego. It also entails a transition from I–it attitudes to I–thou attitudes – to use Buber's terminology.

This does not imply that one acts, wishes to act, or consistently *can* act in harmony with the principle of equality. The statements about biospheric equality must be merely taken as guidelines. Even under conditions of intense identification, killing occurs. The Indians in California, with their animistic mythology, were an example of equality in principle, combined with realistic admissions of their own vital needs. When hunger arrives, brother rabbit winds up in the pot. 'A brother *is* a citizen, but oh, so temptingly nutritious!' – This exclamation is too easy: the complicated rituals which surround the hunt in many cultures illustrate how closely people feel bound to other beings, and how natural it is to feel that *when we harm others, we also harm ourselves*. Non-instrumental acts develop into instrumental.

Immanuel Kant's maxim 'You shall never use another person only as a means' is expanded in Ecosophy 'T' to 'You shall never use any living being only as a means'.

A lack of identification leads to indifference. Distant objects or events which do not seem to concern us are at best relegated to the indifferent background.

The pesticide azodrin reduced the number of certain 'obnoxious' insects to almost zero, which was the intention, but in addition it exterminated the natural enemies of the pest. The result after some time was more unwanted insects than ever. Such accidents have motivated a new slogan: you must know what will occur upon intervention in nature. If you don't know the consequences, don't intervene. But is this realistic? No more than a small fraction of the consequences can ever be known. Our ignorance now and in the near future about the consequences of intervention is appreciably greater than was initially assumed. Our indifference to the environment of life has meant that it is ordinarily experienced merely as a grey background. With identification, all this changes.

Suppose we spread a chemical substance upon a piece of land and take up a single gram of earth. What is happening in this tiny piece of our 'grey background' and what would happen in the event of our intervention? An investigation of just such a small clump of earth revealed that an astounding number of small organisms lived there: among other things 30,000 protozoa, 50,000 algae, 400,000 fungi and 2,500,000,000 bacteria.[1] The fertility of the Earth depends on an unsurveyable, intricate interaction – a crazily complex symbiotic network which embraces all these small living beings.

The greater our comprehension of our togetherness with other beings, the greater the identification, and the greater care we will take. The road is also opened thereby for delight in the well-being of others and sorrow when harm befalls them. We seek what is best for ourselves, but through the extension of the self, our 'own' best is also that of others. The own/not-own distinction survives only in grammar, not in feeling.

Philosophically, the concepts ego, self, and Self (the deep, comprehensive and ecological self) are braided into dissimilar systems which originally were closely associated to the world religions. Because of the reduced influence of these religions in our industrial societies, the philosophies of identification have become almost inaccessible. The hotbed for many kinds of spontaneous religious experience is no longer a cultural gift of the cradle.

It is noteworthy that a 'democracy of life forms' is or was characteristic of some primal societies. Their conception of the human situation is more realistic than that offered in our techno-natural scientific education. While we derobe nature as such of all sensory diversity, and assert that it is really colourless, animism moves in the opposite direction.

While warning against an 'unconscious' plunge into the technocratic society of the future, one of our foremost scientists has remarked: 'We own nature together with our fellows'. But the ideology of ownership of nature has no place in an ecosophy. The Norwegian people or the Norwegian state does not own Norway. The resources of the world are not only resources for human beings. Legally, we can 'own' a forest, but if we destroy the living conditions for life in the forest, we are transgressing the norm of equality.

This egalitarian attitude is manifested when the hunter has a long discussion with the spirit of the bear, and explains apologetically that the larder is bare and that he must now kill the bear to nourish his family. In return, the hunter can remind the bear's spirit that both he and his family will die one day, and turn to dust, and so to vegetation, sustenance for the descendants of the bear. In other words, this is a *realistic* egalitarian attitude, an acknowledgement of the cycles of life and their interconnection in nature.

Wildlife and forest management, and other professions in intimate contact with nature, change people's attitudes. It is only through work, play, and understanding that a deep and enduring identification can develop, an identification deep enough to colour the overall life conditions and ideology of a society.

The egalitarian attitude is not restricted to pre-industrial societies. 'Nature mysticism', as it is often called, is a genuine aspect of Western culture. To identify with all life does not imply an abandonment of our cultural heritage. Moral exhortation, punishment of ecocriminals, economic sanctions, and other negative tools have their place, but the education towards greater and wider identification though widening the Self is a thoroughly positive way.

'That which is not of value to any human being is of no value at all'

Some people who partake positively in important environmental decisions report that they are inhibited by the thought that somehow *any* valuation whatsoever is a human valuation and therefore must be a value *for* humans. They feel that there are philosophical reasons for downplaying or eliminating reference to nature as such, the planet as such, wilderness as such. To avoid irrationality, one must stick to homocentric utilitarian positions: one must point to usefulness *for* humans.

Philosophical reflection convinces us that only humans formulate value statements on this planet. Value statements, like theories of gravitation, are formulated by humans in human language, not by mosquitoes in mosquito language. We may speak of gravitation for us and its absence whether we are in a gravitational field or not. Newton's laws were made by Newton, but stones fall without him.

Our conclusion is quite simple: the mere fact that *humans* say 'this is valuable', does not imply that 'this is beneficial for humans'. It is misleading terminology to maintain that values humanly conceived as valuable are such *for human beings*.

The subjective stance implied by 'good means good for mankind', if applied consistently, easily leads to solipsistic egotism: 'good is *good for me*'. If I give anything, it is because I get satisfaction from it. If I am altruistic, it is solely because I am better off when others are better off. Few have any conception of the entire human population, or of what is good for such a mass of people. Good 'for myself, my family and friends' is perhaps more clearly meaningful for most of us. But we correctly refuse to admit that we, by '*x* is good', mean '*x* is good for myself, my family and friends'.

Common sense can be a guide here. We acknowledge our mixed motives, and realize that our evaluations are more or less egocentric, that we have our own benefit more or less in mind and seldom give priority to others before ourselves. The demarcation lines cannot be drawn, and there are great individual and collective differences. Often, however, we will completely agree in practice. Let us say that we are planning a trip together. Some places will be visited because it is to *A*'s advantage, while we others *see no value in it*, other places may be chosen by *B*, etc. At the same time, we are, as friends, aware that *each* of us thinks it is valuable that we visit a place *someone* thinks valuable to visit. This brings in evaluations of relevance on the meta-plane.

These propositions suggest that to ascribe value to animals, plants, landscapes, and wilderness areas independently of their relation to human utility or benefit is a philosophically legitimate procedure. To relate all value to mankind is a form of anthropocentrism which is not philosophically tenable.

Human nature may be such that with increased maturity a *human* need increases to protect the richness and diversity of life for *its own sake*. Consequently, what is useless in a narrow way may be useful in a wider sense, namely satisfying a human need. The protection of nature for *its own sake* would be a good example of this.

Friluftsliv: exuberance in nature

Contrary to expectation, urbanized life has not killed human fascination with free nature, but only made the access more difficult and promoted mass tourism. There is fortunately a way of life in free nature that is highly efficient in stimulating the sense of oneness, wholeness and in deepening identification.

The words 'outdoor recreation' are often used for the activities more and more people in the industrial societies are engaging in during their leisure time. But in Norwegian, there is a clearer, more value-laden word that refers to the type of outdoor recreation that seeks to come to nature on its own terms: to *touch the Earth lightly*. Literally, 'friluftsliv' means 'free air life', but it has been translated as 'open air life' and 'nature life'.[2] In the following, we retain the original term to indicate a positive kind of state of mind and body in nature, one that brings us closer to some of the many aspects of identification and Self-realization with nature that we have lost.

The satisfaction of the need for outdoor life and the need for machine-orientated technical unfolding cannot take place *simultaneously*. At present, the socio-economic forces in the industrial countries are lobbying in favour of priority for the capital-intensive apparatus: the apparatus-poor life is a hindrance to 'progress'. We should see true *friluftsliv* as a route towards paradigm change.

Friluftsliv plays a more and more important role as the dark shadows of the urban lifestyle of the industrial states have become more evident. The polar explorer and Norwegian national hero, Fritjof Nansen, remarked that '*friluftsliv* is a partial continuation of an aspect of an earlier form of life'. Human beings, until quite recently, have been hunters and gatherers, that is, lived and worked in nature. Much less than one per cent of our history has been devoted to the attempt to live a life characterized by machines and crowded quarters. As recently as the beginning of this century, many prominent futurists, including H.G. Wells, believed that 'progress' would succeed, and that human beings would be completely happy in their new radical form of life.

At the same time, *friluftsliv* caught on: more or less playful kinds of short excursions in nature. These excursions do not serve to procure food, nor do they fit any other characterization as work. Outdoor life has assumed forms which resemble the physical activities in the hunter and gatherer cultures: on water – swimming, diving, rowing, paddling, sailing, fishing; in fields and forests – hiking, camping, skiing, riding, hunting; in mountainous terrain – glacial walks, climbing, cross-country skiing, mountain climbing on skis, fishing, hunting. Where do the competition sports fit in? Nils Faarlund says:

> Competition as a value represents a form of self-realization which is reserved for the select. The competition-motivated lifestyle presupposes 'losers'. Self-realization for the elite presupposes that the others are denied self-realization. Competition as a value is thus excluding and elitist. Outdoor life in the sense of exuberant living in nature presupposes on the other hand the self-realization of others to achieve one's own (i.e.: a presentation of self which does not separate the individual from nature).

> An important element is the necessity of effort. Without effort, no quality, and without quality, reduced enjoyment. Enjoyment of the quality in one's personal life conduct is an autotelic experiencing of value, or inner motivation. Competitive motivation is external motivation and thus a weaker mode of motivation.[3]

With the near future in mind, it is important to stake out guidelines for ethically and ecologically responsible *friluftsliv*. These can be formulated as follows.

1   Respect for all life. Respect for landscape. The elimination of pleasure hunting necessarily follows, except for 'photographic hunting'. Hunting must be restricted to ecosophically justifiable wildlife management. Traceless passage through the wilderness: one leaves no tell-tale 'droppings' in the landscape. No more cairn construction, and no expansion of backwoods urbanization (highways, motels, etc.) of the natural areas.

2   Outdoor education in the signs of identification. Children's (and adults') longing and capacity for identification with life and landscape is encouraged. Conventional goal direction: to get there, to be skilful, to be better than others, to get things done, to describe in words, to have and use new and fancy equipment – is discouraged. The ability to experience deep, rich and varied interaction in and with nature is developed.

3   Minimal strain upon the natural combined with maximal self-reliance. This is a great challenge today. Greater knowledge about the use of local plants and other locally available material allows one quite often to live in nature with local resources. But acquaintance with nature's carrying capacity is simultaneously required. This limits the number of people who can be almost self-sufficient within a given landscape.

4   Natural lifestyle. All-sided forms of togetherness with as much dwelling upon goals as possible, as little as possible upon that which is *solely* a means. The greatest possible elimination of technique and apparatus from the outside.

5   Time for adjustment: those who come from urban life ordinarily have a certain appreciation for peace, stillness, and other aspects which contrast sharply with the stressful lifestyle of the city. After a few days, or a week, a certain *underestimation* usually sets in: the lack of radio, television, cinemas, etc. It takes time for the new milieu to work *in depth*. It is quite normal that several weeks must pass before the *sensitivity* for nature is so developed that it fills the mind. If a great deal of technique and apparatus are placed between oneself and nature, nature cannot possibly be reached.

The foregoing five points are meant to be guidelines. In the eyes of the growth economy, these points are poison. One cannot count on any immediate government efforts to protect the existing basis for ethically and ecologically responsible *friluftsliv*. Recently, though, the Norwegian Ministry of the Environment (*Miljverndepartmentet*) has gone quite far in limiting the notion of *friluftsliv* to what is compatible with these five points. In the growth economy at large, goals and intrinsic values are forgotten in favour of tourism and profitable capital investments.

Extremely powerful forces are attempting to replace *friluftsliv* with mechanized, competitive, and environmentally destructive intrusions into nature. These forces can only be countered through a long contest upon many fronts.

When rampant urbanization began to cripple human life in the rich industrial states, the establishment of national parks and other large free areas was advocated. None the less, the need for elbow room and activity under the open sky has been shown to be much more than a luxury need of the elite. Among many people it has developed into a vital need.

The easily accessible free areas have proven to be insufficient, and quickly assumed an urban façade – line-ups, littering, the devastation of vegetation, fatal curtailment of freedom of movement, luxury residences and luxurious living rather than simple *life*.

In the 1980s, many parks in the USA are so overloaded with people (often Europeans in caravans!) that extremely strict regulations have been introduced. A typical stepwise trend can be traced: forbidden to camp in certain areas – forbidden to camp except in designated areas – camping forbidden; forbidden to prepare food except in cement grilles – forbidden to prepare food outdoors; forbidden to move in steep terrain (erosion) – forbidden to walk off the paths – forbidden to stray from the asphalt – only short sojourns allowed – ticket required every day – 'Entrance forbidden: trespassers will be prosecuted'.

Instead of entering a realm of freedom, one feels that one is in some kind of museum ruled by angry owners.

In a country where *friluftsliv* is accepted as a vital need, such restrictions would be considered an outrage.

Cooperation between the representatives of industry and competitive sports has created an *outfitting pressure*: new so-called improvements appear and are marketed continuously, and norms about equipment replacement are impressed upon and accepted by large sections of the population. A refinement which *can* be important in top competition, but is frivolous in *friluftsliv*, is none the less sold to the well-to-do and more lethargic groups of the public who are susceptible to sales pushes. As equipment to outdoor generalists is much less expensive than specialized equipment, people are encouraged to specialize. Furthermore, it is more profitable to see things which require large capital outlays.

After a gigantic outpour of resources and technique, the barriers are overcome – the happy consumer stretches out on the simple bunk in the log cabin, listens to the birds singing, opens a creaky wooden door to watch the lively salmon jumping in the swirling waters. People swallow the equipment hook, line, and sinker, and lengthen their working day and increase stress in the city to be able to afford the 'latest'. Worn out, and with only a little time to spare, they dash off to the outdoor areas, for a short respite before rushing back to the cities. Still starved, they keep right on biting!

Friluftsliv is a rather concrete theme, but it cannot be separated from metaphysics. So the jump back to philosophy is not unduly long. Understanding of anything in nature begins with direct experience, but this soon stimulates reflection.

Notes

[*] From Arne Naess, *Economy, Community and Lifestyle*, Cambridge University Press, 1989, pp.171–81.

[1] Paul R. Ehrlich and Anne H. Ehrlich, *Population, Resources and Environment*, W.H. Freeman, 1970, p.180.

[2] See Peter Reed and David Rothenberg (eds), *Wisdom and the Open Air: selections from Norwegian ecophilosophy*, Oslo Council for Environmental Studies, 1987.

[3] Nils Faarlund, *On the Setting of Values in Outdoor and Sport*, 1973, ms in Norwegian, unpublished.

'Nature, Self, and Gender: Feminism, Environmental Philosophy and the Critique of Rationalism'

Val Plumwood

Val Plumwood, as Val Routley, one of the authors of Reading 1, criticizes deep ecology not from a 'shallow' human-centred position, but from an alternative form of deep green environmentalism.* She criticizes the failure of deep ecology to recognize the distinctness and independence of things in nature, its assimilation of concern for others to a form of self-concern, and its repudiation of concern based on personal connection.

Most mainstream environmental philosophers continue to view environmental philosophy as mainly concerned with ethics. For example, instrumentalism is generally viewed by mainstream environmental philosophers as a problem in ethics, and its solution is seen as setting up some sort of theory of intrinsic value. This neglects a key aspect of the overall problem that is concerned with the definition of the human self as separate from nature, the location of this self in reason, the connection between this and the instrumental view of nature, and broader *political* aspects of the critique of instrumentalism.

One key aspect of the Western view of nature, which the ethical stance neglects completely, is the view of nature as sharply discontinuous or ontologically divided from the human sphere of reason. This leads to a view of humans as apart from or 'outside of' nature, usually as masters or external controllers of it. Attempts to reject this view often speak alternatively of humans as 'part of nature' but rarely distinguish this position from the obvious claim that human fate is interconnected with that of the biosphere, that humans are subject to natural laws. But on the divided-self theory it is reason, the essentially or authentically human part of the self, and in the sense the human realm proper, that is outside nature, not the human as a physical phenomenon. The view of humans as outside of and alien to nature seems to be especially strongly a Western one, although not confined to the West. There are many other cultures which do not hold it, which stress what connects us to nature as genuinely human virtues, which emphasize continuity and not dissimilarity.[1]

As ecofeminism points out, Western thought has given us a strong human-nature dualism that is part of the set of interrelated dualisms of mind–body, reason–nature, reason–emotion, masculine–feminine and has important interconnected features with these other dualisms.[2] This dualism has been especially stressed in the rationalist tradition. In this dualism what is characteristically and authentically human is defined against or in opposition to what is taken to be natural, nature, or the physical or biological realm. This takes various forms. For example, the characterization of the genuinely, properly, characteristically, or authentically human, or of human virtue, in polarized terms to exclude what is taken to be characteristic of the natural is what John Rodman[3] has called 'the Differential Imperative' in which what is virtuous in the human is taken to be what maximizes distance from the merely natural. The maintenance of sharp dichotomy and polarization is achieved by the rejection and denial of what links humans to the animal. What is taken to be authentically and characteristically human, defining of the human, as well as the ideal for which humans should strive, is *not* to be found in what is shared with the natural and animal (e.g. the body, sexuality, reproduction, emotionality, the senses, agency) but in what is thought to separate and distinguish them – especially reason and its offshoots. Hence humanity is defined not as part of nature (perhaps a special part) but as separate from and in opposition to it. Thus the relation of humans to nature is treated as an oppositional and value dualism.

The process closely parallels the formation of other dualisms, such as masculine–feminine, reason–emotion, and spirit–body criticized in feminist thought,[4] but this parallel logic is not the only connection between human-nature dualism and masculine–feminine dualism. Moreover, this exclusion of the natural from the concept of the properly human is not the only dualism involved, because what is involved in the construction of this dualistic conception of the human is the rejection of those parts of the human character identified as feminine – also identified as less than fully human – giving the masculine conception of what it is to be human. Masculinity can be linked to this exclusionary and polarized conception of the human, via the desire to exclude and distance from the feminine and the non-human. The features that are taken as characteristic of humankind and as where its special virtues lie, are those such as rationality, freedom, and transcendence of nature (all traditionally viewed as masculine), which are viewed as not shared with nature. Humanity is defined oppositionally to both nature and the feminine.

The upshot is a deeply entrenched view of the genuine or ideal human self as not including features shared with nature, and as defined *against* or in *opposition to* the non-human realm, so that the human sphere and that of nature cannot significantly overlap. Nature is sharply divided off from the human, is alien and usually hostile and inferior. Furthermore, this kind of human self can only have certain kinds of accidental or contingent connections to the realm of nature. I shall call this the discontinuity problem or thesis and I argue later that it plays a key role with respect to other elements of the problem.

Although the discontinuity problem is generally neglected by the ethical stance, a significant exception to its neglect within environmental philosophy seems to be found in deep ecology, which is also critical of the location of the problem within ethics.[5] Furthermore, deep ecology also seems initially to be more likely to be compatible with a feminist philosophical framework, emphasizing as it does connections with the self, connectedness, and merger. Nevertheless, there are severe tensions between deep ecology and a feminist perspective. Deep ecology has not satisfactorily identified the key elements in the traditional framework or observed their connections to rationalism. As a result, it fails to reject adequately rationalist assumptions and indeed often seems to provide its own versions of universalization, the discarding of particular connections, and rationalist accounts of self.

Deep ecology locates the key problem area in human–nature relations in the separation of humans and nature, and it provides a solution for this in terms of the 'identification' of self with nature. 'Identification' is usually left deliberately vague, and corresponding accounts of self are various and shifting and not always compatible.[6] There seem to be at least three different accounts of self involved – indistinguishability, expansion of self, and transcendence of self – and deep ecologists appear to feel free to move among them at will. As I shall show, all are unsatisfactory from both a feminist perspective and from that of obtaining a satisfactory environmental philosophy, and the appeal of deep ecology rests largely on the failure to distinguish them.

The indistinguishability account

The indistinguishability account rejects boundaries between self and nature. Humans are said to be just one strand in the biotic web, not the source and ground of all value and the discontinuity thesis is, it seems, firmly rejected. Warwick Fox describes the central intuition of deep ecology as follows: 'We can make no firm ontological divide in the field of existence... there is no bifurcation in reality between the human and non-human realms... to the extent that we perceive boundaries, we fall short of deep ecological consciousness.'[7] But much more is involved here than the rejection of discontinuity, for deep ecology goes on to replace the human-in-environment image by a holistic or gestalt view that 'dissolves not only the human-in-environment concept, but every compact-thing-in-milieu concept' – except when talking at a superficial level of communication.[8] Deep ecology involves a cosmology of 'unbroken wholeness which denies the classical idea of the analysability of the world into separately and independently existing parts'.[9] It is strongly attracted to a variety of mystical traditions and to the Perennial Philosophy, in which the self is merged with the other – 'the other is none other than yourself.' As John Seed puts it: 'I am protecting the rainforest' develops into 'I am part of the rainforest protecting myself. I am that part of the rainforest recently emerged into thinking.'[10]

There are severe problems with these claims, arising not so much from the orientation to the concept of self (which seems to me important and correct) or from the mystical character of the insights themselves as from the indistinguishability metaphysics which is proposed as their basis. It is not merely that the identification process of which deep ecologists speak seems to stand in need of much more clarification, but that it does the wrong thing. The problem in the sort of account I have given, is the discontinuity between humans and nature that emerges as part of the overall set of Western dualisms. Deep ecology proposes to heal this division by a 'unifying process', a metaphysics that insists that everything is really part of and indistinguishable from everything else. This is not only to employ overly powerful tools but ones that do the wrong job, for the origins of the particular opposition involved in the human–nature dualism remain unaddressed and unanalysed. The real basis of the discontinuity lies in the concept of an authentic human being, in what is taken to be valuable in human character, society, and culture, as what is distinct from what is taken to be natural. The sources of and remedies for this remain unaddressed in deep ecology. Deep ecology has confused dualism and atomism and then mistakenly taken indistinguishability to follow from the rejection of atomism. The confusion is clear in Fox, who proceeds immediately from the ambiguous claim that there is no 'bifurcation in reality between the human and non-human realms' (which could be taken as a rejection of human discontinuity from nature) to the conclusion that what is needed is that we embrace an indistinguishability metaphysics of unbroken wholeness in the whole of reality. But the problem must be addressed in terms of this specific dualism and its connections. Instead, deep ecology proposes the obliteration of all distinction.

Thus deep ecology's solution to removing this discontinuity by obliterating *all* division is far too powerful. In its over-generality it fails to provide a genuine basis for an environmental ethics of the kind sought, for the view of humans as metaphysically unified with the cosmic whole will be equally true whatever relation humans stand in with nature – the situation of exploitation of nature exemplifies such unity equally as well as a conserver situation and the human self is just as indistinguishable from the bulldozer and Coca-Cola bottle as the rocks of the rainforest. What John Seed seems to have in mind here is that once one has realized that one is indistinguishable from the rainforest, its needs would become one's own. But there is nothing to guarantee this – one could equally well take one's own needs for its.

This points to a further problem with the indistinguishability thesis, that we need to recognize not only our human continuity with the natural world but also its distinctness and independence from us and the distinctness of the needs of things in nature from ours. The indistinguishability account does not allow for this, although it is a very important part of respect for nature and of conservation strategy.

The dangers of accounts of the self that involve self-merger appear in feminist contexts as well, where they are sometimes appealed to as the alternative to masculine-defined autonomy as disconnection from others. As Jean Grimshaw writes of the related thesis of the indistinctness of persons (the acceptance of the loss of self-boundaries as feminine ideal):

> It is important not merely because certain forms of symbiosis or 'connection' with others can lead to damaging failures of personal development, but because care for others, understanding of them, are only possible if one can adequately distinguish oneself *from* others. If I see myself as 'indistinct' from you, or you as not having your own being that is not merged with mine, then I cannot preserve a real sense of your well-being as opposed to mine. Care and understanding require the sort of distance that is needed in order not to see the other as a projection of self, or self as a continuation of the other.[11]

These points seem to me to apply to caring for other species and for the natural world as much as they do to caring for our own species. But just as dualism is confused with atomism, so holistic self-merger is taken to be the only alternative to egoistic accounts of the self as without essential connection to others or to nature. Fortunately, this is a false choice;[12] as I argue below, non-holistic but relational accounts of the self, as developed in some feminist and social philosophy, enable a rejection of dualism, including human-nature dualism, without denying the independence or distinguishability of the other. To the extent that deep ecology is identified with the indistinguishability thesis, it does not provide an adequate basis for a philosophy of nature.

The expanded self

In fairness to deep ecology it should be noted that it tends to vacillate between mystical indistinguishability and the other accounts of self, between the holistic self and the expanded self. Vacillation occurs often by way of slipperiness as to what is meant by identification of self with the other, a key notion in deep ecology. This slipperiness reflects the confusion of dualism and atomism previously noted but also seems to reflect a desire to retain the mystical appeal of indistinguishability while avoiding its many difficulties. Where 'identification' means not 'identity' but something more like 'empathy', identification with other beings can lead to an expanded self. According to Arne Naess, 'The self is as comprehensive as the totality of our identifi-cations... Our Self is that with which we identify.'[13] This larger self (or Self, to deep ecologists) is something for which we should strive 'insofar as it is in our power to do so',[14] and according to Fox we should also strive to make it as large as possible. But this expanded self is not the result of a critique of egoism; rather, it is an enlargement and an extension of egoism.[15] It does not question the structures of possessive egoism and self-interest; rather, it tries to allow for a wider set of interests by an expansion of self. The motivation for the expansion of self is to allow for a wider set of concerns while continuing to allow the self to operate on the fuel of self-interest (or Self-interest). This is apparent from the claim that 'in this light... ecological resistance is simply another name for self defence'.[16] Fox quotes with approval John Livingstone's statement: 'When I say that the fate of the sea turtle or the tiger or the gibbon is mine, I mean it. All that is in my universe is not merely mine; it is *me*. And I shall defend myself. I shall defend myself not only against overt aggression but also against gratuitous insult.'[17]

Deep ecology does not question the structures of rational egoism and continues to subscribe to two of the main tenets of the egoist framework – that human nature is egoistic and that the alternative to egoism is self-sacrifice.[18] Given these assumptions about egoism, the obvious way to obtain some sort of human interest in defending nature is through the expanded Self operating in the interests of nature but also along the familiar lines of self-interest.[19] The expanded-self strategy might initially seem to be just another pretentious and obscure way of saying that humans empathize with nature. But the strategy of transferring the structures of egoism is highly problematic for the widening of interest is obtained at the expense of failing to recognize unambiguously the distinctness and independence of the other.[20] Others are recognized morally only to the extent that they are incorporated into the self, and their difference denied.[21] And the failure to critique egoism and the disembodied, non-relational self means a failure to draw connections with other contemporary critiques.

The transcended or transpersonal self

To the extent that the expanded Self requires that we detach from the particular concerns of the self (a relinquishment that[22] despite its natural difficulty we should struggle to attain), expansion of self to Self also tends to lead into the third position, the transcendence of overcoming of self. Thus Fox urges us to strive for *impartial* identification with *all* particulars, the cosmos, discarding our identifications with our own particular concerns, personal emotions, and attachments. Fox presents here the deep ecology version of universalization, with the familiar emphasis on the personal and the particular as corrupting and self-interested – 'the cause of possessiveness, war, and ecological destruction'.

This treatment of particularity, the devaluation of an identity tied to particular parts of the natural world as opposed to an abstractly conceived whole, the cosmos, reflects the rationalistic preoccupation with the universal and its account of ethical life as oppositional to the particular. The analogy in human terms of impersonal love of the cosmos is the view of morality as based on universal principles or the impersonal and abstract 'love of man'. Thus Fox reiterates (as if it were unproblematic) the view of particular attachments as ethically suspect and as oppositional to genuine, impartial 'identification', which necessarily falls short with all particulars.

Because this 'transpersonal' identification is so indiscriminate and intent on denying particular meanings, it cannot allow for the deep and highly particularistic attachment to place that has motivated both the passion of many modern conservationists and the love of many indigenous peoples for their land (which deep ecology inconsistently tries to treat as a model). This is based not on a vague, bloodless, and abstract cosmological concern but on the formation of identity, social and personal, in relation to particular areas of land, yielding ties often as special and powerful as those to kin, and which are equally expressed in very specific and local responsibilities of care.[23] This emerges clearly in the statements of many indigenous peoples, such as in the moving words of Cecilia Blacktooth explaining why her people would not surrender their land:

You ask us to think what place we like next best to this place where we always lived. You see the graveyard there? There are our fathers and our grandfathers. You see that Eagle-next mountain and that Rabbit-hold mountain? When God made them. He gave us this place. We have always been here. We do not care for any other place... We have always lived here. We would rather die here. Our fathers did. We cannot leave them. Our children were born here – how can we go away? If you give us the best place in the world, it is not so good as this... This is our home... We cannot live anywhere else. We were born here and our fathers are buried here... We want this place and no other ...[24]

In inferiorizing such particular, emotional, and kinship-based attachments, deep ecology gives us another variant on the superiority of reason and the inferiority of its contrasts, failing to grasp yet again the role of reason and incompletely critiquing its influence. To obtain a more adequate account than that offered by mainstream ethics and deep ecology it seems that we must move toward the sort of ethics feminist theory has suggested, which can allow for both continuity and difference and for ties to nature which are expressive of the rich, caring relationships of kinship and friendship rather than increasing abstraction and detachment from relationship.

Notes

[*] From Val Plumwood, 'Nature, Self, and Gender: Feminism, Environmental Philosophy, and the Critique of Rationalism', in R. Elliot (ed.) *Environmental Ethics*, Oxford University Press, 1995, pp.155–64.

[1] E.g. Bill Neidjie's words, 'This ground and this earth/like brother and mother' (B. Neidjie with S. Davies and A. Fox, *Kakadu Man*, Mybrook P/L, 1985, p.46) may be interpreted as an affirmation of such kinship or continuity. (See also Neidjie, *Kakadu Man*, pp.53, 61–2, 77, 81–2, 88.)

[2] The logic of dualism and the masculinity of the concept of humanity are discussed in Val Plumwood, 'Ecofeminism: An Overview and Discussion of Positions and Arguments', *Women and Philosophy, Supplement to Australasian Journal of Philosophy*, 64, June 1986, pp.120–38; and 'Women, Humanity and Nature', *Radical Philosophy*, 48, 1988, pp.6–24. See also Karent J. Warren, 'Feminism and Ecology: Making Connections', *Environmental Ethics*, 9, 1987, pp.17–18; and 'The Power and Promise of Ecological Feminism', *Environmental Ethics*, 12/2, 1990, pp.121–46.

[3] John Rodman, 'Paradigm Change in Political Science', *American Behavioural Scientist*, 24/1, 1980, pp.54–5.

[4] See e.g. Rosemary Radford Ruether, *New Woman New Earth*, Seabury Press, 1975; Susan Griffin, *Woman and Nature: The Roaring Inside Her*, Harper and Row, 1978; Joan L. Griscom, 'On Healing the Nature/History Split in Feminist Thought', *Heresies*, 4/1, 1981, pp.4–9; Ynestra King, 'Feminism and Revolt', *Heresies*, 4/1, 1981, pp.12–16; Genevieve Lloyd, 'Public Reason and Private Passion', *Metaphilosophy*, 14, 1983, pp.308–26; and 'Reason, Gender, and Morality in the History of Philosophy', *Social Research*, 50/3, 1983, pp.490–513; Alison Jaggar, *Feminist Politics and Human Nature*, Rowman & Allenheld: Harvester, 1983.

[5] None the less, deep ecology's approach to ethics is, like much else, doubtfully consistent, variable, and shifting. Thus although Arne Naess calls for recognition of the intrinsic value of nature, he also tends to treat 'the maxim of self-realization' as *substituting for* and obviating an ethical account of care and respect for nature (Arne Naess, *Ecology, Community, and Lifestyle*, Cambridge University Press, 1988, pp.20, 86) placing the entire emphasis on phenomenology (see also his 'The Shallow and the Deep, Long-Range Ecology Movement: A Summary', *Inquiry*, 16, 1973, pp.95–100; and 'Intrinsic Value: Will the Defenders of Nature Please Rise', in M. Soule (ed.), *Conservation Biology*, Sinauer Associates, 1986). In more recent work, however, the emphasis seems to have quietly shifted back again from holistic intuition to a broad and extremely vague 'biocentric egalitarianism' which places the centre once again in ethics and enjoins an ethic of maximum expansion of Self (see Warwick Fox, *Towards a Transpersonal Ecology: Developing New Foundations for Environmentalism*, Shambala, 1990.

[6] Other critics of deep ecology, such as Richard Sylvan ('A Critique of Deep Ecology', *Radical Philosophy*, 40–1, 1985) and Jim Cheney ('Ecofeminism and Deep Ecology', *Environmental Ethics*, 9, 1987, pp.115–45), have also suggested that it shifts between different and incompatible versions. Ecofeminist critics of deep ecology have included Ariel Salleh ('Deeper than Deep Ecology', *Environmental Ethics*, 6, 1984, pp.339–45); Marti Kheel ('The Liberation of Nature: A Circular Affair', *Environmental Ethics*, 7, 1985, pp.139–49); Janet Biehl ('It's Deep, But is it Broad? An Ecofeminist Looks at Deep Ecology', *Kick It Over*, Special Supplement (Winter 1987)) and Warren ('The Power and Promise of Ecological Feminism').

[7] Warwick Fox, 'Deep Ecology: A New Philosophy of Our Time?', *Ecologist*, 14, 1984, p.7.

[8] Ibid., p.1.

[9] Naess, quoted ibid., pp.3, 10.

[10] John Seed, Joanna Macey, Pat Felming, and Arne Naess, *Thinking Like a Mountain: Towards a Council of All Beings*, New Society Publishers, 1988.

[11] Jean Grimshaw, *Philosophy and Feminist Thinking*, University of Minnesota Press, 1986, pp.182–3. Also published as *Feminist Philosophers*, Wheatsheaf, 1986.

[12] This is argued in R. Routley and V. Routley, 'Social Theories, Self-Management and Environmental Problems', in D. Mannison, M. McRobbie and R. Routley, (eds), *Environmental Philosophy*, ANU Department of Philosophy Monograph Series RSSS, 1980, pp.217–332), where a relational account of self developed in the context of an anarchist theory is applied to relations with nature. Part of the problem lies in the terminology of 'holism' itself, which is used in highly variable and ambiguous ways, sometimes carrying commitment to indistinguishability and sometimes meaning only 'non-atomistic'.

[13] Naess, quoted in Warwick Fox, *Approaching Deep Ecology: A response to Richard Sylvan's Critique of Deep Ecology,* Environmental Studies Occasional Paper 20, University of Tasmania Centre for Environmental Studies, 1986, p.54.

[14] Fox, *Approaching Deep Ecology*, pp.13–19.

[15] As noted by Cheney.

[16] Fox, *Approaching Deep Ecology*, p.60.

[17] Ibid.

[18] Thus John Seed says: 'Naess wrote that when most people think about conservation, they think about sacrifice. This is a treacherous basis for conservation, because most people aren't capable of working for anything except their own self-interest... Naess argued that we need to find ways to extend our identity into nature. Once that happens, being out in front of bulldozers or whatever becomes no more of a sacrifice than moving your foot if you notice that someone's just about to strike it with an axe.' (John Seed, interviewed by Pat Stone. *Mother Earth News*, May/June 1989.)

[19] This denial of the alterity of the other is also the route taken by J. Baird Callicot, who indeed asserts that 'The principle of axiological complementarity posits an essential unity between self and world and establishes the problematic intrinsic value of nature in relation to the axiologically privileged value of self' (J. Baird Callicot, 'Intrinsic Value, Quantum Theory, and Environmental Ethics', *Environmental Ethics*, 7, 1985, p.275.) Given the impoverishment of Humean theory in the area of relations (and hence its inability to conceive a self-in-relationship whose connections to others are not merely contingent but essential), Callicot has little alternative to this direction of development.

[20] Grimshaw, *Philosophy and Feminist Thinking*, p.182. See also the excellent discussion in Warren, 'The Power and Promise of Ecological Feminism', pp.136–8, of the importance of recognition and respect for the other's difference; Lawrence A. Blum, *Friendship, Altruism and Morality*, Routledge & Kegan Paul, 1980, p.75; and Seyla Benhabib, 'The Generalized and the Concrete Other', in E. Kittay and D. Meyers (eds), *Women and Moral Theory*, Rowman and Allenheld, 1987, p.166.

[21] Warren, 'The Power and Promise of Ecological Feminism'.

[22] According to Fox, *Towards a Transpersonal Ecology*, p.12.

[23] This traditional model of land relationship is closely linked to that of bio-regionalism, whose strategy is to engage people in greater knowledge and care for the local areas that have meaning for them and where they can most easily evolve a caring and responsible lifestyle. The feat of 'impartial identification with all particulars' is, beyond the seeking of individual enlightenment, strategically empty. Because it cares 'impartially' for everything it can, in practice, care for nothing.

[24] T.C. McLuhan (ed.) *Touch the Earth*, Abacus, 1973, p.28.

'Transpersonal Ecology and the Varieties of Identification'

Warwick Fox

In this Reading,* Fox elaborates and defends the ideas of Arne Naess, and in particular the idea of wide identification. The term 'transpersonal' implies the ideal of transcending one's personal (individual) identity. The Reading develops the idea of cosmologically based identification, at the expense of personally based identification, since only the former can support impartial concern for all natural things.

Three bases of identification

How does one realize, in a this-worldly sense, as expansive a sense of self as possible? The transpersonal ecology answer is: through the process of identification. As Naess says: 'The ecological self of a person is that with which this person identifies. This key sentence (rather than definition) about the self, shifts the burden of clarification from the term "self" to that of "identification". Or rather "process of identification".'[1] How, then, does one proceed in realizing a way of being that sustains the widest and deepest possible identification? I suggest that there are three general kinds of bases for the experience of commonality that we refer to as identification; three general kinds of ways in which we may come to identify more widely and deeply. I refer to these bases of identification as *personal*, *ontological*, and *cosmological*.

Personally based identification refers to experiences of commonality with other entities that are brought about through personal involvement with these entities. This is the way in which most of us think of the process of identification most of the time. We generally tend to identify most with those entities with which we are often in contact (assuming our experiences of these entities are of a generally positive kind). This applies not only to concrete entities (e.g., the members of our family, our friends and more distant relations, our pets, our homes, our teddy bear or doll) but also to those more abstract kinds of entities with which we have considerable personal involvement (our football or basketball club, the individual members of which may change from year to year; our country). We experience these entities as part of 'us', as part of our identity. An assault upon their integrity is an assault upon our integrity.

In contrast to personally based identification, ontologically and cosmologically based forms of identification are transpersonal in that they are not primarily a function of the personal contacts or relationships of this or that particular person. There is, of course, a sense in which *all* forms of identification beyond one's egoic, biographical, or personal sense of self can be described as *transpersonal*. However, the point here is that personally based identification is, as its name suggests, a far more personal – or, alternatively, a far less *trans*personal – form of identification than either ontologically or cosmologically based identification, since it is a function of the personal contacts or relationships of this or that particular person, whereas, as we shall see below, the latter two forms of identification are not.

Ontologically based identification refers to experiences of commonality with all that is that are brought about through deep-seated realization of the fact *that* things are. (I am using the complex and variously employed term *ontology* in this context to refer to the fact of existence per se rather than to refer to the question of what the basic aspects of existence are or how the world is.) This is not a simple idea to communicate in words! Moreover, I do not intend to say very much about this idea since, in my view, it properly belongs to the realm of the training of consciousness (or perception) that is associated, for example, with Zen Buddhism, and those who engage in such training continually warn about the limits of language in attempting to communicate their experientially based insights. Martin Heidegger is a notable Western philosopher who does attempt to convey such insights in words, but then, although deeply rewarding, he is also notorious for the difficulty of his language. It is interesting to note in this connection, however, that upon reading a book by the Zen master D.T. Suzuki, Heidegger is reported to have said, 'If I understand this man correctly, this is what I have been trying to say in all my writings'.[2]

The basic idea that I am attempting to communicate by referring to ontologically based identification is that the fact – the utterly astonishing fact –that things *are* impresses itself upon some people in such a profound way that all that exists seems to stand out as foreground from a background of non-existence, voidness, or emptiness – a background from which this foreground arises moment by moment. This sense of the specialness or privileged nature of all that exists means that 'the environment' or 'the world at large' is experienced not as a mere backdrop against which our privileged egos and those entities with which they are most concerned play themselves out, but rather as just as much an expression of the manifesting of Being (i.e., of existence per se) as we ourselves are. We have perhaps all experienced this state of being, this sense of commonality with all that is simply by virtue of the fact *that* it is, at certain moments. Things *are!* There is something rather than nothing! Amazing! If we draw upon this experience we can then gain some insight into why it is that people who experience the world in this way on a regular or semi-regular basis (typically as the result of arduous spiritual discipline) find themselves tending to experience a deep but impartial sense of identification with *all* existents. We can gain some insight into why such people find themselves spontaneously inclined 'to be open for the Being [the sheer manifesting] of [particular] beings' and, hence, why, for them, 'the best course of "action" is to let beings be, to let them take care of themselves in accord with their own natures'.[3]

For those who cannot see any logical connection between deep-seated realization of the fact that things *are* and the experience of deep-seated commonality with – and thus respect for – all that is, I can only reiterate that these remarks cannot and should not be analysed through a logical lens. We are here in the realm of what Wittgenstein referred to as the mystical when he said, 'It is not *how* things are in the world that is mystical, but *that* it exists'.[4] If one seriously wishes to pursue the question of ontologically based identification then one must be prepared to undertake arduous practice of the kind that is associated with certain kinds of experientially based spiritual disciplines. (Roger Walsh captures what is of central interest about these disciplines in this context by referring to them as *consciousness disciplines* in order to distinguish them 'from the religious dogma, beliefs, and cosmologies to which most religious devotees adhere, and from the occult popularisms of both East and West'.[5] Those who are not prepared to do this – that is, most of us – are no more in a position to dismiss the fruits of such practice than are people who would dismiss the fruits of scientific research without being prepared to undertake the training that is necessary to become a scientist or at least to understand the general features of scientific procedure.[6])

Cosmologically based identification refers to experiences of commonality with all that is that are brought about through deep-seated realization of the fact that we and all other entities are aspects of a single unfolding reality. This realization can be brought about through the empathic incorporation of *any* cosmology (i.e., any fairly comprehensive account of *how* the world is) that sees the world as a single unfolding process – as a 'unity in process', to employ Theodore Roszak's splendid phrase.[7] This means that this realization can be brought about through the empathic incorporation of mythological, religious, speculative philosophical, or scientific cosmologies.[8] I am not meaning to assert by this that these various kinds of accounts of how the world is are equal in epistemological status, only that each is *capable* of provoking a deep-seated realization that we and all other entities are aspects of a single unfolding reality. Consider, for example, the world-views of certain indigenous peoples (e.g., of some North American Indians), the philosophy of Taoism, or the philosophy of Spinoza.

For many people in the modern world the most viable – perhaps the only truly viable – source of cosmological ideas is science. Yet, despite this, there are many other people (including many who are formally trained in science or who simply have a general interest in science) who seem unable or unwilling to see science in a cosmological light. For them, science is all about prediction, manipulation, and control ('instrumental rationality') and cosmology is seen as something that belongs to mythology, religion, or speculative philosophy, or else as a highly specialized sub-discipline of physics that deals with the evolution and structure of the physical universe. But the anthropocentrically fuelled idea that science is all about prediction, manipulation, and control is only half the story. As George Sessions says, 'Modern science... [has] turned out to be a two-edged sword'.[9] The other side of science is its importance for understanding our place in the larger scheme of things (and it is scarcely necessary to add that this aspect has had profoundly *non*-anthropocentric implications). This side of science is its cosmological aspect. Considered from this side, modern science can be seen as providing an account of creation that is the equal of any mythological, religious, or speculative philosophical account in terms of scale, grandeur, and richness of detail. More specifically, modern science is providing an increasingly detailed account of the physical and biological evolution of the universe that compels us to view reality as a single unfolding process.[10]

The most obvious feature of the physical and biological evolution of the universe as revealed by modern science is the fact that it has become increasingly differentiated over time. This applies not just at the level of biological evolution but also at the level of the physical evolution of the cosmos. If we think of this process of increasing differentiation over time diagrammatically then it is natural to depict it as a branching tree. Indeed, this is precisely the way in which evolutionary theorists think of biological evolution.[11] In general terms, ancestral species do not change *into* newer species; rather, newer species radiate out (branch away) from ancestral species, which can continue to exist alongside the newer species. This 'budding off' process occurs when populations of a particular kind of organism become in any way reproductively isolated (e.g., through geographical divergence or through divergence in breeding seasons) and then undergo changes in their genetic composition, primarily as a result of natural selection, to the point where members of one population are no longer capable of interbreeding with members of the other population.[12] But it is not only phylogenetic development (the evolution of species) that must be depicted as a continually branching tree. The image of a branching tree is just as relevant to other forms of development that involve increasing differentiation over time, whether it be ontogenetic development (the evolution of individual organisms from a cell to maturity) or the evolution of the universe itself from *nothing* to its present state some fifteen billion years later.[13] As the science writer Stephen Young explains in a brief recent introduction to the importance of the tree metaphor in science generally: 'Trees are indispensable to science. From physics to physiology, they serve as metaphors, expressing in a word details that would otherwise occupy a paragraph ... The theory of evolution is unthinkable without trees. Elsewhere within science, afforestation continues apace. If trees did not exist, scientists would have to invent them.'[14]

Even if our present views on cosmological evolution (including phylogenetic and ontogenetic evolution) turn out to stand in need of modification in crucial respects, we still have every reason to believe that the particular views that supersede these views will be entirely in conformity with the far more general idea that all entities in the universe are aspects of a single unfolding reality that has become increasingly differentiated over time. The justification for such confidence lies not only in the fact that *all* the evidence that bears on this question across *all* scientific disciplines points in this general direction, but also in the fact that even the most radical scientific (i.e., empirically testable) challenges to our present scientific views also point in this general direction. What is at issue in scientifically framed debates about the evolution of the universe or the evolution of life is only the question of the *mechanisms* of evolution (i.e., the mechanisms that underlie the increasing differentiation of the universe over time), not the fact of evolution per se.

[...]

If we empathetically incorporate (i.e., have a lived sense of) the evolutionary, 'branching tree' cosmology offered by modern science then we can think of ourselves and all other presently existing entities as leaves on this tree – a tree that has developed from a single seed of energy and that has been growing for some fifteen billion years, becoming infinitely larger and infinitely more differentiated in the process. A deep-seated realization of this cosmologically based sense of commonality with all that is leads us to identify ourselves more and more with the entire tree rather than just with our leaf (our personal, biographical self), the leaves on our twig (our family), the leaves we are in close proximity to on other twigs (our friends), the leaves on our minor sub-branch (our community), the leaves on our major sub-branch (our cultural or ethnic grouping), the leaves on our branch (our species), and so on. At the limit, cosmologically based identification, like ontologically based identification, therefore leads to impartial identification with *all* particulars (all leaves on the tree).

Having said this, it must immediately be noted that, as with ontologically based identification, the fact that cosmologically based identification tends to be more *impartial* than personally based identification does not mean that it need be any less deeply felt. Consider the Californian poet Robinson Jeffers! For Jeffers, 'This whole [the universe] is *in all its parts so beautiful*, and is felt by me to be so intensely in earnest, that I am *compelled* to love it' (emphases added).[15] Although Jeffers may represent a relatively extreme exemplar of cosmologically based identification, it should nevertheless be clear that this form of identification issues at least – perhaps even primarily? – in an orientation of steadfast (as opposed to fair-weather) friendliness. Steadfast friendliness manifests itself in terms of a clear and steady expression of positive interest, liking, warmth, good will, and trust; a steady predisposition to help or support; and, in the context of these attributes, a willingness to be firm and to criticize constructively where appropriate. Indeed, if a particular entity or life form imposes itself unduly upon other entities or life forms, an impartially based sense of identification may lead one to feel that one has no real choice but to *oppose* – even, in extreme cases, to terminate the existence of – the destructive or oppressive entity or life form. Even here, however, an impartially based sense of identification leads one to oppose destructive or oppressive entities or life forms in as educative, least disruptive, and least vindictive a way as possible.

Over time, steadfast friendliness often comes to be experienced by the recipient as a deep form of love precisely because it does not cling or cloy but rather gives the recipient 'room to move', room to be themselves. In the context of this book, it may be of particular interest to add here that Arne Naess seems to me to be an exemplar of steadfast friendliness – and of course I am not only talking here about his relationship with me over the years, but of his orientation toward the world in general. It is also interesting to note that Naess has himself written a paper on the importance of the concept of friendship in Spinoza's thinking in which he notes that 'the intellectual sobriety of Spinoza favours *friendship rather than worship*' and that, for Spinoza, 'friendship is the basic social relation' between members of a free society.[16] Naess concludes this paper by explicitly linking the theme of friendship in Spinoza's philosophy with 'the ecological concept of symbiosis as opposed to cut-throat competition'. 'Both in Spinoza and in the thinking of the field ecologist', says Naess, 'there is respect for an extreme diversity of beings capable of living together in an intricate web of relations'.[17]

Notwithstanding the eloquent testimonies to cosmologically based identification that have been offered by Spinoza, Gandhi, Jeffers, Naess, and many others (even Einstein, for example), many people find it difficult to think of identification in anything other than personally based terms. For these people, cosmologically based identification approximates to something like going out, encountering every entity in the universe (or, at least, on the planet) on a one-to-one basis, and coming to identify with each entity on the basis of that contact. But this simply represents an example of personally based identification that has been blown up into universal (or global) proportions. In contrast, cosmologically based identification means having a lived sense of commonality with all other entities (whether one happens to encounter them personally or not) in much the same way as, for example, leaves on the same tree would feel a sense of commonality with each and every other leaf if, say, we assumed that these leaves were all conscious and had a deep-seated realization of the fact that they all belonged to the same tree. In summary, then, personally based identification proceeds from the person – and those entities that are psychologically, and often physically, closest to the person – and works outward to a sense of commonality with other entities. In contrast, cosmologically based identification proceeds from a sense of the cosmos (such as that provided by the image of the tree of life) and works inward to each particular individual's sense of commonality with other entities. In vectorial terms, this contrast in approaches means that we can think of personally based identification as an 'inside-out' approach and cosmologically based identification as an 'outside-in' approach.

One may gain or seek to cultivate a cosmologically based sense of identification in a wide variety of ways. Even if we exclude mythological, religious, and speculative philosophical cosmologies and restrict ourselves to the cosmology of modern science, these ways of coming to embody a cosmologically based sense of identification can range from approaches such as the ritualized experientially based work being developed by John Seed and Joanna Macy under the title 'Council of All Beings',[18] to participation in theoretical scientific work (a number of the very best scientists have had a profound sense of cosmologically based identification); to more practically oriented involvement in natural history (many naturalists and field ecologists, for example, effectively come to experience themselves as leaves on the tree of life and seek to defend the unfolding of the tree in all its aspects as best they can); to simply developing a deeper personal interest in the scientific world model and in natural history along with one's other interests.

[...]

I want to turn now from the emphasis that is placed in transpersonal ecology on ontologically and, especially, cosmologically based forms of identification and consider the relative lack of emphasis that is placed on personally based identification. In contrast to the other two forms of identification, there *is* a fundamental theoretical reason why transpersonal ecologists do not emphasize personally based identification. Specifically, the fact that personally based identification refers to experiences of commonality with other entities that are brought about through personal involvement with these entities means that this form of identification *inevitably* leads one to identify most with those entities with which one is most involved. That is, one tends to identify with *my* self first, followed by *my* family, then *my* friends and more distant relations, *my* cultural or ethnic grouping next, *my* species, and so on – more or less what the socio-biologists say we are genetically predisposed to do. The problem with this is that, while extending love, care, and friendship to one's nearest and dearest is laudable in and of itself, the *other* side of emphasizing a purely personal basis for identification is that its practical upshot (*my* self first, *my* family and friends next, *my* cultural or ethnic grouping next, *my* species next, and so on) would seem to have far more to do with the *cause* of possessiveness, greed, exploitation, war, and ecological destruction than with the solution to these seemingly intractable problems.

I can hardly stress the importance of this last point enough. Personally based identification can slip so easily – and imperceptibly – into attachment and proprietorship. Anybody who doubts that personally based identification is a potentially treacherous basis for identification need only reflect on the way in which romantic love between two people – a paradigmatic example of intense personally based identification – can sometimes collapse into acrimonious divorce; or the truth in the old adage about family fights often being the worst fights; or the fact that we will do things to 'others' (or allow things to be done to 'them') that we would never do (or allow to happen) to 'one of us'. Yet again and again ecophilosophical discussants are all too prepared to extol the virtues of what effectively amounts to personally based identification while simply ignoring the possessive, greedy, exploitative, warmongering, and ecologically destructive drawbacks that can also attend this particular basis of identification.

Notes

* From Warwick Fox, *Towards a Transpersonal Ecology: developing new foundations for environmentalism*, Shambala, 1990, pp.249–67.

[1] Arne Naess, 'Self-realization: An Ecological Approach to Being in the World,' p.35.

[2] Quoted in William Barrett, 'Zen for the West,' in *Zen Buddhism: Selected Writings of D. T. Suzuki*, ed. William Barrett (Doubleday/Anchor Books, 1956), p.xi. There is a whole literature on the similarities between Heidegger's thought and Eastern thought, espcially Zen. For a guide to much of this literature, see the papers and books listed at note 3 in Michael Zimmerman, 'Heidegger and Heraclitus on Spiritual Practice,' *Philosophy Today* 27 (1983): 87–103. Special mention should be made here of Zimmerman's own book on Heidegger entitled *Eclipse of the Self: The Development of Heidegger's Concept of Authenticity* (Ohio University Press, 1981), which explores the relationship between Heidegger's thought and Zen in its final section (pp.255–76). In addition to the papers and books cited by Zimmerman in 'Heidegger and Heraclitus,' see the following inspirational papers by Hwa Jol Jung: 'The Ecological Crisis: A Philosophic Perspective, East and West,' *The Centennial Review* 18 (1974): 1–28.

[3] Michael Zimmerman, 'Toward a Heideggerean Ethos for Radical Environmentalism,' *Environmental Ethics* 5 (1983): 99–131, pp.102 and 115.

[4] Ludwig Wittgenstein, *Tractatus Logico-Philosophicus,* trans. D.F. Pears and B.F. McGuiness (Routledge and Kegan Paul, 1961), proposition 6.44.

[5] Roger Walsh, 'The Consciousness Disciplines and the Behavioral Sciences: Questions of Comparison and Assessment,' *American Journal of Psychiatry* 137 (1980): 663–73, p.663.

[6] On this general point, see Ken Wilber's insightful essays 'Eye to Eye' and 'The Problem of Proof,' which constitute the first two chapters of his book *Eye to Eye: The Quest for the New Paradigm* (Anchor Books, 1983).

[7] Theodore Roszak, *Where the Wasteland Ends: Politics and Transcendence in Postindustrial Society* (Faber and Faber, 1973), p.400.

[8] On the general question of the empathic incorporation of cosmologies or 'world models,' see Alex Comfort, *Reality and Empathy: Physics, Mind, and Science in the 21st Century* (Albany: State University of New York Press, 1984). By *empathy,* Comfort means an 'incorporation going beyond intellectual assent' (p.xviii). See also Stephen Toulmin, *The Return to Cosmology: Postmodern Science and the Theology of Nature* (University of California Press, 1982), esp.the final chapter in which Toulmin explicitly links the cultivation of a cosmological sense of things – or what I am referring to as cosmologically based identification – with the development of 'a genuine piety... toward creatures of other kinds: a piety that goes beyond the consideration of their usefulness to Humanity as instruments for the fulfilment of human ends' (p.272).

[9] George Sessions, 'Ecocentrism and the Greens: Deep Ecology and the Environmental Task,' *The Trumpeter* 5 (1988): 65–69, p.27.

[10] One could drown in the number of semi-popular and more technical books that could be cited at this point! A gentle approach might be more effective; thus, for a highly readable, comprehensive, *single* volume overview of the scientific view of the world, see Isaac Asimov's exemplary guide *Asimov's New Guide to Science*, rev. ed. (Penguin Books, 1987). For an excellent systems-oriented overview of the scientific view of the world, see Ervin Laszlo, *Evolution: The Grand Synthesis* (Shambala, 1987).

[11] See, for example, Richard Dawkins, *The Blind Watchmaker* (Penguin Books, 1988), esp.ch. 10: 'The One True Tree of Life.'

[12] See Mark Ridley, *The Problems of Evolution* (Oxford University Press, 1985), ch. 8: 'How Can One Species Split into Two?'

[13] For overviews of recent work on the origins of the physical cosmos, see Paul Davies, *God and the New Physics* (Penguin Books, 1984): Paul Davies, *Superforce: The Search for a rand Unified Theory of Nature* (Unwin Paperbacks, 1985); John Gribbin, *In Search of the Big Bang: Quantum Physics and Cosmology* (Corgi Books, 1987); Alan H. Guth and Paul J. Steinhardt, 'The Inflationary Universe,' *Scientific American,* May 1984, pp.90–102; Stephen W. Hawking, *A Brief History of Time: From The Big Bang to Black Holes* (Bantam Books, 1988); and Heinz R. Pagels, *Perfect Symmetry: The Search for the Beginning of Time* (Bantam Books, 1986).

[14] Stephen Young, 'Root and Branch in the Groves of Academe,' *New Scientist,* 23/30 December 1989, pp.58–61, at pp.58 and 61.

[15] Quoted in Bill Devall and George Sessions, *Deep Ecology: Living as if Nature Mattered,* p.101.

[16] Arne Naess, 'Friendship, Strength of Emotion, and Freedom,' in *Spinoza Herdacht 1677– 1977* (no further details), pp.11–19, at p.13

[17] Ibid., p.19.

[18] See John Seed, Joanna Macy, Pat Fleming, and Arne Naess, *Thinking Like a Mountain: Towards a Council of All Beings* (New Society Publishers, 1988).

'Environmental Verses'

'Going, Going'

Philip Larkin

With wry gloom Larkin foresees the final disappearance of a countryside
that, though itself far from being wild nature, is still natural by contrast
with the encroaching concrete.

I thought it would last my time –
The sense that, beyond the town,
There would always be fields and farms,
Where the village louts could climb
Such trees as were not cut down;
I knew there'd be false alarms

In the papers about old streets
And split-level shopping, but some
Have always been left so far;
And when the old part retreats
As the bleak high-risers come
We can always escape in the car.

Things are tougher than we are, just
As earth will always respond
However we mess it about;
Chuck filth in the sea, if you must:
The tides will be clean beyond.
– But what do I feel now? Doubt?

Or age, simply? The crowd
Is young in the M1 café;
Their kids are screaming for more –
More houses, more parking allowed,
More caravan sites, more pay.
On the Business Page, a score

Of spectacled grins approve
Some takeover bid that entails
Five per cent profit (and ten
Per cent more in the estuaries): move
Your works to the unspoilt dales
(Grey area grants)! And when

You try to get near the sea
In summer ...
        It seems, just now,
To be happening so very fast;
Despite all the land left free
For the first time I feel somehow
That it isn't going to last,

That before I snuff it, the whole
Boiling will be bricked in
Except for the tourist parts –
First slum of Europe: a role
It won't be so hard to win,
With a cast of crooks and tarts.

And that will be England gone,
The shadows, the meadows, the lanes,
The guildhalls, the carved choirs.
There'll be books; it will linger on
In galleries; but all that remains
For us will be concrete and tyres.

Most things are never meant.
This won't be, most likely: but greeds
And garbage are too thick-strewn
To be swept up now, or invent
Excuses that make them all needs.
I just think it will happen, soon.

25 January 1972

From 'Letter to Lord Byron'

W.H. Auden

Auden pokes gentle fun at an earlier (pre-war) generation of 'greens',
before that term was invented.

The mountain-snob is a Wordsworthian fruit;
   He tears his clothes and doesn't shave his chin,
He wears a very pretty little boot,
   He chooses the least comfortable inn;
   A mountain railway is a deadly sin;
His strength, of course, is as the strength of ten men,
He calls all those who live in cities wen-men.

I'm not a spoil-sport, I would never wish
   To interfere with anybody's pleasures;
By all means climb, or hunt, or even fish,
   All human hearts have ugly little treasurers;
   But think it time to take repressive measures
When someone says, adopting the 'I know' line,
The Good Life is confined above the snow-line.

Besides, I'm very fond of mountains, too;
   I like to travel through them in a car;
I like a house that's got a sweeping view;
   I like to walk, but not to walk too far.
   I also like green plains where cattle are,
And trees and rivers, and shall always quarrel
With those who think that rivers are immoral.

Not that my private quarrel gives quietus to
   The interesting question that it raises;
Impartial thought will give a proper status to
   This interest in waterfalls and daisies,
   Excessive love for the non-human faces,
That lives in hearts from Golders Green to Teddington;
It's all bound up with Einstein, Jeans, and Eddington.

It is a commonplace that's hardly worth
    A poet's while to make profound or terse,
That now the sun does not go round the earth,
    That man's no centre of the universe;
    And working in an office makes it worse.
The humblest is acquiring with facility
A Universal-Complex sensibility.

For now we've learnt we mustn't be so bumptious
    We find the stars are one big family,
And send out invitations for a scrumptious
    Simple, old-fashioned, jolly romp with tea
    To any natural objects we can see.
We can't, of course, invite a Jew or Red
But birds and nebulae will do instead.

The Higher Mind's outgrowing the Barbarian,
    It's hardly thought hygienic now to kiss;
The world is surely turning vegetarian;
    And as it grows too sensitive for this,
    It won't be long before we find there is
A Society of Everybody's Aunts
For the Prevention of Cruelty to Plants.

I dread this like the dentist, rather more so:
    To me Art's subject is the human clay,
And landscape but a background to a torso;
    All Cézanne's apples I would give away
    For one small Goya or a Daumier.
I'll never grant a more than minor beauty
To pudge or pilewort, petty-chap or pooty.

'Pied Beauty'

Gerard Manley Hopkins

The poet gives thanks for the variegated beauty of nature, and creates a mild puzzle for an atheistical reader: can she join in?

Glory be to God for dappled things –
    For skies of couple-colour as a brinded cow;
    For rose-moles all in stipple upon trout that swim;
Fresh-firecoal chestnut-falls; finches' wings;
    Landscape plotted and pieced – fold, fallow, and plough;
    And áll trádes, their gear and tackle and trim.

All things counter, original, spare, strange;
    Whatever is fickle, freckled (who knows how?)
    With swift, slow; sweet, sour; adazzle, dim;
He fathers-forth whose beauty is past change:
              Praise him.

'Binsey Poplars'

felled 1879

Gerard Manley Hopkins

A poignant example of attachment to a particular cherished scene.

My aspens dear, whose airy cages quelled,
Quelled or quenched in leaves the leaping sun,
All felled, felled, are all felled;
　　Of a fresh and following folded rank
　　　　Not spared, not one
　　　　That dandled a sandalled
　　Shadow that swam or sank
On meadow and river and wind-wandering weed-winding bank.

　O if we but knew what we do
　　　When we delve or hew –
　　Hack and rack the growing green!
　　　Since country is só tender
　　To touch, her being so slender,
　　That, like this sleek and seeing ball
　　But a prick will make no eye at all,
　　Where we, even where we mean
　　　　To mend her we end her,
　　When we hew or delve:
After-comers cannot guess the beauty been.
　Ten or twelve, only ten or twelve
　　Strokes of havoc únselve
　　　The sweet especial scene,
　　Rural scene, a rural scene,
　　Sweet especial rural scene.

Answers to Exercises

Premise 1	If only the conscious features of an experience have value, then experiences with identical conscious features would be identical in value.	**EXERCISE 6**
Premise 2	Being in a wilderness and plugging in to the experience machine give experiences with identical conscious features.	
Premise 3	The two experiences are not identical in value.	
Conclusion	Not only the conscious features of an experience have value.	

---

1   Each soldier, reasoning independently, must conclude that it is best to run, whatever the other does. Tom's reasoning is: either Dan will stay or he will run; if he stays my best chance of survival is to run; if he runs my best chance of survival is to run too. Therefore ...   **EXERCISE 10**

2   The essential assumptions are (a) there are only two possible actions: to run or to stay; (b) neither soldier is concerned about the fate of the other; (c) their choices are independent, i.e. each must choose without knowing how the other will choose.

3   Tom reasons: either Dan keeps the agreement or he doesn't; if he keeps it, then my best chance of survival is to break it; if he breaks it, then my best chance of survival is to break it too. Therefore ...

4   It would prevent them from acting on the prudential reasoning that would lead each of them to act in the way that produces the non-optimal result.

5   The suggested alternatives are (a) the knowledge that desertion would be severely punished; (b) 'psychological substitutes' for physical chains or external deterrents, i.e. internal constraints, such as loyalty to a code of honour, or a disposition to abide by agreements, that would have the same deterrent effect.

6   It alters the prudential calculation. Tom reasons: if I run this time, Dan is less likely to expect me to stay next time, so would run; whereas if I stay he

will be encouraged to stay next time. He knows that if he runs this time and I have stayed, I shall probably run next time, so he has reason to stay. And he knows that I know. But there is a risk. It is in this situation that an agreement-keeping tendency can tip the balance.

EXERCISE 13

1 It is 'life-enhancing' because it is 'other-acknowledging': that is, wonder opens the mind to the appreciation of other beings, and counteracts self-absorption. It is associated with – helps to encourage – moral virtues.

2 Respect, compassion, gentleness and humility.

3 Gratitude.

EXERCISE 17

1 (a) implies that X has a conscious desire to be well-nourished; (b) implies that it is good for X to be well-nourished.

2 In (a) X can be replaced by 'a human being' and, probably, by 'a mouse', but not by 'a dandelion'. In (b) X can be replaced by any of the three.

3 A value concept is objective if it refers to a state that is of value *to* a being, whether or not it is valued *by* that being. A value concept is subjective if its application entails that the state it refers to is valued *by* the being in question.

4 Since, according to Taylor, the concept of the good of a being is an objective value concept, it can be applied to beings that lack consciousness and so cannot value anything.

EXERCISE 21

1 *Sense 1*: 'the aggregate of the powers and properties of all things'; 'the sum of all phenomena, together with the causes that produce them.'

'all the powers existing in either the outer or the inner world and everything which takes place by means of those powers.'

Contrast (not stated): what is not of the outer or inner world – the supernatural.

Sense 2: 'what takes place without the agency of man'.

Contrast: whatever takes place by human agency.

2 (i) We can act in accordance with nature in the first sense – Mill thinks that we have no alternative.

(ii) In the second sense we can follow nature by *imitating* it or by not trying to improve it. Mill thinks the former immoral and the latter irrational.

3   Religion inhibits attempts to improve nature by suggesting that it is as good as it could be.

4   Unclear.

5   A sense in which 'nature' is 'a term of ethics', meaning not what is but what ought to be.

Answers to revision test

Chapter 1

1 (iii)

2 (i) and (ii) false; (iii) true

3 (i)–(iii) false; (iv) true

4 (ii) and (iii)

Chapter 2

1 (iii)

2 (ii) and (iii)

3 (a) (i) (ii) and (iv); (b) (ii) (iii) and (iv)

4 It is not tradeable, i.e. not exchangeable, for something of equivalent value.

Chapter 3

1 (iii) and (iv)

2 (iii) and (iv)

3 (iv) is true, the others are all false.

4 (i) false; (ii) true; (iii) false; (iv) false; (v) true; (v) false; (vii) true

Chapter 4

1 (i) false; (ii) true; (iii) non-instrumental; (iv) respect, compassion, gentleness, gratitude, humility

2 (i) A disinterested, as opposed to an instrumental, use.

(ii) Science can develop the disinterested use of the senses, which is a characteristically human capacity whose development is necessary to a fulfilled human life.

Chapter 5

1   (a) (i) only; (b) (i), (iii) and (v); (c) (i) and (iv)

2   (i) false; (ii) true; (iii) true; (iv) false

Chapter 6

1   (i) Universal nature (all phenomena).

(ii) Wild (non-human) nature.

(iii) By imitating it and by refraining from improving it.

2   A is invalid: the conclusion does not follow from the premise. B is invalid too. The remedy in each case is to provide an additional premise: for A, 'It is permissible for human beings to do what is natural for them'; for B, 'It is wrong for human beings to do what is unnatural for them'.

3   (i) false; (ii) true

4   false

Chapter 7

1   (i) (ii) and (iv) only. (iii) and (v) form part of Naess's view, but not Taylor's.

2   Pro: (i), (ii), (vi), (viii).

Con: (v), (vii), (iv) (iii).

Bibliography

Adams, W.M. (1996) *Future Nature*, Earthscan.

Attfield, R. (1981) 'The Good of Trees', *Journal of Value Enquiry*, 15.

Axelrod, R. (1984) *The Evolution of Co-operation*, Penguin.

Cooper, D.E. and Palmer, J.A. (eds) (1992) *The Environment in Question*, Routledge.

Elliot, R. (ed.) (1995) *Environmental Ethics*, Oxford University Press.

Fox, W. (1990) *Towards a transpersonal Ecology: developing new foundations for environmentalism*, Shambala.

Frankena, W.K. (1979) 'Ethics and the Environment', in Goodpaster and Sayre (eds) (1979).

Goodpaster, K.E. and Sayre, K.M. (eds) (1979) *Ethics and Problems of the 21st Century*, University of Notre Dame Press.

Hardin, G. (1968) 'The Tragedy of the Commons', *Science*, 162; reprinted in Hardin and Baden (1977).

Hardin, G. and Baden, J. (eds) (1977) *Managing the Commons*, W.H. Freeman and Co.

Hare, R.M. (1987) 'Moral Reasoning about the Environment', *Journal of Applied Philosophy,* 4, reprinted in Hare (1989).

Hare, R.M. (1989) *Essays on Political Morality,* Oxford University Press.

Hepburn, R. (1984) *Wonder and Other Essays*, Edinburgh University Press.

Howarth, J. (1996) 'Neither Use nor Ornament: a consumers' guide to Care', Thingmount Working Paper 96–05, Department of Philosophy, University of Lancaster.

Hume, D. (1975 edn) *An Enquiry Concerning the Principles of Morals,* edited from the 1777 edn by L.A. Selby-Bigge, revised by P.H. Nidditch, Oxford University Press.

Kant, I. (1873 edn) *Critique of Practical Reason and Other Works,* Abbott, T.K. (trans.), Longmans.

Kant, I. (1948 edn) *The Moral Law*, H.J. Paton (trans.), Hutchinson.

Lean, G. (1997) 'It may be our last chance', *Independent on Sunday*, 30 November.

Lovejoy, A.O. (1948) '"Nature" as an aesthetic norm', in *Essays in the History of Ideas*, John Hopkins Press.

Mackie, J.L. (1977) *Ethics: Inventing right and wrong*, Penguin.

Mannison, D.S., et al. (eds) (1980), *Environmental Philosophy*, Department of Philosophy, Research School of Social Sciences, Australian National University, Canberra.

Midgley, M, (1983) 'Duties Concerning Islands' in Elliot (1995).

Mill, J.S. (1963–77 edn) *Principles of Political Economy*, in *Collected Works*, vol. 3, University of Toronto Press.

Mill, J.S. (1963–77 edn) 'Nature', in *Collected Works*, vol. 10, University of Toronto Press.

Miller, F. and Sartorious, R. (1979) 'Population Policy and Public Goods', *Philosophy and Public Affairs*, vol. 8, no 2, pp.148–74.

Naess, A. (1973) 'The Shallow and the Deep, long-range Ecology Movement', *Inquiry*, vol. 16, pp.95–100.

Naess, A. (1989) *Economy, Community and Lifestyle*, Cambridge University Press.

Norton, B.G. (1989) 'The Cultural Approach to Conservation Biology', in Western and Pearl (1989), pp. 241–6.

Nozick, R. (1974) *Anarchy, State and Utopia*, Blackwell.

O'Neill, J. (1993) *Ecology, Policy and Politics: Human Well-being and the Natural World*, Routledge.

Passmore, J. (1980) *Man's Responsibility for Nature*, 2nd edn, Duckworth.

Pearce, D., Markandya, A. and Barber, E.B. (1989) *Blueprint for a Green Economy*, Earthscan Publications Ltd.

Pearce, D. (1992) 'Green Economics', *Environmental Values*, vol. 1, no 1, pp. 6–8.

Plumwood, V. (1991) 'Nature, Self, and Gender: Feminism, Environmental Philosophy, and the Critique of Rationalism', in Elliot (1995).

Regan, T. (1983) *The Case for Animal Rights*, University of California Press.

Rodman, J. (1977) 'The Liberation of Nature', *Inquiry*, 20, pp.83–145.

Rolston III, H. (1979) 'Can and Ought We to Follow Nature?', *Environmental Ethics*, 1; reprinted in Rolston (1989).

Rolston, III, H. (1989) *Philosophy Gone Wild*, Prometheus Books.

Routley, R. and V. 'Human Chauvinism and Environmental Ethics' in Mannison et al. (1980), pp.129–31.

Schweitzer, A. (1949) *Civilization and Ethics*, 3rd edn, A.C. Black.

Scruton, R. (1996) *Animal Rights and Wrongs*, Demos.

Singer, P. (1973) 'Animal Liberation', *New York Review of Books*, 5 April, pp.17–21.

Singer, P. (1975) *Animal Liberation: a new ethics for our treatment of animals*, Random House.

Singer, P. (1993) *Practical Ethics*, 2nd edn, Cambridge University Press.

Singer, P. (1997) *How are we to live?*, Oxford University Press.

Stone, C. (1974) *Should Trees Have Standing? Toward Legal Rights for Natural Objects*, Toga Publishing Company.

Sumner, L.W. (1996) *Welfare, Happiness and Ethics*, Oxford University Press.

Sylvan, R. and Bennett, D. (1994) *The Greening of Ethics,* The White Horse Press.

Taylor, P.W. (1981) 'The ethics of respect for nature', *Environmental Ethics,* vol. 3, no 3; reprinted in Zimmerman (1993).

Taylor, P.W. (1986) *Respect for Nature: A Theory of Environmental Ethics,* Princeton University Press.

Vadnjal, D. and O'Connor, M. (1994) 'What is the Value of Rangitoto Island?' *Environmental Values,* 3, pp.369–80.

Warburton, N. (1996) *Thinking from A to Z,* Routledge.

Warnock, G.J. (1971) *The Object of Morality,* Methuen.

Western, D. and Pearl, M.C. (eds) (1989) *Conservation in the Twenty-first Century,* Oxford University Press.

Williams, B. (1995) *Making Sense of Humanity and other philosophical papers,* Cambridge University Press.

Wilson, E.O. (1994) *The Diversity of Life,* Penguin.

Zimmerman, M.E. (ed.) (1993) *Environmental Philosophy,* Prentice Hall.

Index